George Buchanan Gray

Studies in Hebrew Proper Names

George Buchanan Gray

Studies in Hebrew Proper Names

ISBN/EAN: 9783337316259

Printed in Europe, USA, Canada, Australia, Japan

Cover: Foto ©Andreas Hilbeck / pixelio.de

More available books at **www.hansebooks.com**

STUDIES

IN

EBREW PROPER NAMES

BY

G. BUCHANAN GRAY, M.A.

LECTURER IN HEBREW AND OLD TESTAMENT THEOLOGY IN MANSFIELD COLLEGE

LATE SENIOR KENNICOTT SCHOLAR IN THE UNIVERSITY OF OXFORD

LONDON

ADAM AND CHARLES BLACK

1896

PREFACE

THE present volume has grown out of an essay written for the Senior Kennicott Scholarship in 1893. During the past three years I have been able to make the collection of data for my arguments more complete and more exact—more especially by a closer examination of the textual tradition of the names. Comparatively little has been done in the way of a systematic treatment of the text of the Old Testament proper names, although in the recent dictionary by Siegfried and Stade good service has been rendered by giving under the various names the Greek equivalents, which frequently indicate the degree of uncertainty attaching to particular instances. The notes to Kittel's edition of Chronicles (in Haupt's Bible) also afford valuable help; but my own notes were practically complete before this appeared. Under the circumstances I am hopeful that, apart from the arguments and theories of my book, the notes on the text of the names (contained chiefly in Appendix II., but also scattered throughout the book) will be found of help by other workers in this subject. I should explain that I have examined the testimony of the versions for all *hapax legomena* to which I have had occasion to refer, and for many other names which appeared to be of questionable genuineness. Where a form is cited from the LXX. it may be understood that none of the MSS. represented by Swete's edition, nor the Lucian recension as printed by Lagarde gives a variant presenting any material (*i.e.* more than orthographic) difference from the form cited, unless the contrary is distinctly stated or implied. For the text of the Targums, the Samaritan and the Syriac, I have used Walton; for the last also Lee's text. I need scarcely add that I am not unmindful of the necessarily provisional character of all work of this kind in the present stage of Old Testament textual criticism; but even now several names in the Massoretic text ought to be dismissed as the result of transcriptional or other error, and others are, entirely or in particular usages, so questionable that they should be used in argument only with extreme caution. I have made it my aim, though possibly without uniform success, to give the benefit of the doubt (when the evidence was evenly balanced) to readings (as also to etymologies) unfavourable to my arguments, or at least in all important cases to draw attention to the uncertainty; the arrangement of Appendices II. and III. will moreover render it easy for any one to test in detail the character of the data for the several arguments.

The original essay has been amplified in almost every part, and was re-written in the latter part of last year; but the main line of argument and the chief conclusions, though they have been generally strengthened, have not been greatly modified by my more recent investigations. One or two details with regard to changes may be referred to: in Chapter II. the section dealing with compounds in 'Am has been modified and very greatly enlarged; the discussion of the geographical names in Ba'al is new, so also is the geographical analysis of the animal names (pp. 105 ff.); in Chapter III. the analysis of the names in the Priestly Code is much more detailed, and consequently the conclusions I have felt myself justified in drawing are much more definite. Three years ago little more than the peculiarity of these names was clear to me; the causes of it were obscure. Some obscurity in details remains and probably must do so; but Dillmann's comments (especially on Num. i.), which then weighed with me, have ceased to incline me to the opinion that the whole or even the main cause of this peculiarity of the names might be their antiquity. The application of my results to test the historical character of individual sections of Chronicles (pp. 226-242) is also fresh, and may, I hope, throw some light on the obscure section (cc. i.-ix.) with which that book opens. But I would explain that any abruptness and positiveness of expression which may mark that part of my book is due to the desire for brevity, not to the attribution of undue importance or certainty to the results.

In discussions where so much often turns on the form of the name, it has seemed desirable to give the Hebrew characters rather than a transliteration. On the other hand where the form is of less importance, and especially in summarising sections, I have frequently preferred to give the recognised English equivalent rather than a more exact transliteration.

The name of Nestle is indissolubly associated with the subject of Hebrew proper names: from his monograph on the subject and from his subsequent contributions I have derived the greatest assistance. My indebtedness to the writings of other scholars, notably Nöldeke, Robertson Smith, and Wellhausen, has also been great, as the references in the notes will sufficiently indicate.

Finally, I must give myself the pleasure of thanking all those from whom I have received help through personal communication; and more especially would I record here my warm gratitude to Professor Driver for the constant encouragement and frequent advice which I have received from him, to Dr. Neubauer who, under circumstances which have rendered the act one of singular kindness, has read large parts of my book while it has been passing through the press, and given me the benefit of many valuable suggestions, and to my colleague, Mr. Thatcher, who has assisted me in a most welcome manner by reading the proof-sheets and favoured me with numerous criticisms which have enabled me materially to improve the exposition of my subject.

G. BUCHANAN GRAY.

MANSFIELD COLLEGE, OXFORD,
August 1896.

TABLE OF CONTENTS

CHAPTER III

CHAPTER IV

APPENDIX I

APPENDIX II

APPENDIX III

LIST OF ABBREVIATIONS

CIS = Corpus Inscript. Semiticarum.
JA = Journal Asiatique.
JBL(it) = Journal of Biblical Literature.
J Ph = Journal of Philology.
KAT = Schrader's Keilinschriften u. das Alte Testament. (Citations are from the second German edition, the pagination of which is given in the margin of Whitehouse's translation.)
MT = Massoretic Text.
OT = Old Testament.
P(T)SBA = Proceedings (Transactions) of the Society of Biblical Archaeology.
REJ = Revue des Études Juives.
RP = Records of the Past.
TSK = Theologische Studien u. Kritiken.
de Vogüé = de Vogüé's Syrie Centrale.
WZKM = Wiener Zeitschrift für Kunde des Morgenlandes.
ZATW = Zeitschrift für die alttestamentliche Wissenschaft.
ZDMG = Zeitschrift d. Deutschen Morgenländischen Gesellschaft.

CHAPTER I

METHOD AND LIMITS OF THE ENQUIRY

HEBREW proper names, in common with those of other early peoples, are more than symbols: they were conferred not merely for purposes of distinction, but because of an idea they expressed. This underlying idea can still, in the case of many names, be easily detected, and its appropriateness is in some cases apparent. But, apart from this, the fact that the names were once significant, and were conferred because of their significance, could be proved by reference to narratives of a well-known type, in which the circumstances that gave rise to the names of particular children are recorded. Sarah calls her child "Laughter" (Isaac) because of the laughter of joy or astonishment which his birth occasions; and Rachel records the fact that Benjamin's birth was to cost her her life by calling him "Son of my Sorrow" (Ben-oni).[1] To the value of these narratives as proof of custom, it is clearly immaterial whether they are strictly historical

[1] Gen. xxi. 1-7; xxxv. 18. Cf. further *e.g.* Gen. iv. 1, 25; xxx. 6 ff.; Hos. i.

or not; it is sufficient to recollect that they form part of the earliest extant Hebrew literature. We may safely infer, therefore, that the early Hebrews were determined in their choice of names for their children by the wish to express some thought or emotion. But was this wish the only determining factor? The question is an important one, if we are to estimate at all accurately the extent to which the ideas underlying proper names represent fresh and vigorous popular thought and imagination in the period to which they belong. In later times other considerations unquestionably had great weight in the choice of a name—probably in most cases much greater weight than the meaning of the name. Did these also exist in the earlier periods, or did they not?

Among the customs prevalent in later times the most important was that in accordance with which the child received the name of the father, grandfather, or some other kinsman. This custom was clearly well established by the first century A.D.; a departure from it already occasions surprise. When Elizabeth chooses for her child the name "John," her friends protest —"There is none of thy kindred that is called by this name," and when Zacharias ratifies the choice, "they marvelled all."[1] A proof of the prevalence of this custom from a more distinctly Jewish source[2] may be found in the record of Hillel's descendants from the first

[1] Luke i. 59-61.

[2] Cf. also Ber. (*Talm. Pabli*) 18*b* as cited below, p. 31.

century B.C. downwards. In his family, for several centuries, the grandson generally bears the same name as the grandfather; the genealogy runs,—in every case from father to son,—Hillel, Simon, Gamaliel, Simon, Gamaliel, Simon, Judah, Gamaliel, Judah, Gamaliel, Judah, Hillel, Gamaliel, Judah, Gamaliel.[1] We can probably trace the same custom somewhat earlier in the name of Jesus the son of Sirach, who was "grandchild to Jesus of the same name with him,"[2] and in the Asmonaean family, in which the names Hyrcanus, Alexander, and Aristobulus recur. Mattathias son of John and grandson of Simeon named one of his five sons after his father, and another Simon[3] after his grandfather. These instances carry us back to the first and second centuries B.C. In the high-priestly family we find the custom of naming the grandson after the grandfather establishing itself from the close of the fourth century B.C. onwards; the genealogy from 332 to 165 B.C. runs, Onias, Simon, Onias, Simon, Onias.[4] The *son* of the last is, however, also named Onias.[5]

[1] *Vide* Graetz, *Geschichte der Juden* (2nd edit.), iv. 480 ff.

[2] Ecclus. 1st Prologue *ad init.*

[3] The two Greek forms *Συμεών* and *Σίμων* imply the same Hebrew original שמעון.

[4] *Vide e.g.* Schürer, *The Jewish People in the time of Jesus Christ*, I. i. 188, where the references to Josephus may be found.

[5] To what I have said in the above paragraph I here add the following remarks:—(1) The preference for naming the child after its grandfather was common to the (later) Jews and

The custom of naming after a kinsman is thus proved for later times by the unmistakable implication of the narrative in Luke, and by numerous instances from genealogies. But among the early Hebrews it was unknown. This negative state-

many other peoples. Gesenius drew attention to the prevalence of the custom among the Phoenicians, *Monumenta Phoenicia*, p. 100. In the Carthaginian Inscriptions instances are very numerous, *vide e.g. CIS*, i. 7, 47, 138, 496, 498, 507, 509, 530, 541, 566, 579, 593. For Nabataean instances cf. *CIS*, ii. 307 : חלצת בר זבדי בר חלצת בר זבדי ; see also Nos. 164, 323 (first century A.D.). At Palmyra in the first to third centuries A.D. the custom must have been very common: instances in the Palmyrene inscriptions are unusually numerous, see *e.g.* De Vogüé, 1, 3, 4, and the genealogies drawn up by him, on pp. 45, 51. There are, unfortunately, too few early inscriptions to show whether this custom was prevalent among these peoples at an earlier period than among the Jews. The Zinjerli inscriptions refer to two Panammus (D. H. Müller, *Altsem. Inschriften von Sendschirli*, p. 6), but in the present state of decipherment we can draw no very certain conclusions as to their relationship. The line of the kings of Damascus in the tenth to eighth centuries B.C. can be clearly traced for the most part, and with some probability completely established: *vide* Winckler, *Alttest. Untersuchungen*, pp. 61 ff.; here the three Benhadads of whom the O.T. speaks might appear at first sight to illustrate the custom, but Winckler has shown that Benhadad II. is identical with Benhadad I., and the O.T. narratives (1 K. xix. 15, 16; 2 K. viii. 8, 15) suggest that Hazael, father of the later Benhadad, was not a son of the earlier: in any case we have no direct statement that they were related. The earlier lists of the Syrian kings (1 K. xi. 23; xv. 18) show no trace of the custom. Löw (*Beiträge zur jüd. Alterthumskunde*, ii. 94) suggests that the Jews derived the custom from the Greeks; the date at

ment can, it is true, only be proved by the *argumentum e silentio;* but for the non-existence of a custom no other form of argument is possible. The argument is in the present case twofold: in the first place, the early Old Testament narratives contain *numerous* accounts of the naming

which we first find traces of it among the Jews so far favours this view. May we also from the terms of the Introd. to Ecclus. assume that even in the second century it had not yet become very prevalent? However this may be, I hope the instances cited may suffice to show that where the custom existed we can trace it, and therefore, where we cannot trace it, we have a right to conclude it did not exist. (2) The custom of naming the son after the *father* was always much rarer. Gesenius indeed argued (*l.c.*) that among the Phoenicians the elder son received the name of the grandfather, the younger that of the father. But the evidence for this is scanty: cf. Bloch, *Phoen. Glossar*, p. 19 n. And this is the more striking when it is remembered that the number of cases in which the names of father and son are known are far more numerous than those in which the names of grandfather, father, and son are known. Löw (*op. cit.* p. 96) has on this account cast discredit on the narrative in Luke i. 59-61, on the ground that the son was never named at least after the *living* father. But this is questionable; we have the case of Onias IV. the son of Onias III. and the numerous Abba bar Abbas (Ber., 18*b* cited below, p. 31); cf. also Edersheim, *Life and Times of Jesus*, i. 157. Instances from the inscriptions will be found in *CIS*, i. 122, 153, 550 (Phoen.); ii. 174, 311 (Nabataean). (3) The child was commonly called after ancestors remoter than the grandfather: for the Jews, cf. the line of Gamaliel given above; for the Phoenicians, *CIS*, 550, 626 (three instances of naming after the great-grandfather), 659, 776, 808; for the Nabataeans, *CIS*, i. 182.

of children; but in none is it recorded that the child received the name of a kinsman, and in none is any surprise expressed because the name is freely chosen without regard to the names already existing in the family. These Old Testament narratives thus stand in direct contrast to that in Luke i. 59-61. Again, we have several genealogies in the early Old Testament narratives, and, especially in the books of Samuel, find numerous members of the same family mentioned; but we fail (except in the single instance of Maacah as the name of Absalom's mother and daughter) to discover among these traces of such a custom. Thus, of the twenty-one kings of Judah, all of the family of David, no two bear the same name; and this is the case also with the various dynasties of the northern kingdom. In other cases where the genealogy is given up to, or beyond, the grandfathers, we also find that the same name does not recur (see Zeph. i. 1; Zech. i. 1; Jer. xli. 1, 2; 1 S. ix. 1, xiv. 3; 2 K. ix. 2, xxii. 3 [cf. ver. 12, and Jer. xli. 2], 14). In brief, later narratives and later genealogies agree in testifying to the existence of the custom of naming after a relative; early narratives and early genealogies agree in showing that this custom had not yet arisen. We may, I think, safely infer that the custom first arose among the post-Exilic Jews, probably not much earlier than the close of the fourth century B.C.[1]

[1] Instances of names recurring in families at an earlier date occur in the Chronicler's genealogies, especially in ch. vi.; but

Another custom very similar to the one just discussed consisted in giving to children names of famous persons, in some cases Jewish,[1] in others

this is only one instance out of many in which the evidence of the Chronicler is directly at variance with that of earlier sources. For the significance of this, see below, pp. 172 f. A few apparent instances in the earlier literature must, however, be considered. (1) Abner the son of Ner. Could we assume that Abner meant "father of Ner," and implied that the person so named actually had a son named Ner, we should have a well-attested early instance of the son named after the grandfather. But this deduction is illegitimate, see below, p. 66 ff. (2) Ahimelech, Abiathar, Ahimelech (1 S. xxx. 7; 2 S. viii. 17) is only an apparent instance. The succession is due to intentional misplacement; *vide* Wellhausen on 2 S. viii. 17, and Winer, *Bibl. Realwörterbuch*, *s.v.* Ahimelech. (3) The succession Jehoiada, Benaiah, Jehoiada, is due to textual corruption; *vide* Bertheau on 1 Chr. xxvii. 34. Real instances of the same name recurring in the same family are these: Jonathan's son, and Saul's son by his concubine Mizpah, were both named Meribaal, 2 S. xxi. 7 f.; one of Absalom's daughters bore the same name as his sister, Tamar, 2 S. xiv. 27, xiii. 1; the first of these is a mere coincidence, the second may be something more, especially since another of Absalom's daughters was named after her grandmother, Maacah, 1 K. xv. 2, 2 S. iii. 3; the case of Maacah is quite isolated, and it is noticeable that the elder Maacah was a foreigner—Geshurite.

[1] See the list in Zunz, *Namen der Juden*, p. 23; on the particular case of Simon cf. J. B. Lightfoot, *Galatians*, p. 269. The influence of Ecclus. xliv. ff., and especially xliv. 1-12, on the development of this custom may have been considerable. Another closely related custom was that of naming children after those from whom the parents had received a favour: cf. Chol. 47*b*; Jebam. 105*a* (cited by Lightfoot, *Works*, 1684, ii. 387).

foreign.[1] Certain names of persons living within a century of the Return may probably be due to this cause, but nothing suggests that the custom existed in pre-Exilic times. This custom also appears to have become prevalent only from the Greek period onward.

The prevalence of either of these customs would naturally tend to diminish the consciousness of the actual meaning of the name; consequently, where they prevail, we can only argue with caution and within limitations from the continued existence of a name to the existence at the time of its conferment of the idea implied in it.[2] It is important, therefore, to have proved that neither of these customs was prevalent, if even existent, among the pre-Exilic Hebrews; from their names we are justified in inferring their ideas.

I have been able to trace only one custom which in any way controlled the free choice of names on the ground of their meaning. This is the custom of giving children names *related in form* to those of their kinsmen. Coincidences of this kind are, I believe, too numerous to be accidental. A few instances will illustrate the kind of similarity referred to. At

[1] *E.g.* Alexander; cf. Zunz, *op. cit.* p. 11, especially the tradition cited by him on p. 36.

[2] On the other hand the creation of new names at a time when it has become customary not to create but to borrow, will testify so much the more to the strength of the idea implied. Interesting instances are the Syrian Christian names compounded with Jesus, *e.g.* Abhd-Ishō', Dādh-Ishō', Ishō'-dādh and Ishō'-yābh; see Wright, *Syriac Literature* (index).

Palmyra we find *Nebo*zebed and Tarhibol sons of Bar*nebo*, son of *Nebo*zebed.[1] Among the Phoenicians, 'Azru*ba'al* son of Maher*ba'al*, son of Hanni*ba'al*.[2] Among the Sabaeans, *Samah*karib son of *Samah*'afiḳ, son of *Samah*yafi', and the brothers *Zaid* and *Zaid*'il.[3] These instances, among various peoples,[4] illustrate what appears to have been a custom. Among early Hebrew names also we find some similar instances. Thus *Ahi*tub names two of his sons *Ahi*jah and *Ahi*melech;[5] *Ahi*noam is the daughter of *Ahi*maaz;[6] three members of the family of Saul receive names containing the element *bôsheth*;[7] the kings of Judah receive almost invariably names compounded with *Yah*.[8]

Possibly, therefore, in some cases, and to a certain extent, the selection of a child's name was controlled by the desire that it should *resemble* that of the father or some other relative; but it is clear that so long as only one part of a compound name was thus fixed without immediate reference to its meaning, those who

[1] De Vogüé, *Syrie Centrale*, 73.

[2] *CIS*, i. 477; cf. also 472, 502, 629, 856.

[3] *CIS*, iv. 37; cf. also 20. Comparison might also be made with the Arabic custom of giving children names of similar sound, *e.g.* the well-known instance of Hasan and Husein.

[4] The illustrations given in the text are all from Semitic names; on the same custom among the Greeks, *vide* Bechtel and Fick, *Die griechischen Personennamen*, p. xi.

[5] 1 S. xiv. 3; xxii. 9.

[6] 1 S. xiv. 50.

[7] See below, pp. 121 f., 124.

[8] See below, pp. 260 f.

chose the name must yet have been fully conscious of the meaning of the whole.

There is thus every reason for believing that the Hebrews, as a general rule, and in the earlier periods always, conferred on their children names which were appropriate to the occasion in virtue of their inherent significance. Often the giving of the name was an opportunity for the parents to express their religious thoughts in the form of gratitude for the past, or hope for the future; and these feelings might be prompted by private and family circumstances, or by the larger interests of public life.[1] At other times the names given possessed a purely secular reference, and perpetuated the memory of some physical characteristic of the child, or some emotion of the parents. Names of the first class, when their meaning can be rightly interpreted, cannot but throw light on Hebrew religion and more especially on the *popular* religion, while names of the second class contribute much material for Hebrew *Culturgeschichte.* The first class has already received a somewhat full treatment from Nestle;[2] the second class has been treated more briefly, yet pregnantly, by Friedrich Delitzsch,[3] and quite recently at greater length by Grunwald.[4]

[1] For the former cf. Genesis iv. 1, 25; for the latter 1 S. iv. 21.

[2] In *Die israelitischen Eigennamen nach ihrer religionsgeschichtlichen Bedeutung*, Haarlem, 1876.

[3] In *Proleg. eines neuen hebr.-aram. Wörterbuch zum A.T.* ch. vi.

[4] *Die Eigennamen des alten Testaments in ihrer Bedeutung für*

But Nestle has attempted what Delitzsch did not—to treat the names historically, to show how the names in use in particular periods throw light on the stage of the development of religion then attained. Not to do this is, indeed, to leave the names but half used; but the doing of it successfully is beset by numerous difficulties.

First among these is the uncertain date of some of the O.T. writings which contain the richest stores of proper names. Thus Nestle wrote assuming that the Priestly Code[1] belongs to the earliest Hebrew literature. During the last twenty years this assumption has become much more questionable, and cannot wisely be made the starting point of any fresh attempt to deal with the subject. But were it possible to start from the contrary assumption that P is post-Exilic, the difficulty would be but half surmounted. The Priestly Code, though compiled late, might yet, in the matter of proper names, embody much more ancient sources; and the same is the case with the undoubtedly late work of the Chronicler (Ezra, Nehemiah, and Chronicles).

We are thus faced by this difficulty: of the two writings which contain the larger part of the proper names of the O.T. one is undoubtedly late, and, in

die Kenntniss des hebräischen Volksglaubens, von M. Grunwald, Breslau, 1895.

[1] This will be cited by the symbol P.

the opinion of an increasing number of scholars, the other is the same; yet one refers all, the other a large proportion, of the names in question to the earlier periods of Hebrew history. Now, if these names which have come down to us only in works of late or uncertain date were yet derived by the compilers of these works from genuine ancient sources, and are in consequence real records of the periods to which they are referred, any historical treatment of O.T. proper names which neglects them will thereby be vitiated; if, on the other hand, they are schematic inventions of the compilers, or names current in later times, and referred by these compilers without sufficient authority to earlier periods, to treat them as early will lead to equally erroneous results. One thing will become clear from the subsequent detailed discussions; in some important respects conclusions will differ almost to the extent of being mutually contradictory, according as we include or exclude the testimony of these late or uncertain writings in drawing our inferences. This being the case, before we can reach final and satisfactory conclusions on several important points, we shall be obliged to examine carefully the names in P and Chronicles, and to determine as far as possible their historical value.

Another difficulty arises from the fact already established — that names were not hereditary in early times. This being so, we can use a name occurring at a particular period to show that the idea embodied in it was then existent; but we cannot, from the mere non-existence of a particular name in earlier or later writers, argue as to the date of the origin or decay of the idea. A canon of limitation in inference thus comes into force—single names justify positive conclusions only.

But the same fact also suggests a method of investigation which can in a measure overcome the limitation and obtain negative as well as positive conclusions. This method will consist in dealing not with single names, but with *classes of names*. In certain cases it is possible, without depending too much on ambiguous etymologies, to group together certain names in clearly defined classes, such, for example, as those which contain the divine name אל or יה. Now, if we find the names of such classes confined to certain periods, or increasing or diminishing in number in the course of centuries, we can argue with considerable probability to the approximate date of the origin and decay of the idea common to the names of the class in question, and to its comparative prevalence in different periods.

In this connection another point of some importance in the subsequent discussions may be referred to. The enormous number of different personal names and the comparative rarity in early times of the recurrence of the same name prove that they were created with great facility; but the fact that the same name is borne by several people—sometimes by several contemporaries[1]—suggests that current names were not infrequently adopted instead of fresh ones being created. This, no doubt, indicates the general diffusion of the idea at the period in question; but it may be questioned whether in such cases the idea expressed by the name was so vividly present in the individual instances to the minds of the parents or others conferring it as when a fresh name was created for the occasion; and it seems probable that, in this way, the transition to the later custom of giving a name simply or chiefly because it had previously been borne by some relative, benefactor, or famous man, was made easy.

In view of this it will not be surprising if, here and there, traces be found of an ancient class of names in a late period: the less surprising, if it be remembered that a new meaning[2] more in consonance with later modes of thought could in some instances be easily read into an old name of which the original idea had been forgotten or had ceased to appeal to the persons concerned. There can be little doubt that the custom of creating fresh names was controlled by a conservative tendency in respect to the name form: old forms disappeared indeed, yet gradually, with the

[1] For instances see App. 3 A, No. 16 B, No. 43, *e.g.* II.

[2] Cf. the numerous cases of false etymologies of proper names in the O.T.; and also the note (pp. 153 f.) on the probable change in meaning in יואל. Cf. further, but with caution, Güdemann's essay *Die superstitiöse Bedeutung des Eigennamens* in the *Festschrift* to M. Steinschneider (Leipsic, 1896).

gradual obsolescence of an idea: for the same reason new forms only arose at the demand of fresh and vigorous thought.

Other difficulties in the way of an historical treatment remain to be noticed. One of the chief of these is due to the ambiguous character of the genealogies and lists: granted that the genealogies in Chronicles and P are derived from accurate and early sources, what do they mean? Is one justified in starting from some known person in a genealogy, counting backwards or forwards by generations, and so fixing the date of any given unknown person in the same genealogy? A very little comparative study shows that this is impossible; generations are often omitted, sometimes added, so that at best only within limits, often the widest, could unknown persons be thus dated.

But this is not the only ambiguity, nor, perhaps, for the present investigation the most serious. To what do the names refer? In dealing with Semitic genealogies, this is a question not only justified, but necessitated; for the genealogical scheme was employed not only for *individuals*, but also for *families* or *clans*;[1] and, in the latter case, the order is geographical quite as much as chronological. Genealogies of this latter type we find, by common consent, in Genesis x.: straightforward pedigrees of individuals, on the other hand, we clearly find in 1 Chron. iii.; unfortunately in

[1] Cf. *e.g.* Wellhausen, *De Gentibus*, p. 4 ff.: Kuenen, *Religion of Israel*, i. 109 ff., 176-182.

many cases, especially in the early chapters of Chronicles, it is doubtful to which class particular lists belonged—whether in reality, or even in the intention of the compiler; it is often equally obscure to what period the compiler himself referred them. Any satisfactory discussion of O.T. proper names must rest on a recognition of these ambiguities; at the same time any method which succeeds in solving the doubts and determining the date and character of any or all these lists, must unquestionably advance the study of the subject.

I have said that many O.T. names are clearly and by general admission those of clans or families. In such cases another canon of limitation in inference holds good: clan names occurring in a particular period only establish for the idea involved a *terminus ad quem;* they show that at an undefined *previous* period the idea had existed, they do not prove the existence of the same at the period of mention.[1]

[1] This is sufficiently manifest where clan or tribal names may be assumed, on account of their similarity in form and general significance to personal names, to be derivative from that of an individual of bygone times, whether a common ancestor or a distinguished leader or chief; on the latter cause of tribal names cf. Nöldeke in *ZDMG*, 1886, pp. 157-159. But the same canon equally applies in the case of names which we have no reason for believing were even originally borne by individuals. A tribal name would not be abandonéd because its origin had been lost sight of, or its meaning had become obscure.

Personal names easily, if slowly, changed with changing ideas, because the process of giving these names was constantly going on, and the lives of individuals are short; but the lives of clans may be, and often are, long, and their names, derived from far past times, may bear silent and long unobserved testimony to ideas unfamiliar and even repugnant to later generations; for a whole clan or family could only discard its ancient name with difficulty, and consequently it was only in the rarest cases that it actually did so.[1]

The canon just established for clan names clearly applies equally to place names.[2] But in the case of these still further caution has to be observed. Many, perhaps most, of the names of towns and places in the O.T. go back to times before the Hebrew conquest of Palestine; for the conquest of a country is seldom followed by a wholesale change in the names of its towns, etc.[3] In consequence, therefore, of the extreme probability of most of the place names being Canaanite, not Hebrew, in origin, they will be cited chiefly for comparative purposes.

The chief difficulties have now been stated, and

[1] Cf. Wellhausen, *Die Reste des arabischen Heidenthums*, p. 6.

[2] Except indeed in such a case as that of 2 K. xiv. 7, where the name of the place can be chronologically fixed as definitely as those of persons.

[3] Reminiscences of changes in place names are found in O.T., cf. *e.g.* Gen. xxviii. 19; Num. xxxii. 38; yet on both these passages, especially the latter, cf. Dillmann.

the method they necessitate has been indicated. The classes of names, the history of which will be examined in the following discussions, are as follows:—

I. Names containing an element denoting some form of kindred:

1. אב = father.
2. אח = brother.
3. עם = kinsman, uncle.
4. דד = kinsman, uncle, חם = father-in-law, and אם = mother.
5. בן = son, and בת = daughter.

II. Animal names.

III. Names containing an element denoting some form of dominion:

1. מלך.
2. בעל.
3. אדן.

IV. Names containing a divine name:

1. אל.
2. יה.
3. שדי.

It may at first sight seem that the classification is made too much on the ground of mere external resemblance; but in the first instance this will perhaps be found best. It is not necessary that all the names in any single class be ultimately considered homogeneous. It must be left to the analysis to show whether they are so or not.

In dealing with each class, the first effort will be to determine the chronological distribution of its members: two questions will call for answer:—

1. Were names of the class *created* in all periods?
2. Were they equally distributed over all periods?

The discussion will be directly concerned only with O.T. names; but references to later Jewish names will be made when they throw light on points that arise. In addition to chronological, geographical and ethnographical distribution is of great importance, and the existence of numerous names of foreigners in the O.T. demands attention. In this connection and within the limits of the classes to be discussed, reference must frequently be made to extra-biblical Semitic names as confirmatory of and supplementary to the biblical records. These foreign names are especially valuable in that they throw light on the extent to which many names and the ideas they contained were common to Israel and the surrounding nations.

On the basis of the results as to chronological and geographical distribution, conclusions special to the class will be drawn and suggestions made within the various sections dealing with the various classes of names; more general conclusions depending on the total results and on the examination into the historical value of the names peculiar to P and Chronicles will be reserved, and discussed in the concluding chapters.

To complete this introductory chapter, it only remains to explain the scheme of the chronological analysis. The very nature of the case forbids us to expect instances of any special class in every half century of the history. For the case stands thus: in the Hexateuch and Judges we find a large number of names referred, by earlier or later tradition, to the most ancient period of Hebrew history, from the Exodus to the establishment of the Monarchy. In the books of Samuel we have a large number of names of persons contemporary with Saul and David; to these the books of Chronicles add considerably. The books of Kings and the prophetic writings are our earliest sources for names of persons living between David and the Exile: here again the whole number is considerable, but within this whole period the only shorter period for which any large number of names could be cited is the reign of Josiah. In this period also the additional names recorded by the Chronicler are numerous. Finally, the books of Ezra and Nehemiah contain long lists of individuals, as well as of families, living in the post-Exilic period.

These then must constitute the periods for the following discussions: — (1) The Early or Pre-Davidic Period—I.; (2) The Davidic Period—II.; (3) The Period of the Later Kings—III.; (4) The Post-Exilic Period—IV.

In certain cases, to render clear the real course of the development, it will be further necessary to subdivide the long period of the later kings into two divisions—(1) down to the close of the eighth century, (2) from the beginning of the seventh century.

For reasons stated above it will be necessary to distinguish between names attested by the earlier writings and those only found in the late or uncertain writings. The need for this distinction only disappears in the case of names assigned to Period IV.

Finally, the general significance of the division should be noted. Names of the first period should reflect the religion and thought of the still unsettled and ununited tribes; those of the second period may be expected to show signs of the effect of national unity and success; those of the third ought to illustrate the influence of the prophets; and those of the fourth the influence of the realisation of the prophetic teaching in the Exile.

Consequently, names equally distributed throughout these periods may naturally be expected to contain ideas peculiarly characteristic of an unsettled and unorganised people, but not incapable of being harmonised with the conditions of settled life, and the higher teaching of the prophets; names frequent in the earlier periods, sporadic or non-existent in the later, should contain ideas in one way or another at variance with the new conditions of life or with the prophetic teaching; and, lastly, names sporadic or non-existent in the early periods, but increasingly frequent in the later, should somewhat directly reflect the teaching of the great religious leaders.

CHAPTER II

DETAILED EXAMINATION OF THE CHIEF CLASSES OF PROPER NAMES

I

THE compound names in which one element denotes some form of kindred consist of the three clearly distinguishable classes in which this element is אב (father), or אח (brother), or בן (son); of some at least of the names compounded with עם in the sense of "uncle," and of a few names compounded with חם (husband's father), and דָד or דוֹד (uncle).

1

NAMES COMPOUNDED WITH אב (FATHER)

A list of all names of this class found in the O.T. with particulars of the different persons by whom they are borne will be found in Appendix II. p. 277. Before proceeding to analyse their use it will be convenient to justify here certain admissions to and omissions from that list.

1. Lagarde[1] questions the inclusion in this class of many apparent instances on the ground that אבן = אב (cf. ابن) = בן. He bases this conclusion chiefly on the transliteration of the LXX. in certain cases, *e.g.*—

אבנר = 'Αβεννήρ.
אבשלום = 'Αβεσσαλώμ.
אבישי = 'Αβεσσαί.
אבישוע = 'Αβεσσουέ.

This is not convincing; for (1) the reduplicated ν and σ in these cases may quite as probably be due to euphonic as to etymological reasons; it is to be observed that this ν of the hypothetical אבן is only found where the second element of the word begins with ν or σ (in the latter becoming of course σ by assimilation); and (2) the reduplication in Greek may possibly represent a long vowel sound; cf. אלישע = 'Ελισσαιέ (LXX. Lucian); 'Ελασσά = אלה ש(מש)א:[2] in other words, 'Αβεννήρ may represent אֵבִינֵר as well as אֵבְנֵר. When in addition to this we find, judging from the clear instances, that the formation of names by prefixing בן was not common among the Hebrews,[3] we have good reasons for rejecting Lagarde's suggestion, and retaining the names in question in the present class.[4]

[1] *Bildung der Nomina*, p. 75.

[2] So Baethgen, *Beiträge*, 303; but De Vogüé, p. 50, with greater probability explains אלהשא = אלהנשא.

[3] See below, pp. 72 ff.

[4] A suggestion of Halévy's, unlike Lagarde's, would largely

2. אבי is read only in 2 K. xviii. 2; in the parallel passage, 2 Chr. xxix. 1, the same person is named אביה. I have preferred the reading in Kings for the following reasons:—(*a*) *as against* אביה, the versions in Kings all support אבי:[1] (*b*) in Chronicles, on the other hand, Origen's LXX. and the Vulg. alone support *MT* in reading אביה; the other versions are ambiguous, but the Syriac suggests אבי.

3. ישבאב (1 Chr. xxiv. 13 only) has been retained in the list with much hesitation. The versions cast great doubt on its genuineness, the Vulg. *Isbaab* alone approximating to *MT;* possibly LXX. A Ἰσβάαλ points to the true reading—אִישְׁבַּעַל. In any case it must be regarded as textually uncertain; it is unique in its formation among names containing אב.

4. יואב. This word is *probably* composite, in which case the second element is אב; for this probability, cf. the converse name אביה, and the parallel יואח, which can scarcely be anything but the converse

increase the number of compounds with אב. He explains (*R.E.J*, x. pp. 1 ff.) a number of names beginning with בְּ as mutilated forms of compounds with אב: thus בְּנָיִ = אבי־נוי ; בצלאל = אבי־צלאל. I am not convinced by Halévy's argument, and have not thought it safe to adopt his theory for my argument. He founds his theory in large part on the assumption that the names contain the name of the actual father, and this I show below to be improbable.

[1] Trg. and Vulg. directly support אבי; Syr. ܐܒܝ; LXX. Ἀβου, with variants in some MSS. Ἀβουθά, Ἀβούθ, *vide* Field's *Hexapla*, *i.l.*

of אחיה. We know of no root יאח. At the same time the *possibility* that יואב is a derivative from the root יאב should be kept in view.[1] In מואב, on the other hand, in spite of Gen. xix. 37 and the preceding narrative, we probably have a derivative and not a compound word.[2] Consequently יואב has been included in, מואב excluded from, the list of names compounded with אב.

5. אבים is probably not a genuinely different name from אביה which appears in the parallel passages.[3] It appears to be a scribal correction in Kings, where it occurs five times in a few consecutive verses (1 K. xiv. 31; xv. 1, 7 *bis*, 8). In Chronicles the name is always written אביה, as it appears still to have been in Kings when the early versions were made; for in each of the passages the LXX. reads 'Αβιού, Syr. ܐܒܝܐ. Consequently אבים has not been treated as a distinct name, but will be found under אביה.

6. אבי־עלבון (2 S. xxiii. 31) has been omitted, the name (אבאל) which appears in the parallel passage in Chronicles being given instead.[4] Against Wellhausen's suggestion that the original reading in both places was אבי־בעל, of which אביאל in Chronicles is an euphemistic correction, is the fact that Chronicles does not

[1] Cf. Nöldeke in *ZDMG*, 1888, p. 477.

[2] Cf. *TSK*, 1892, p. 573; Lagarde, *Bildung der Nomina*, p. 90.

[3] For a defence and explanation of the form אבים, cf. however Jastrow in *JBL*, xiii. (1894), p. 114.

[4] For the justification for this, *vide* Klostermann or Driver on 2 S. xxiii. 31.

appear to have been subjected to the revision which replaced בעל in proper names by אל.[1]

With the above exceptions the names given in the list clearly[2] contain the element אב, however uncertain in some cases the meaning of the whole name may be. If Lagarde's view of אבנר, etc., discussed above, be accepted, then the evidence for the inference drawn below is diminished; otherwise it will be found that the evidence for the inference is on the whole increased by a different estimate of the uncertain instances from that just made.

There are in all thirty-one[3] well-attested names of this class recorded in the O.T. Of these, three (שנאב, אבידע, אבימאל) occur only as names of foreigners, and four others (אביאסף, אביהוד,[4] אביטוב, and אבישור) are certainly or probably found only as names of families. The remaining twenty-four are borne by forty-one

[1] Geiger, *ZDMG*, 1862, p. 730.

[2] A few unimportant cases of textual or other uncertainty will be found noticed in the notes in the Appendix.

[3] The two forms אבירם and אברם (App. 18, 27) being counted as a single name. The number would be thirty-two, if the LXX. B preserves the true reading in 1 Chr. viii. 4; Ἀβεισάμας clearly implies אבישמש, a name which never occurs in *MT*. On the other hand אבישוע, read here by *MT* and LXX. A Luc. Syr., Vulg., occurs also in another connection in 1 Chr. v. 30, where *MT* has also the support of LXX. B.

[4] Wellhausen (*Gött. Nachrichten*, 1893, p. 480) suggests that אחוד is an abbreviation of this name; it is the name of a Benjamite individual of Per. I. (Judg. iii. 6), and of a Benjamite tribe (1 Chr. vii. 10).

Israelite individuals. The following table shows the chronological distribution of these names, and the nature of the evidence on which it rests. In this as in similar tables the first column (to the left) gives the number attested by the certainly pre-Exilic records, the second those attested by Chronicles but not by the certainly pre-Exilic writings, the third column those attested by P, and the fourth the totals:—

In Period I. persons bearing these names number	8 + 2[1] + 4	= 14
" II. " " "	15[2] + 4[3]	= 19
" III. " " "	6[4] + 1	= 7
" IV. " " "		1
		41

The one instance in Period IV. deserves notice. אביחיל, the name of Esther's father, occurs twice in *MT* (Esth. ii. 15, ix. 29), but in both passages the LXX. reads Ἀμειναδάβ, which is the regular LXX. equivalent in Samuel for אבינדב, and elsewhere for עמינדב. The instance is therefore textually uncertain. But even if the *MT* is correct, אביחיל is probably not an instance of this class freshly coined in this period.[5] Although

[1] One is textually doubtful. See App. 28 *c*, with footnote.

[2] Or 16, if ישי (= אישי) is an abbreviation of אבישי. So Wellhausen, *Bücher Sam.* p. 95.

[3] One of these is the uncertain ישבאב; see p. 24.

[4] In detail these occur as follows:—in tenth century, 2; in ninth century, 2; in eighth century, 1; in seventh century, 1.

[5] Similarly, if we accept the statement of Mt. i. 13, that Zerubbabel had a son named Abiud (contrast 1 Chr. iii. 19), we may infer from 1 Chr. viii. 3 that אביהוד though current was not newly coined after the Exile.

it is found only in P and Chronicles, yet it occurs once (1 Chr. ii. 29) in what Wellhausen regards as a pre-Exilic source,[1] and in the midst of names which I shall subsequently show to be of early origin. See p. 234; cf. also p. 238 on 1 Chr. v. 14, where the name also occurs.

With three exceptions[2] *all names*[3] *of the class borne by individuals in the O.T. are referred in the literature to a period as early as the Davidic.*[4] This fact, combined with the nature of the chronological distribution of the persons bearing names of the class, justifies the following conclusion:—

Names compounded with אב were freely formed in Israel down to the time of David; but the *formation* must have become obsolete long before the Exile. Old names of the class continued to be occasionally used, but even they fell into disuse by the close of the Exile. Briefly, the formation is an ancient one, which became extinct within the O.T. period.

In addition to the forty-one names of individuals

[1] *De Gentibus*, p. 23. A further instance of this class in Period IV. is furnished by אואל (Ezra x. 34), if, according to the alternative explanation of the *Oxf. Lex.*, it = אבואל; but this would certainly be an old name; cf. 1 S. ix. 1.

[2] The name just discussed, אחאב, borne by a king in the early part of the ninth century, and אבי, by a woman in the eighth.

[3] Of the twenty-five names in question we have the evidence of the early writings for twenty; and in the case of only five are we dependent on the later writings or P.

[4] See table in App. II. 1.

on which the above conclusion is based, names of this class occur in thirteen instances of what are certainly or probably clans or families. For the date of the conferment of these names we have thus only a *terminus ad quem*;[1] in the case of one—Abiezer, the name of a clan in the time of Gideon[2]—this must have been early. This instance thus adds directly to the evidence for the antiquity of the class. The remaining instances are found in P or certainly post-Exilic compilations. All, therefore, that we can say with certainty in these cases is that the names were given at some undefined period prior to the fifth or the third century as the case may be.[3] Clearly no argument can be drawn from these instances against the above conclusion. On the other hand, the less certain may fairly be judged by the more certain; and it may be considered *probable*, in the light of the above conclusion, that these names, and consequently the families bearing them, are pre-Exilic in origin. The degree of probability on this account can be better judged in the light of subsequent discussions. But

[1] Cf. above, p. 16 f.

[2] Judg. vi. 34.

[3] Assuming that we cannot assign P with certainty to an earlier period than the fifth, Chronicles to an earlier period than the third century. To any one who is prepared to accept a pre-Exilic date for P (in which one of these family names occurs), or for the sources of the Chronicler (who records most of the rest), the proof of the antiquity will be complete; he will not hesitate then to conclude that the two families mentioned in Ezra-Neh. derived their names from ancient times.

one or two other points in favour of a tolerably early origin of these families, and of the names as applied to them, may be noted here.

1. The *names* of five of these families, three Abiahs and two Joabs, are *unquestionably* ancient in origin; the only question is whether they may not have been *current* much later also. Three individuals named Abiah, and one named Joab, living in or before the tenth century, are mentioned in the early writings; no individual bearing either of these names is known to have lived at a later date.

2. Some of the rest, judged by analogy, are *probably* ancient; for the second element in some of these names is known to have entered into other names at an early period. Thus, corresponding to Abi*tub* we have Ahi*tub*, to Abi*shua*,[1] Eli*shua*, to Abi*hud*, Ammi*hud* (a Geshurite), all in Period II.[2]

If any of the names in 1 Chr. ii.-ix., classified in the appendix as chronologically uncertain, and treated just above as family names, should be considered personal, I would, at the present point, only observe that we have no reason for regarding the persons so

[1] For the great antiquity of אבישוע, and that probably as a Palestinian name, cf. Winckler, *Geschichte Israels*, p. 130 f.

[2] Perhaps we might further compare with אבישור, אחישָר, the name of a person living in the tenth century. Were the second parts of אבישור and אחישר originally different? Or is the difference one simply of punctuation? On אביחיל see above, p. 27; the only remaining name אביאסף has no close analogy to other early names.

named as belonging to a late period of the history. Subsequently I hope to show that these names of uncertain origin and character confirm the conclusion based on the names of individuals; meantime it must suffice to note that they in no way manifestly conflict with it.

With that conclusion, moreover, an examination of later post-biblical Jewish names finds nothing inconsistent, and is so far confirmatory. These post-biblical names give no new instance of the formation; further, with two or three exceptions no old names of this formation were even used by the later Jews. The only frequent name having similarity to those discussed in this section is אבא. This is frequently prefixed to another name as a kind of title;[1] Abba Saul, Abba José are well known Rabbis; but that it was also very often given as a name by itself we learn from the Talmud, where we read, "Some one said, I wish to see Abba: he received the answer, there are many Abbas here; he said, I want to see Abba bar Abba: he received the answer, there are also many Abba bar Abbas here: finally he said, I want to see Abba bar Abba, the father of Samuel."[2] But Abba is a simple, and not a compound name, and therefore essentially different from at least most of

[1] Cf. Mat. xxiii. 9; Schürer, *op. cit.* ii.[1] 316 (Germ. ed. ii. 258).

[2] Ber. (*Talm. Babli*) 18*b*, cited by Levy, *Neuhebr. und chald. Wörterbuch*, s.v. אבא.

the O.T. names, the only one with which it might be compared being אבי. In some cases [1] Abba is *joined* with the name to which it is prefixed, the result being a name apparently resembling the O.T. name; but the resemblance is only apparent.

The only other late Jewish names which are certainly or possibly identical with names in the O.T. are אבויה, אביי, and אחאב.[2] The first of these is probably the O.T. אביה, although Levy does not suggest this in his dictionary: if it is, we must account for it as being a case of naming a child after a famous man.[3] The second of the above names may be a variant form of the first,[4] or an Aramaic translation of נחמני,[5] in which case it may at once be dismissed from consideration here, or equivalent to *πατρίκιος*.[6] In the last case it belongs to a class, to which probably the third name given above also belongs, of names denoting some form of relationship. These are essentially different from names which combine a term denoting relationship with some other term to form a

[1] *E.g.*; אבמרי = אבאמרי; *vide* Levy, *s.v.* אבא. (In these and similar cases, to avoid unnecessary multiplication of references, I shall not cite the sources if they can readily be found in Levy, to whose work I have chiefly turned for information on these matters.)

[2] The last is only known through the Greek Ἀχίαβος, nephew of Herod; Jos. *Ant.* xvii. 7.

[3] See above, pp. 7 f. [4] Zunz, *Namen der Juden*, p. 22.

[5] Levy, *s.v.* אבי״.

[6] Nöldeke in *WZKM*, 1892, pp. 306 ff.

whole that does not denote relationship.[1] Of the really characteristic O.T. formation, I find therefore at most but one instance (אבויה) in use, and even that not in frequent use, among the later Jews. When we bear in mind the tendency to revive old names [2] this fact must be considered strongly confirmatory of the conclusion based on the chronological distribution of the names in the O.T.

I conclude this section with instances showing how widespread was this formation of proper names among the Semitic peoples.

The O.T. mentions the following foreigners with names of this class: אבידע a *Midianite*, אבימאל a *Joktanid*, אבימלך, king of *Gerar*, and שנאב, king of *Admah*, all referred to the earliest period, and the first three on the authority of the early writings. A-bi-mil-ki was king of Tyre in the fifteenth century B.C.[3] Abi-baal was father of Hiram, king of *Tyre*, in the tenth century B.C.[4] In *Assyria* names of this class are not uncommon.[5] These instances show that as in Israel so elsewhere the formation was an early one; but long after the Jews had discarded names be-

[1] See below, p. 83. [2] Zunz, *Namen der Juden*, pp. 22 ff.

[3] Index to Tell-el-Amarna Tablets (Brit. Mus.). Cf. also Abiṣarru (of Tyre?) cited by W. Max Müller, *Asien u. Europa*, p. 194.

[4] For other early Phoenician names of the class, see Schrader, *KAT*, gloss. *s.v.* אב.

[5] Schrader, *KAT*, p. 150; Friedr. Delitzsch, *Prolegomena*, p. 202; R. P. (New Series), iii. p. ix.

longing to it, they continued in frequent use among different Semitic peoples as we see from the (later) inscriptions. In the *Phoenician* inscriptions we find אבבעל,[1] אבחלל[2]; in the *Himyaritic*[3] inscriptions אבכרב, אבועלי, אבואד, אבידע and ידעאב; in the *Aramaic* אבסלי[4] (Egypt, 482 B.C.), כחשאב and [א]ברהם[5] (second or third century B.C.) and אביטב.[6] On the negative side, I may add that I have failed to find instances in the Palmyrene inscriptions, and Ledrain[7] certainly cites no names *beginning* with אב. In Arabic, as is well known, names with *Abu* prefixed are very numerous; but these are of an entirely different type, being formed from the name of the actual son of the bearer of the name. The argument that this is not the case in Hebrew will be found below, pp. 66 ff.

2.

Names compounded with אח (Brother)

The list of these names will be found in Appendix II. 2, pp. 279 f. Before proceeding to analyse the list, some uncertain instances must be referred to.

[1] *E.g. CIS*, 378, and very frequently.

[2] *JA*, 1883, p. 157. Less certain instances are אבקם read by Derenbourg three times in *Les Inscrip. Phéniciennes* (*Revue d'Assyriologie*, 1885), Nos. 1, 2, 46, but in the two former, at least, questionably according to *CIS*, i. 105, 106; and אבנבעל, on which, see p. 79.

[3] *CIS*, iv. 20, 24; 6; 69; *ZDMG*, 1873, p. 648.

[4] *CIS*, ii. 122.

[5] Both uncertain; *CIS*, ii. 120.

[6] *Ib.* 123.

[7] *Dict. des noms propres Palmyréniens.* Paris, 1887.

1. אֵחִי and אֲחִירָם. These two forms occur in two parallel lists—the former in Gen. xlvi. 21, the latter in Num. xxvi. 38. The same family appears to be intended by אחר, 1 Chr. vii. 12, and אחרח, 1 Chr. viii. 1. אחירם is the genuine name and is therefore given in the list; אחי is a mere corruption[1] and is therefore excluded from it.

2. אחין occurs only in 1 Chr. vii. 19. The versions differ as to the precise form. As in any case the name is not a compound, it may safely be dismissed from the discussion. For the significance of the form, if genuine, see p. 83.

[1] The proof of this is conclusive. (1) אחי occurs in a passage (Gen. xlvi. 21) which there is good reason for considering corrupt; for the LXX. suggests that several words have fallen out of the text; of the three consecutive names אחי וראש מפים none occur in any of the other Benjamite genealogies nor, indeed, elsewhere at all, and for the word אחי we have the variants אחים, Sam. T. and V.; Ἀγχείς, LXX. (2) On the other hand אחירם occurs in a passage free from suspicion of serious corruption and has itself the virtual support of all versions, the LXX. Ἰαχειράν (B), Ἀχιάν (F) being the most divergent, and (3) the text in Genesis can be explained by the known laws of textual corruption if the reading in Numbers is original, but the converse is not the case. Assuming the originality of the text in Numbers, the original text in Genesis ran אחירםשפופם, whence the present corrupt text in Genesis אחיוראשמפים arose by the following processes :—A wrong division of words, a repetition of י read the second time as ו, a confusion of ם with א and of פ with ם. For illustrations of these errors, see Driver, *Samuel*, pp. xxx. ff., lxx. f., and Reinke, *Die Veränderungen des hebr. Urtextes des A.T.* p. 62.

In the following instances the names are well attested in reference to certain persons and are therefore included in the list; but the reference of them to other people is due to textual corruption and therefore merely apparent. Thus

1. אחיה in three different connections is corrupt, viz., in 1 Chr. xi. 36, the correct text of which is preserved in 2 S. xxiii. 34;[1] in 1 Chr. xxvi. 20, where it is a corruption for אחיהם (LXX.);[2] and in 1 Chr. ii. 25, where it is a corruption of אחיו, a reading virtually supported by LXX. and Syr.[3]

2. אֲחִי, 1 Chr. v. 15, is a now unintelligible fragment of something that has fallen out, for the versions show extraordinary variations, and in *MT* אחי abruptly breaks the order of a list proceeding regularly from father to son.

3 אַחְיוֹ, in 1 Chr. viii. 14, is an error for אֶחָיו.[2] In 2 S. vi. 3, 4, the name is also open to some doubt; but on the whole the passage seems to require a proper name:[4] I have therefore retained it.

Difficulties are also connected with the application of the names Ahitub and Ahimelech, but these are exegetical and not critical. (1) Ahitub. The question arises—To how many different persons is it given? It appears as the name (*a*) of a grand-son of Eli,

[1] Driver, *Samuel*, p. 284. [2] Bertheau, *ad loc.*

[3] Wellhausen, *De Gentibus*, p. 15, footnote.

[4] Driver, *Samuel*, p. 204. On the text and etymology see, however, also Jastrow, *JBL*, xiii. (1894), p. 101.

1 S. xiv. 3; (*b*) a priest in the time of David, 1 S. xxii. 9; (*c*) the father of Zadok, 2 S. viii. 17; and (*d*) the father of Meraioth, Neh. xi. 11. Now (*c*) is probably = (*d*), a link having been added to the genealogical scheme in Nehemiah. Further, Wellhausen[1] identifies (*c*) with (*a*), and Bertheau[2] (*a*) with (*b*). I have therefore only taken account of one person of the name; but if a different view be taken, it will only strengthen the conclusion drawn below.

(2) Ahimelech. I take account of two persons only; but, again, if Wellhausen's view of 2 S. viii. 17 be not accepted, and we assume in consequence that there was a third person of the name, my conclusion is so far strengthened.

We find then twenty-six different names compounded with אח in the O.T.; of these five occur only as names of foreigners, or families, or in the ambiguous genealogies in Chr. i.-ix. The remaining twenty-one are borne by thirty-three Israelite individuals, the chronological distribution being thus:—

In Period I. persons bearing names of this class number				0+2+5=	7
,, II.	,,	,,	,,	11+2	=13
,, III.	,,	,,	,,	11+2	=13
,, IV.	,,	,,	,,		0
					33

Possibly to Period IV. we might assign אחימן: but (1) the name is doubtfully attested in the only

[1] Note on 2 S. viii. 17, in *Die Bücher Samuelis*.
[2] *Die Bücher der Chronik*, p. 57.

place where it occurs, 1 Chr. ix. 17—the versions, with the exception of the Vulg., not supporting *MT*—and is omitted from the parallel passage in Neh. xi. 19; and (2), even if the text be correct, it is probably a family name.

Of the eleven persons in Period III., most lived in the earlier half of the period, and six as early as the tenth century; five of them bear names which had been already current in Period II. The six fresh names make their appearance as follows:—Ahinadab and Ahishar in the tenth century, Ahab and Hiel in the ninth, Joah in the eighth and Ahikam in the seventh.

Thus, *with two exceptions*[1] *all*[2] *names of the class borne by Israelitish individuals have already appeared as early as the ninth century.* From this fact, combined with the chronological distribution of persons bearing the names, I conclude that—

Names compounded with אח, apparently having been in use from the earliest times among the Hebrews, were frequent in the time of David and his immediate successors; from that time fresh names of the class were less freely formed till perhaps as late as the seventh century, after which the *formation* became obsolete, and even the existing names fell almost, if not entirely, into disuse.

[1] Joah in the eighth and Ahikam in the seventh century.

[2] For the twenty-one names in question we have the evidence of the early writings for fifteen; of the remaining six, two are peculiar to P, one to Chr., and three are common to P and Chr.

I need not repeat, with reference to *family* names of this class, what was said in the last section;[1] it will be sufficient quite briefly to state their number and character. Of the ten families bearing names of this class, the only one which is certainly post-Exilic bears a name—Ahijah, Neh. x. 27—which is unquestionably ancient; a family, referred by P to Period I., bears a name (Ahiram, Num. xxvi. 38) which may very well have been in use in early times among the Hebrews, as it certainly was among their neighbours, and as the parallel name Abiram certainly was among themselves. The remaining eight family[2] names occur in 1 Chr. ii.-ix.; two are certainly ancient, Ahijah and Ahio; a third is Ahiram, which has just been referred to. The analogy of ʽAmmihud favours the antiquity of Ahihud; the remaining names are without significant analogies.

It will probably be admitted that here again there is nothing in these names of uncertain date and character to call in question the conclusion based on the names of definite date and character.

An examination of the post-biblical Jewish names has much the same result as in the case of the names compounded with אב. Several persons bear names denoting some form of kinship, such as אחא, אחאי, אחבי (= אחאבא), אחדבוי (= אחדאבא); but only one

[1] P. 28 ff.

[2] On the alternative to their being family names, see above, p. 30 f.

of the compound names continues in use, and this is Ahijah,[1] which existed as a family name in Period IV. Perhaps in a Sinaitic inscription we find one other trace of the revival at a late date of an old name of this class in Hiel, which Euting infers from the nature of the inscription to be a Jewish name.[2] Thus the one, or at best two instances, of the characteristic O.T. formation found in later times is no proof of the continued consciousness of the idea originally expressed by the name. We may safely conclude that these later Jews gave and received the name Ahijah simply on the ground of its biblical associations.

We have evidence, biblical and non-biblical, that names compounded with אח also were widely spread over the Semitic world; and from the inscriptions we see that they held their own to a later date among some other Semitic peoples than among the Hebrews. The early writings of the O.T. mention a Canaanite (13*a*)[3] in Period I., a Hittite (12*b*) and a Tyrian (21*b*) in Period II., and another Tyrian (21*c*) in the tenth century, with names of this class. Aḫimilki was king of Ashdod in the seventh century;[4] an earlier Aḫimiti[5] had been king of the same place. In Assyria

[1] "*N. pr.* mehrerer Personen in verschiedenen Zeiten," Levy, *s.v.* אחיה; cf. also *s.v.* חי״א.

[2] Euting, *Sin. Inschriften*, No. 370.

[3] The numbers refer to the place of the name in Appendix II. 2, where the references are given.

[4] *KAT*, 355.

[5] *Ib.* 162.

names of this formation were not infrequent: Friedr. Delitzsch[1] cites Aḫû-dûru, Aḫû-nûru, Aḫû-le'te. The element aḫi appears also very frequently in such Assyrian names as Sin-aḫi-irba, Marduk-nâdin-aḫ;[2] but these are quite dissimilar to the Hebrew names, "aḫ" in these cases clearly being the object of the verb, which it certainly is not in any of the existing Hebrew names.

In inscriptions which carry us down to later times we find the *Phoenician* names חמלך, חמלכת, חמנכת and חרם;[3] *Aramaic* אחלכד, אחוני;[4] *Himyaritic* אחכרב;[5] *Palmyrene* אחיתור.[6]

3.

Names Compounded with עם

The two groups of names already discussed are homogeneous to this extent, that there is no reason for believing that the elements אב and אח ever mean anything else than "father" and "brother" respectively.

[1] *Prolegomena*, p. 202; Ahi-nuri is the name of a Babylonian in the sixth century, *RP*², i. 160.

[2] *ZDMG*, 1872, 118-130.

[3] For references see Bloch, *Phoen. Glossar.* He also cites (but without adding an interpretation) חיתם from Derenbourg, *Les Inscrip. Phéniciennes* (*Revue d'Assyr.* 1885), No. 29. Derenbourg treats the name as a compound with אח, but the occurrence side by side with it of the fem. חיתמת suggests that both names may be derivatives and not compounds.

[4] *CIS*, ii. 93, 154.

[5] *Ib.* iv. 69.

[6] *PSBA*, viii. (1885) p. 29.

The only notable difference that has yet emerged is that between the names which as a whole define a relative, and those in which the term of relationship is merely a part in a whole which does not define a relative. Important questions as to the full and exact meaning of these names remain to be considered, but the treatment of them hitherto has been much facilitated by this general homogeneity. The names compounded with עם, which we shall next examine, are less numerous than the foregoing, but far more heterogeneous; the greater heterogeneity in formation and usage is certain, and it remains to be seen whether they are not correspondingly heterogeneous in meaning; this in itself is probable enough, for עם is a more ambiguous word than either אב or אח.

Instead of relegating these names to the Appendix, it will for several reasons be more convenient to present them here classified and annotated so far as is necessary to indicate the etymological or textual uncertainty of certain members of the class. Out of a total of about twenty names compounded with עם, six occur only as names of places; these are

יבלעם [1]	יָקְמְעָם	ירקעם [2]
יקדעם [2]	יקנעם	עֲמְעָד [2]

[1] Judg. i. 27; Jos. xvii. 11; 2 K. ix. 27; in 1 Chr. vi. 55 *MT* (but not LXX.) בלעם. Cf. also Egypt. transliteration Y-b-ra-ʿa-mu̥; W. Max Müller, *Asien u. Europa*, p. 195.

[2] These names each occur but once; the versions cast no

Another of these names (בן־עמי)[1] occurs only of a

serious doubt on the correctness of the forms, so far at least as the element עם is concerned; in the case of יקדעם and יקמעם the initial י also is certain. The LXX. forms are usually somewhat corrupt, but the only case where a different Hebrew word is suggested (Ἀμιὴλ for עמיאל) is no doubt the result of a Greek copyist's confusion of the similar letters Λ and Δ. In each case, therefore, we may safely argue from the *MT* form. (Throughout this section I shall cite references only for special purposes; in other cases they can easily be found by reference to the lexicons.)

[1] To the number of names used only of foreigners we ought to add עמיחור, if this form can be textually proved, and בלעם if it be a compound, not a simple word. Ammihur was a Geshurite contemporary of David (2 S. xiii. 37), and Balaam is the name of the well-known heathen prophet (Num. xxii. ff.); the latter is by a textual error given also as the name of a town (*vide* p. 42 n. 1). But עמיחור rests entirely on the authority of K'tib in the only passage where it occurs; K'ri and VV. read עמיהוד, a name which occurs more than once elsewhere; in favour of עמיחור is the fact that it is the rarer name and therefore the harder reading; against it, that it may have arisen under the influence of the ending of the next word but one following—גשור. As to בלעם; the hypothesis that the word is compound is *unnecessary;* it can be quite naturally explained as a derivative from the root בלע; cf. Stade, *Hebr. Grammatik*, § 293; and also Wellhausen (*De Gentibus*, p. 37) on the connection between the forms √, √+ י, √+ ָן, √+ ָם. The form בֶּלַע is a not infrequent name. If then we are to accept a derivation that treats the word as compound, a good case must be made out. Against the older view (*e.g.* Gesenius, *Thesaurus*) that בלעם = "not a people," it is unnecessary to argue at length; no names compounded with בַּל (= not) are known, and Hosea i. 9 is certainly not to the point here. More attractive is a derivation more

foreigner, and another (אניעם[1]) only in the genealogical lists in 1 Chr. (vii. 19).

This leaves about a dozen names of the class ascribed in the O.T. to Hebrew individuals, and of these, six[2] occur in the early writings, as follows:—

עמינדב[3] of 1 person in Period I.
עמיאל „ 1 „ „ II.

recently suggested (*e.g.* Neubauer, *Studia Biblica*, i. 226) that the component parts are בעל = בַּל and עם, the meaning being "'Am (a god) is lord." The *probability* of the correctness of this derivation depends, firstly, on proving the existence of a god 'Am; and, secondly, on establishing clear parallels *in early times* among *Canaanites and Hebrews* of the abbreviation of בעל into בל. I shall have occasion to discuss both these points below (pp. 52 f., 123). But in any case I see no good reason for preferring this derivation to the one given above. Eerdmans discovers עם also in מִלְכֹּם = מלך עם = 'Am is king: see his *Melekdienst*, p. 112, cited in Ges.-Buhl, *s.v.* מלכם.

[1] This name occurs only once, but *MT* is (virtually) supported by all VV. The current interpretation is "lamentation of the people"; I do not know that this is very probable. In spite of the present orthography, the word is perhaps a derivative from נעם; cf. Nab. אנעם, *CIS*, ii. 191, Ar. أَنْعَمُ.

[2] Or seven, if (see Wellhausen, *Isr. u. jüd. Gesch.* p. 24) עמשי (= 'Ammishai) is a parallel to אבישי.

[3] Ruth iv. 19. If Ruth be regarded as a post-Exilic work, עמינדב, which occurs elsewhere of this person only in Chronicles, should be struck out of the above list. But I see no reason to question the antiquity of this genealogy; cf. below, Ch. III.

אליעם[1]	of	2[2] persons	in Period	II.
יתרעם	„	1 person	„	II.
רחבעם	„	1 „	„	III. 10th cent.
ירבעם	„	2 persons	„	III. 10th and 8th cent.

On the authority of P we should add to the foregoing list of Hebrew names of individuals in עם[3]—

[1] Each of the two persons named Eliam is mentioned but once in *MT* (2 S. xi. 3 ; xxiii. 34). In 2 S. xi. 3, the Vg. alone of the versions supports *MT*, and, moreover, the same person in 1 Chr. iii. 5 is named עמיאל. In spite of this, *MT* in 2 S. xi. 3 is right. The Syr. and LXX. variants taken together support *MT* ; thus ܥܡܝܐܝܠ supports the last part, Ἐλιάβ the first part of the name read in *MT*. Each version has substituted a more familiar for an uncommon name. The variant in the parallel passage in Chr. *may* be due to the fact that the person in question actually possessed names of the two forms (cf. יהויכין and יכניה); but I am more inclined to think it is a scribal substitute for a name which, as applied to a man, would on any interpretation have a meaning repugnant to the later Jewish consciousness. Ammiel = people of God, on the other hand, could create no repugnance, though as the name of an individual it is of questionable suitability. In 2 S. xxiii. 34 the LXX only differs, and *MT* requires no further defence. The name אליעם occurs on a Phoenician inscription found in Sardinia—*CIS*, 147.

[2] One, perhaps, a foreigner ; in 2 S. xi. 3, Eliam is father of the wife of a Hittite.

[3] To the names cited from *P*, some would add a third, עמרם, regarding it as parallel to אברם, אחירם. This is possible, but far from certain. עמרם may be a derivative from the root עמר ; cf. Hebr. עמרי, Aram. עמרן (*CIS*, ii. 114), Ar. عامر, عمرو, عمر, عمران. Cf. p. 43, n. 1.

עמישדי borne by 1 person in Period I.
עמיהוד[1] „ 3 persons „

Another person mentioned in P bears the already familiar name of 'Ammiel.

Three further names of the class are found only in Chronicles :—

ישבעם[2] borne by 2[3] persons in Period II.
עמיזבד „ 1 person „ „
יָקְמְעָם[3] „ 1 „ „ „

Names of this class already referred to occur in Chr. of persons not mentioned elsewhere, as follows :—

Amminadab is the name of 2 persons, one in Period I. the other in Period II.
Ammiel is the name of 1 person in Period II.

[1] Probably this occurs in Samuel as the name of a *foreign* contemporary of David, p. 43.

[2] The name occurs in three passages only—1 Chr. xi. 11, xii. 6, xxvii. 2. In the first it is unquestionably an error for אישבעל—which is read by many MSS. of the LXX. ; see Driver on 2 Samuel xxiii. 8. I see no convincing reason for supposing that this error is other than accidental ; the name ישבעם may therefore be quite correctly read in the other two passages where the LXX. scarcely offers a real variant. If, indeed, with Bertheau (on 1 Chr. xi. 11) we identify the persons mentioned in 1 Chr. xi. 11 and xxvii. 2, we should have to correct the latter passage also ; but I see no ground for the identification.

[3] This name only occurs in 1 Chr. xxiii. 19, and xxiv. 23 ; in the former passage LXX. reads 'Ικεμιάς, in the latter 'Ιοκόμ (B), and 'Ικεμιά (A), thus suggesting יקמיה. But the other versions on the whole support *MT*.

I summarise the foregoing evidence in a table corresponding to those given in the preceding sections:

Period I.	Hebrew individuals bearing names in עם number			1 + 1 + 5	= 7
,, II.	,,	,,	,,	4 + 6	= 10
,, III.	,,	,,	,,	3 + 0	= 3
,, IV.	,,	,,	,,	...	= 0[1]
					20

This may be stated in the form of a conclusion thus:—

Names of individuals compounded with עם were formed in ancient times, but ceased to be (spontaneously) formed or used[2] as early as about the eighth century.

The antiquity of the formation is certain; the date of its obsolescence depends on the real origin of the names peculiar to P and Chr.; but it will probably be allowed that these doubtful names are either ancient, or, if post-Exilic, *artificial* formations.

It is, however, important to observe to how large an extent we depend on the late and uncertain writings for our knowledge of these names and their relative frequency; the following table shows the number and prevalence of names borne by *persons*

[1] Or one, if Amram be included in the class; see above, p. 45, n. 3. In any case the man of this name mentioned, Ezr. x. 34, may have owed his name to the custom discussed above, pp. 7 f.

[2] On Amram (Ezr. x. 34) see preceding note. Amram is also a frequent name among the Amoraim and Tannaim—*vide* סדר הדורות (Warsaw, 1889-1892), ii. 303. On the other hand there appears to be no good evidence in any single instance of a name certainly compounded with 'Am being current among the later Jews.

living at a definite period before the Exile, in אב, אח, and עם, and the kind of evidence on which they rest:—

	Names.				Persons.				
	Early Writings.	Chr. & P.		Total.	Early. Writings.	Chr.	P.		Total.
אב	19	5	=	24	29	7	4	=	40
אח	15	6	=	21	22	6	5	=	33
עם	6	5	=	11	8	7	5	=	20

The foregoing conclusion and comparisons are concerned only with names of individuals; but one of the heterogeneous features of names in עם as a whole is due to the fact that several of the names are names of towns. In contrast to this there is no single instance of a town name among compounds with either אב or אח. Moreover, five[1] out of the six names of towns belong to a formation, to which at most only one[2] of the fifty-seven names in אב and אח belongs.

This point brings us to the heterogeneity of formation in names compounded with עם; the following scheme will illustrate this, and at the same time also the extent of similarity and dissimilarity in this group of names to those in אב and אח. It takes no account of foreign names, and mentions or refers to town names only in brackets.[3]

[1] Another Palestinian town name of the same formation occurring frequently in Egyptian inscriptions is Ynu'm = ינועם (Meyer, *ZATW*, 1886, p. 7).

[2] The textually uncertain ישבאב, p. 24.

[3] The instances in עם in each class, the instances in אב and אח also in classes 2 and 3 are cited exhaustively.

1. עם is followed by a noun in עמיהוד, עמיאל, עמישדי, ? (עמעד [1]).
   אב " " " אביהוד, אביאל, etc.
   אח " " " אחיהוד, חיאל, etc.

To this formation the great majority of names in אב and אח conform.

2. עם is preceded by a noun in אליעם, אניעם,[2] יתרעם.[3]
   אב " " " אליאב, יואב, אחאב,[4] אהליאב.
   אח " " " יואח.[5]
3. עם is followed by a verb[6] in 3rd pf. in עמיזבד, עמינדב.
   אב " " " " אבירם, אבינדב, אביאסף, אבינן.
   אח " " " " אחירם, אחינדב, אחיסמך, אחיקם.[7]
4. עם is preceded by a verb in 3rd s. impf. in ישבעם, ירבעם, יקמעם (and five town names).
5. עם is preceded by a verb in 3rd s. pf. in רחבעם.

---

[1] I classify this here without in any way committing myself to the view that עד = eternity, or indeed that it is a noun at all.

[2] P. 44, n. 1.

[3] Probably to be classed here; compare the converse form in אב, אביתר. Meyer (*ZATW*, 1886, p. 7), however, classes it with ירבעם; cf. class 5 below.

[4] P. 32.

[5] The rarity of this class compared with the preceding and the peculiarity of the few instances are noticeable; of the eight instances, four have as their first element a divine name: on three of the rest, see the preceding notes; the remaining instance אהליאב is peculiar to P.

[6] Many of the instances of this class may rather belong to class 1. Thus עמינדב (and the parallels) may mean עם is generous. But the verbal character of the last element in at least one or two of the names seems clear, *e.g.* אחיקם.

[7] On אחישר, see p. 30, n. 2. אחבן and אחיאם scarcely belong to the class.

The last two classes are peculiar[1] to the names in עם; and these classes absorb four out of the thirteen personal names, or ten out of the whole group of nineteen. To render clear the greater heterogeneity and the peculiarity of these names, I add the following comparisons:—

13	personal	(or clan)	names	in עם	are	divided	into	5	formations.
26	"	"	"	אח	"	"		3	"
31	"	"	"	אב	"	"		3	"

In the personal and clan names of the three groups, the elements אב, אח, and עם are prefixed or postfixed as follows:—

	Prefixed.	Postfixed.
אבי . . .	25	6
אחי . . .	25	1
עם . . .	5	8

The first of these last tables might lead us to divine that עם is after all only in appearance a common element; and the second should prevent any hasty inference that as a class the names in עם are entirely analogous in significance to the names in אב and אח.

It remains to be seen how far the ambiguity of the word עם can be limited in the individual names containing it, and with what probability any can be classified among names containing a word of relationship

[1] Unless we include here ישבאב, but cf. p. 24.

The following meanings have been attributed to עם in some or all of the proper names containing it.

1. People.—So generally interpreted in all names till recently, and generally still in some.[1]
2. Kinsman.—The evidence for this meaning of the word in Hebrew briefly stated is—(1) the regular use of Ar. عَمّ in the sense "paternal uncle"; (2) phrases like נאסף אל עמיו; cf. the parallel נאסף אל אבותיו. This meaning is therefore secured to the word in Hebrew independently of the evidence of the proper names, and is now generally accepted.[2] In certain of the proper names also עם is now by many interpreted "kinsman."[3]

[1] *E.g. Oxf. Hebr. Lex.*, *s.v.* אחיעם; Meyer, *ZATW*, 1886, p. 7.

[2] Opinion differs as to whether the word means definitely "uncle" or not; but it is unnecessary to discuss the point here. A meaning at least as definite as kinsman, in contrast to the wider term, people, is claimed by Krenkel, *ZATW*, 1888, 280 ff.; Nöldeke, *ZDMG*, 1886, 172 f. (in criticism of R. Smith, *Kinship*, p. 58), cf. Wellhausen, *Gött. Nachrichten*, 1893, 480 f.; Driver, *Deuteronomy*, p. 384; Dillman, *Genesis*, p. 262; and in the new dictionaries of Gesenius-Buhl and Siegfried-Stade this meaning is definitely recognised.

[3] The possibility of this meaning in some names is admitted by Nestle, *Eigennamen*, 187 n. It is accepted by Krenkel (*l.c.*) for עמיאל, עמיהוד, עמינדב, עמרם, אליעם, and בן־עמי; and apparently by Buhl, for all names *beginning* with עם, see *Lex. s.vv.*; cf. also Siegfried-Stade, p. 523*a* (top). Grunwald (*Die Eigennamen des A.T.*, p. 46 f.) so explains the names just referred to, and also the six place names.

3. "'Am" or "'Ammi" is considered to be the proper name of a god.[1] For this, apart from proper names, we have this evidence: (1) "Emu" is the name given to the god Nergal by the Shuhites on the W. of the Euphrates;[2] (2) the same god may be mentioned in Num. xxii. 5, if the meaning really is Balak sent "to Pethor, which is by the River (*i.e.* Euphrates), to the land of the children of 'Ammo";[3] (3) the chief god of the Ḳataban

[1] Suggested in connection with the similar Himyaritic names (*vide infra*) so long ago as 1872 by Lenormant (*Lettres Assyriologiques*, 1st series, ii. 84); criticised by Praetorius, *Neue Beiträge zur Erklärung der himyarischen Inschriften*, p. 25. So far as I am aware the suggestion was first made with reference to Hebrew names by Derenbourg in *REJ*, ii. 123 f.; accepted by Neubauer, *Studia Biblica*, i. 225, and Sayce, *RP* (second series), iii. p. xi. Derenbourg only explains names beginning with עמי and also the name בן־עמי thus, apparently regarding the ' as a part of the (hypothetical) divine name; he says, "Le *yod* dans le composé Amminadab . . . ne peut être ni le pronom de la première personne, ni une lettre de liaison, comme dans Malkisedek et d'autres noms propres." Neubauer, however, also finds the divine name in Rehoboam, Jeroboam, and Balaam. As to the last two, at least, Sayce agrees with Neubauer.

[2] *Western Asia Inscriptions*, ii. 54, 65 (referred to by Sayce, *l.c.*).

[3] Cf. Sayce, *l.c.* The position of the "sons of Ammo" corresponds to that of the Shuhites who call Nergal "Emu." But the above translation is very much open to doubt. The reading of the VV. עמון need not be pressed; but on other grounds the text is doubtful, see Dillmann. Further, in

Arabs was called 'Amm.[1] This proves that the term 'amm had virtually become the proper name of a god among some peoples dwelling in districts somewhat remote from, though not out of communication with, Palestine; but there is no direct evidence that this had also happened in Palestine.

The chief reasons against taking עם in all these names in the most obvious sense of "people" is the difficulty of interpretation in certain cases — most apparent in אליעם,[2] but as names of individuals, also in other cases, *e.g.* עמיאל etc.—and the parallelism that exists between several of these names and those in אב, אח, and יה. From this parallelism have arisen the other two modes of interpretation,[3] between which in itself it is not decisive, as will be seen by the following comparative table. The asterisk denotes that the names in question occur (of Hebrews) only in writings of uncertain or late date, and brackets are used where the similar element is transposed:—

I.

יואל חִיאל אביאל עמיאל

a straightforward prose narrative, would the people be termed sons of its god?

[1] Hommel in *ZDMG*, 1895, p. 525, n. 1.

[2] The only interpretation (people's god) suggested in the *Oxf. Lex.* is most advisedly marked "?".

[3] Cf. on the one hand Krenkel, on the other Derenbourg and Neubauer, as cited above, pp. 51 f.

עמיהוד*	אביהוד*	אחיהוד*	(הודיה*)	
עמישדי*				
				Moabite
עמינדב	אבינדב	אחינדב	יהונדב	כמושנדב [1]
עמיזבד*			יהוזבד	
אליעם	אליאב		אליה	
יתרעם	(אביתר)			
אניעם*				
[עמרם*	אברם	אחירם	יהורם].	

II.

רחבעם		רחביה*	
ירבעם			ירבעל
ישבעם* ?	ישבאב [2]	(יהוישיב*)	
יקמעם*		יקמיה*	

In the formations common to עם, אב, and אח, the parallels in favour of עם denoting "kinsman," or being a divine name balance one another;[3] at first sight the

[1] Moabite king in eighth century. *KAT*, 288.

[2] Very uncertain, see p. 24.

[3] In consequence, the argument for a god "'Ammi" in the particular form which it assumes with Derenbourg, falls through. His argument can be summarised thus: in the name of Kemoshnadab, king of Moab, Kemosh is the proper name of the god of Moab; ∴ in Amminadab, king of Ammon, Ammi is the proper name of the god of Ammon. It will be clear from the above parallels that the same line of argument would make אבי and אחי *proper* names of a deity. Derenbourg's remaining argument is a little stronger, and based on the parallelism of Ben-ammi and Ben-hadad; but it is very questionable whether

parallels in the remaining names with names in יה appear to incline the balance in favour of עם being a divine name. But the balance of probability is at best very slight, and on other grounds it seems to me most likely that in the names parallel to names in אב and אח the element עם means "kinsman." For if we assume that "'Am" is a divine name in *all* the preceding instances, it follows that there must have been a very considerable cult in Israel of a god of whom we hear nothing, while on the other hand we find no instances whatever of Israelite names compounded with either Chemosh or Ashtoreth whom we are distinctly told the Israelites did at times worship.[1] The positive and main argument is, however, derived from the parallels in other languages, especially the Himyaritic.

In Himyaritic we have a whole series of proper names beginning with עם;[2] most if not all are followed by a verb in the pf.; this is a formation which is also

the original form of Ben-hadad contained the element "Ben" or the divine name "Hadad" (*vide* Winckler, *Alttest. Untersuchungen*, pp. 68 ff.); and further, was Ben-ammi ever really the name of a person? Moab at once lent itself to etymological sport; is not Ben-ammi merely an argument back from בני־עמון with a slight alteration of form to bring out the parallel to the author's conception of the meaning of Moab?

[1] 1 K. xi. 5-7.

[2] *E.g.* עמכרב *CIS*, iv. 73: עמאנס (man's name) *CIS*, 13—also the name of a god of the heathen Arabs, see Wellhausen, *Skizzen*, iii. 20 f.; עמצדק *CIS*, 37. For further examples, including those given above, *vide* Mordtmann in *ZDMG*, 1877, 87; and Praetorius, *ib.* 1872, 427; and *Neue Beiträge*, p. 25.

found, though somewhat infrequently, in Hebrew words compounded with עם, אב, and אח. But the significant feature of these names in Himyaritic is that they correspond in form to other Himyaritic names containing elements denoting kinship, viz. אב father, and חל [1] maternal uncle, thus, *e.g.*

עמכרב אבכרב חלכרב דדכרב (*CIS*, iv. 5)
עמאמר אבאמר חלאמר

The meaning "uncle" for עם in these Himyaritic names is so generally accepted that I need not argue the point afresh. In other languages also we find that compounds in עם exist side by side with names containing manifest terms of kinship. Phoenician names in אב and אח have already been cited above; we find also אלעם; [2] this name occurs in a Sardinian inscription; on other inscriptions [3] from the same island we find instances of names in אח. In the list of the so-called first Babylonian dynasty of eleven kings, most of whom bear Semitic though non-Babylonian names,[4] we find Ammi-Saduga (= עם-צדוק) and Ammi-Satana,[5]

[1] Halévy's explanation (*JA*, 1872, p. 533) of this word in proper names as = force (cf. Hebrew חיל) has met, I think, with no acceptance. [2] *CIS*, i. 147. [3] *Ib.*, 143, 149.

[4] *RP* (second series), iii. p. ix ff.; Winckler, *Geschichte Israels* (1895), 130; Hommel in *ZDMG*, 1895, pp. 524 ff.

[5] Both Sayce and Winckler find another name compounded with עם in this list in the name Ḥammurabi. But may not this rather be compounded with חם = husband's father? So far as the guttural is concerned, I suppose this is quite possible; for the reduplicated מ, perhaps *MT* חמואל preserves a real parallel

but also Abi-išu'a (= אבישוע), and Sumu-abi (שמו־אב).

Again, Schrader[1] quotes from inscriptions "in the districts of the middle Euphrates" (as instances of names of Canaanite type) Aḫiramu, Aḫijababa, and Ammiba'la.

I am not aware of any cases in which names in עם can be cited from any language or for any country without it being possible to cite parallel names in אב or אח or the like, except in the solitary case of Amminadab the Ammonite; this exception cannot be regarded as serious, since the number of Ammonite names which survive is so small.

In view therefore of the facts that עם signifies kinsman (and particularly "paternal uncle"), that names in עם closely correspond in several languages to names in אב, אח, etc., that in Himyaritic, where these names are particularly frequent, we have several parallel names compounded with חל = "maternal uncle," that the names exist in many districts where we have no independent evidence for the existence of a god with the proper name "'Am," and the improbability of the cult, even if it existed at all among the Hebrews,

(yet *vide infra*, p. 64). If this be correct, we should in this list of eleven have two names (Ḥammurabi and Abi-išu'a) containing elements denoting kinship, parallel to the names in "Amm." Sayce, however, thinks it probable that Ammi and Khammi in these names, as in some of the Hebrew names (*vide supra*), are names of a god.

[1] *KAT*, 110.

of a god manifestly of so little importance leaving its impress on so many Hebrew names, we may, it seems to me, conclude with some confidence that in Hebrew names compounded with עם and parallel in form to names compounded with אב or אח, עם signifies "kinsman." These names are עמינדב, עמיאל, אליעם, mentioned in the early writings; if early, עמישדי, עמיהוד, and עמיזבד, peculiar to the late and uncertain writings, but all referred to Periods I. or II., בן־עמי certainly and יתרעם possibly belong here also.

This still leaves eleven names for consideration. The five town names in which עם is preceded by an imperfect form a small group by themselves. We have no reason for interpreting the word in these names "kinsman":[1] quite the reverse; comparison with אב and אח names renders this interpretation unlikely, for in all probability the אב and אח classes afford no instance[2] of a formation in which the imperfect precedes, and certainly no instance of town names. In these names we have either the name of a god, or a reference to "people." But there is nothing in the names to necessitate the hypothesis of a god otherwise unknown in the districts where these towns are situated: it is true several town names are formed by an imperfect followed by אל, but, so far as I am aware, we have no instance of the proper name of a deity taking the place of אל in this formation. The inter-

[1] As Grunwald does, *Eigennamen*, p. 47.

[2] At most one instance; the very uncertain ישבאב, p. 24.

pretation of these names is difficult on account of the first as well as the second elements; but the safest starting-point is to assume that עם has here its usual significance, "people."

The three personal forms ירבעם, ישבעם, and רחבעם are difficult; Hebrew[1] analogy does not favour interpreting עם by "kinsman." Nor is it satisfactory to argue as to the first two from the probably far more ancient place names of similar form. It will subsequently[2] appear that Hebrew *personal* names in which a divine name is preceded by an imperfect are comparatively late formations; we do not find them in the early literature referred to a period earlier than the eighth century. In ירבעם of the ninth century, and ישבעם, if correctly attributed by the Chronicler to the tenth century, we ought not therefore to look for a divine name. "'Amm" as a divine name or in the sense "kinsman" being, according to analogy, unlikely, we retain the meaning "people" in these names also with confidence.

If a case could be made out independently for the god "'Amm"[3] we might well connect the name רחבעם

[1] Cf. the table (II.) p. 54. In Himyaritic we have at least one case of the pf. followed by אב, *e.g.* ירעאב (*ZDMG*, 1873, p. 648); but this ought not to weigh greatly with us in considering the Hebrew רחבעם. [2] Pp. 215 f.

[3] Even among the Ammonites, for Rehoboam's mother was an Ammonite, 1 K. xiv. 21; cf. Neubauer, *op. cit.* p. 225. Neubauer also suggests the possibility of Jeroboam being a foreigner, *e.g.* a Nabataean.

with his (cf. רחביה, a name, however, peculiar to Chronicles). But this is unnecessary; it is certainly probable enough that Solomon recorded the national prosperity of his time in naming his son "The people is enlarged."[1] The only two names that now remain are אניעם and עמעד;[2] these still appear to me obscure, for the *place* name עמעד, the *personal* Phoenician name אבעד (cf. Is. ix. 5) is an analogy that scarcely justifies an inference.[3]

4.

Names compounded with דד or חם .

In any case these names are few in number; with reference to most of them there is also room for difference of opinion as to the interpretation of the elements in question.

The word דד is used in the larger sense of "loved one," but also in the more restricted sense of "uncle" as *e.g.* in 2 K. xxiv. 17. In Syriac the sense *patruus* exists, and also that of *avunculus*.

The sense "uncle" is accepted in the corresponding names דדכרב[4] (Himyaritic) and דדעלה[5] (Aramaic) by

[1] For the phrase, cf. a similar one Is. liv. 2; Dt. xxxiii. 20.

[2] P. 44, n. 1; p. 49, n. 1.

[3] Cf., however, Grunwald, *Eigennamen*, p. 47.

[4] *CIS*, iv. 5.

[5] *Ib.*, ii. 107. Cf. 110 if the name is there rightly deciphered דדבי.

the editors of *CIS*. The former of these corresponds to a series of names containing a term of kinship.[1]

In the light of this established use of the word דד and these Semitic parallels I will briefly review the few possible instances Hebrew affords.

(1) אלדד.[2] The interpretation "a kinsman (uncle) is God" is rendered probable by the parallels אליעם, אליאב.

An alternative interpretation is "God has loved";[3] this is not quite free from objection. The Semitic verb "to love" is ودّ, Sab. ודד: this is well attested in Hebrew by the derivatives ידיד and ידידת as well as by several proper names. But neither Hebrew, Syriac, nor Arabic possesses a verb medial waw in this sense. Another interpretation[4] is "Dad is God"—a name similar to Elijah = Yah is God—Dad being a form of the name of the Syrian god Hadad.[5] Much of what has been urged against "'Amm" being a divine name in Hebrew holds good in this case also.

[1] P. 56.

[2] *MT* (also LXX.) punctuates the second syllable with kametz; if the interpretation suggested be correct, this should be changed to ḥolem.

[3] So *Oxf. Lex.*, *s.v.* where Himyaritic ודדאל is cited as parallel. Muller, however, in his comparison of Hebrew and Himyaritic names compares only ידדיה, and not אלדד, with ודדאל; *ZDMG*, 1883, p. 15. But cf. Nöldeke, *ZDMG*, 1888, p. 479.

[4] Neubauer, *Studia Biblica*, i. 226.

[5] *RP*², i. 109, n. 2.

Of the three interpretations just mentioned, the first appears to me most probable. The name occurs of

(*a*) a prophet in Period I. Num. xi. 26 (JE),

(*b*) in the form אלידד of a Benjamite prince in Period I. Num. xxxiv. 21 (P).

(2) דודיה. Here also the sense "kinsman" seems to me likely in view of the parallels אביה, אחיה. The usual interpretation (Yah's beloved) adopts the wider sense of the word.

The name occurs in one passage only (2 Chr. xx. 37),[1] where it designates a man of the ninth century.

(3) מידד, if really a compound, might perhaps be compared with אחומי; or, if the original form was מודד (cf. LXX. Μωδάδ), with מואב. But it is, in either case, quite as likely a simple derivative from the root ידד.[2] The name occurs only in Num. xi. 26 f. (JE) of a prophet in Period I.

(4) בלדד occurs only as the name of the Shuhite in the book of Job. In this name also דד pro-

[1] Present Hebrew text דודוהו; but the above form is unquestionably the true one; note LXX. (Lucian) Δουδιου: cf. Nestle, *Eigennamen*, p. 70.

[2] Cf. Nestle in *TSK*, 1892, 573, and König, *Hebr. Sprache*, ii. p. 485, on the orthography.

bably signifies uncle,[1] if, as is usually assumed, the first part of the word = Bel. It would then be a parallel form to אלדד, and to בלעם, if the latter word is really compound.

(5) אשדוד is probably a derivative from שדד;[2] in any case there are no analogous forms in אב, אח, etc.

Apparently therefore compounds with דד (= uncle) are a rare parallel formation in Hebrew, as in Himyaritic and Aramaic, to the names in אב, אח, and עם; like these latter, names in דד are ancient and early became obsolete.[3]

Combinations with חם = father-in-law are rarer still, but Hebrew furnishes one fairly certain example, and possibly one or two more. In Himyaritic also the word enters into proper names, as *e.g.* in the frequently recurring חמעתת.[4]

The clearest instance in Hebrew is חמוטל—the

[1] For other interpretations, cf. under אלדד above, p. 61.

[2] Stade, *Hebr. Gram.* § 258.

[3] In Syriac these names have a later history, the two compounds with Jesus (Dadh-īsho and Ishō-dadh) being frequent. The sense "uncle" can scarcely have been consciously retained here: either the more general sense "beloved" is implied, or the names are formed to some extent mechanically according to an established scheme. For a similar phenomenon in Greek, *vide* Bechtel and Fick, *Griech. Personennamen*, p. vii. f.

[4] *CIS*, iv. 12, with references. Renan (*REJ*, v. 175) also cites the above and other Himyaritic names as parallels to the Hebrew; but connects the element חם with the sense to protect.

name of a queen-mother of the seventh century—parallel to אביטל. We probably have a parallel to the series אביאל, חיאל, עמיאל in חמואל; *MT*, it is true, dagheshes the מ in the only place where the name occurs; but the LXX. reads Ἀμουήλ. *Possibly* a parallel to אבידן lies concealed in חֶמְדָּן[1] which might be read חֲמִדָן; this last is, however, an Edomite name.[2]

5.

Names Compounded with בן or בת

Exclusive of instances, such as ben-Jesse—used of David several times in Samuel—and ben-Remaliah,[3] which consist of prefixing *ben* to the name of the father of the person mentioned, probably as an indica-

[1] Gen. xxxvi. 26: at 1 Chr. i. 41 חמרן—through confusion of ר and ד.

[2] There are no clear instances of אם, "mother," in compounds. The most probable is אחיאָם, the name of one of David's heroes, which would be exactly parallel to אחאב. Halévy (*REJ*, x. p. 6) thinks that אֵם lies concealed also in מואב, מרים, אבים (if textually established), and possibly also in מיכל and אבימאל (="father of the mother of God"), with which last compare Him. אבמעתתר and Nab. חביאמה = brother of the father of his mother. Wellhausen (*Isr. u. jüd. Gesch.*, p. 24) suggests that אִמִּינון (so pointed: cf. 2 S. xiii. 20) = my mother is the serpent. The *hap. leg.* שִׁמְאָם [xiii. 20] 1 Chr. ix. 38, might be an instance (cf. Sumu-Abi, p. 57); but the VV do not support the ם. In the parallel passage *MT* has שמאה—also a difficult form, for there is no root שמא.

[3] Is. vii. 4.

tion of contempt,[1] these names number,[2] apparently, sixteen. I classify [3] them at once as follows:—

Foreign.	Tribal and Clan.	Personal.
בן־הדד	בן־זחת	בן־אבינדב
בן־עמי	בן־חנן	בן־גבר
בת־שבע [4] ?	בנימין	בן־דקר
בתשוע	ראובן	בן־חור
בתיה		בן־חסד

Besides the fourteen foregoing we have בן־אוני and בן־הנם which will be discussed more particularly below.

In formation, it will be seen, this group of names is homogeneous, but for the one name ראובן; all the rest are formed by prefixing בן to a substantive. This in itself throws some doubt on the old interpretation of Reuben, "See ye! a son," which in another respect leaves the name without analogy; for, although some few cases exist in which a verb in the imperative *singular*, addressed to God, enters into compound

[1] Gesenius, *Isaiah*, i. 278 f.

[2] Excluding (1) לבן חיל 2 Chr. xvii. 7, which is a textual error; read with LXX. and Syriac לְבְנֵי חיל; (2) בניני, also a textual error; see Ryle on Neh. x. 11.

[3] With the exception of Ben-hadad, the name of three or more probably only two (Winckler, *A.T. Untersuchungen*, p. 62) Syrian kings, and Benjamin, the name of the tribe, a clan (1 Chr. vii. 10), and two contemporaries of Ezra (Ezra x. 32; Neh. iii. 23), each of the above names is used of but one person or clan; it is therefore unnecessary to cite references.

[4] Probably to be classed as foreign, since it is the name of the wife of a Hittite (2 S. xi. 3).

names,[1] there are none in which the imperative *plural* is so used. Olshausen[2] cites two simple names as consisting of an imp. pl., but even these are certainly capable of another explanation. The etymology of Reuben is very obscure;[3] but the connection with בן = a son, is most improbable.

The exact significance of the remaining fifteen names is not always clear; but there is good reason for believing that the Ben is used metaphorically, in other words that the names do not, as in the case of the frequent Arabic names in Ibn, contain the name of the father; Ben-deker, *e.g.*, does not imply that the father's name was Deker. It is true in several cases the second elements in these words occur independently as proper names of individual men or clans, viz., Hur, Abinadab, Geber, Hanan, Zoheth, Sheba, and Shua; but that is because these names in themselves express much the same idea; thus a child might equally well be called "Hero," or "son of a hero" (Geber or Ben-geber). The instance in which it

1 שובאל, אליפלהו; names similar in form to these are not infrequent in Assyrian; see Schrader in *ZDMG*, 1872, pp. 125 f.

2 *Hebr. Sprache*, 277 *g*; the names cited are עירו, רעו.

3 Probably the word is not compound; cf. Baethgen, *Beiträge*, p. 159; *CIS*, iv. 37[5] note. If Josephus (Ρούβηλος) and Syr. (ܪܘܒܝܠ) really preserve a more original form of the word, Lagarde's bold suggestion (*Onomastica Sacra*, II. 95) that it is = راابل, a broken plural of the form עֲרֹעֵר, اصابع, and means "lions," appears to me rather more probable than that the name is compounded with בעל.

seems most likely that the name of the actual father appears is Ben-abinadab, and in view of the connection in which the name occurs, even this instance is uncertain. The positive reasons for interpreting "son," "daughter," figuratively are these:—

1. In some cases the names *cannot* contain the name of the actual father, since this is known to have been different from that implied in the compound name. This can be proved of some of the O.T. names; the father of Bath-sheba was not Sheba, but Eliam; the father of Bithiah was Pharaoh. Any one who regards the patriarchal stories as historical may recall here also Benjamin (and Ben-oni) and Ben-ammi. Ben-hadad I. is son of Tab-rimmon; the later Ben-hadad is son of Hazael.[1] We have, it is true, Bath-shua the daughter of Shua; but this looks like a name which was simply constructed by the Chronicler on the basis of the early narrative.[2] In Genesis we read of "a daughter of a certain Canaanite whose name was Shua"; the Chronicler abbreviates this into "Bath-shua the Canaanitess." May not the circumlocution of the

[1] References for the foregoing 2 S. xi. 3; 1 Chr. iv. 18; Gen. xxxv. 18, xix. 38; 1 K. xv. 18; 2 K. xiii. 3. No great stress must be laid on the cases of the Ben-hadads on account of the uncertainty of the name (*vide infra*); although at least they prove that to the Hebrews it was quite natural to prefix Ben to something other than the name of the father; so far also the narratives of the births of Benjamin and Ben-ammi are clearly to the point here, however we regard them historically.

[2] Gen. xxxviii. 2; 1 Chr. ii. 3.

earlier writer be due to the fact that he does not wish to imply that the woman's actual name was Bath-shua? In the remaining cases we know nothing independently of the fathers of the people in question; whatever we think of the case of Bath-shua, therefore, we ought to conclude that it is more likely that in unknown cases the compounds do not contain the name of the father, than that they do. Further numerous instances might be cited from the inscriptions to show that the parallel names of cognate peoples are not compounded with the name of the actual father; most important, as being most contemporaneous with the O.T. names, is an instance in the Zinjerli inscriptions; the father of *Bar*-rekûb is Panammu.[1]

2. In several parallel foreign names[2] the second

[1] D. H. Müller, *Die altsem. Inschriften von Sendschirli* (Vienna, 1893), p. 6. Other instances where the names are manifestly not compounded with the name of the father will be found in *e.g.* *CIS*, i. (Phoenician) 47, 69, 93, 727; these are בן־חדש, the name of a man, and בתנעם, בתשלם, and בתבעל, names of women. It is possible that בן־מלקרת in a Phoenician inscription from Cyprus, published by Rev. G. A. Cooke in the *Academy* (January 16, 1896), is another man's name of the type; cf. my letter on the point in the *Academy* of February 1, p. 100. See also *CIS*, ii. 185 (Nabataean); De Vogüé, 29, 73, 84 (where compare also the note; Palmyrene). Cf. also the name Bar-Hebraeus where the second element is not the *proper* name of the father; Wright, *Syriac Lit.* pp. 265 f.

[2] *E.g.* ברנבו, De Vogüé, 73 (Palmyrene, 114 A.D.); בתבעל, *CIS*, i. 727, and frequently; ברעתא, *TSBA*, vi. 438 (where further

element is the name of a god; within the O.T. Ben-hadad and Bithiah may be instances of this.

3. The frequency of idiomatic phrases in which בן is used metaphorically, and some of which are quite parallel to Hebrew or other names of the class. It will be sufficient to recall a few instances; with בן חיל = "valorous," compare the proper name בן־גבר; with בן הכות = "worthy of being smitten," the proper name בן דקר; with terms of age expressed by means of בן, the somewhat similar combination found in a very frequent Phoenician proper name—בן חדש = "born on the new moon."[1] In certain Aramaic names this idiomatic use of בר is clearly recognised.[2]

These names, then, are probably[3] as homogeneous in the character of the ideas they express as they are in

instances are cited). Cf. further *CIS*, ii. 185 n.: Robertson Smith, *Kinship*, 206, 220; *Rel. Sem.*[2] 45. If, as seems probable, ברקוס (Ezra ii. 53) = "son of the god Kos" (for whom cf. Baethgen, *Beiträge*, pp. 11, 108; or *KAT*, 150), the name is clearly of foreign (Aramaic) origin, though attaching to a family of Hebrews (Nethinim).

[1] For Syriac parallels (*e.g.* Bar-Ṣaumā = "born in Lent"), cf. Wright in *PSBA*, ix. 48.

[2] Acts iv. 36.

[3] The new *Oxf. Lex.* still finds in some of these names the name of the father, thus בן־חור = "son of Chur." Such interpretations ought at least to be queried. Others are no doubt correctly interpreted, *e.g.* בן־חסד (= "son of mercy"); but why not in these cases add a reference back to the section of the article בן giving its idiomatic usage? Curiously enough בת־שוע is interpreted (with a query) "daughter of opulence."

outward form; that is to say after the removal from the original list of the etymologically uncertain Reuben and the possibly fictitious Bath-shua. Even now, however, the distribution of these names is peculiar; four are foreign, three tribal, five (or, including Ben-oni and Ben-hinnom, seven) are personal; but the five personal names are all contained in a single list of Solomon's officers. Before considering this last peculiar feature, it will be best to examine more carefully the foreign and tribal names.

Some uncertainty attaches to most of the foreign names. Ben-hadad is quite probably merely an erroneous Hebrew translation[1] of Bir-'idri in which Bir is a divine name and 'idri = Hebrew עזר: then compare אליעזר. I have myself raised a question as to the reality of בן־עמי; it may be a purely artificial form rather than a genuine Ammonite name. The foreign origin of Bath-sheba is only probable. Bath-shua the Canaanitess has been omitted as being fictitious (as a proper name) or as being exceptionally compounded with the name of the father. Bithiah remains the only tolerably certain instance of names of this class in O.T. belonging to persons directly stated or implied to be foreigners. Yet there can be no doubt that this class of names was in use among the neighbouring peoples; from the Zinjerli Inscription

[1] Winckler, as cited p. 65 n. 3; De Vogüé (*CIS*, ii. p. 186) also proposes an interpretation (Hadad has built) that would remove בן־הדד from this class.

(of the ninth century B.C.) I have already cited Bar-rekûb; it also contains the similar name Bar-ṣûr. From other inscriptions—mostly, it is true, much later—and from Syriac literature, a great number of instances might be cited.[1] Whatever may have been the case earlier, in later times the formation was peculiarly prevalent in Aramaic.

I pass to the tribal names. Benjamin is derived from a pre-historic period of the Hebrews; we can attach what weight we please to his connection with the *Syrian* Rachel. Clearly Ben-oni must be treated in connection with Benjamin. But had the name ever a real existence as the name of a child? If we accept the narrative (Gen. xxxv. 18) at all, then we must remember that the name was conferred by the *Syrian* Rachel. But it is probably a mere after-growth of the legend that the birth of Benjamin cost Rachel her life; for when once this legend became current, Benjamin must have appeared a singularly inappropriate name. The name subsequently appears as that of two individuals in the fifth century; they may very probably have been named after the patriarch, since the custom of naming after famous men certainly began about this time.[2] A Benjamite clan

[1] See the references cited above, p. 68, notes 1 and 2. Add Wright, *Syriac. Lit.* (Index, *s.v.* Bar), or, more fully, Payne Smith, *Thesaurus*, *s.v.* ܒܪ.

[2] Pp. 7 f. with references: add Reuss, *Geschichte der Heiligen Schriften* (*A.T.*), 2nd edit., p. 505.

is also named Benjamin. The remaining two clan names—Ben-zoḥeth and Ben-ḥanan—both occur in the genealogy of the Hezronites, a very mixed people with many foreign (*e.g.* Midianite and Edomite) affinities.[1]

Hitherto we have found no good evidence that names of this class were created by the Hebrews or even borne by Hebrew individuals in any historical period; and yet we have already considered all but six of this kind of names found in O.T. One even of these six is of unknown origin; for we cannot be sure that בן־הנם was a man's name, since we only find it in the name of the valley of Ben-hinnom. The etymology of הנם is obscure, but בן־הנם may very well be simply an adjectival phrase; this hypothesis can account, by the analogy of well-established Hebrew idiom, for the different forms of the name of the valley, thus

with	גיא בן ה׳	cf.	קרן בן שמן	Is. v. 1
„	גיא הנם	„	איש דברים	
„	גיא בני הנם	„	בני מות	1 S. xxvi. 16.

But if this explanation be rejected[2] and Ben-hinnom regarded as a man's name, we do not know when he lived—it must have been as early as the seventh century—or whether he was Hebrew or foreigner.

[1] Wellhausen, *De Gentibus*, p. 37.

[2] It has been accepted by many, *e.g.* Graf. *Der Prophet Jeremia*, p. 128.

We are now in a position to notice the great peculiarity of the fact that all names of the class borne by individuals[1] in historical times not stated or implied to be foreigners occur in a list of Solomon's officers. This list consists of only twelve names; it can scarcely be by a mere accident that five out of twelve officers of Solomon have names of a class otherwise unknown in connection with Hebrew individuals of historical times. But the cause of the peculiarity is obscure; and considering the paucity of the data at our command, any explanation must be offered with diffidence. But may not this peculiarity in the names be due to the fact that some or all of these victualling officers were *foreigners?* The reasons in favour of this may be briefly summed up thus:—

1. If these five persons were Israelites, it remains inexplicable that out of a particular list of twelve officers of Solomon, five bear names of a class unknown among the far more numerous names of the time of David,[2] or again of the later kings.

2. It is known that David had foreigners among his officers, *e.g.* Ittai the Gittite, Uriah the Hittite, the Cherethites and Pelethites.

3. The great extension of territory under David and Solomon must have brought many foreigners into notice.

[1] Except the two post-Exilic Benjamins, on whom *vide* p. 71.

[2] The persons mentioned in 1 K. iv. belong to a later generation than David; cf. verses 11, 15, and Thenius on 1 K. iv. 7-19.

4. The particular duties of these officers must have been unpopular—cf. the (later, Deuteronomic) account of a king, 1 S. viii. 11 ff.—and may well have been entrusted to foreigners rather than Hebrews.

5. There is only one distinctively Hebrew name in the list—יהושפט.[1]

6. This form of name is known to have been in use among the surrounding peoples.[2]

One thing at all events is clear — names compounded with בן were never frequent, even if they existed at all, among the Hebrews, and were never coined after the ninth century.

This conclusion is scarcely affected even if we include in this class certain names beginning with ב supposed to be an abbreviation of בן. The suggestion does not appear to me probable.[3] But I note that of the seven names cited in the *Oxford Lexicon* (*s.v.* בן) as having been interpreted "son of . . ." three[4] are names of foreigners, another—Baana[5]—is the name

[1] But on this point too much stress must not be laid; we find only nine out of forty-five Hebrew names mentioned in 2 S. ix.-xx. containing יה. Cf. below, p. 185.

[2] Cf. above, pp. 70 f.

[3] Cf. also Halévy, *REJ*, x. p. 2.

[4] בעלים, an Ammonite; בשלם, a Persian; ברשע, king of Gomorrah. In the last as in ברע have we names compounded with בר = Bir in Bir-ʿidri? Cf. p. 70. With ברשע we might then compare אלישע or אֲבִישַׁע.

[5] With this should be compared the Nabataean בענו, *CIS*, ii. 220.

of two more of Solomon's victualling officers; while the rest[1] are applied to quite, or comparatively, unknown but probably Hebrew families or persons.

As I have suggested above (p. 23) the distribution of the clear instances of names in בן is against Lagarde's suggestion that Absalom, Abner, Abishai, and Abishua contain בן in the form of אבן (= son).

An important question common to all the foregoing groups of names remains to be discussed—In what relation do the two elements in these compounds stand to one another, are they related as construct and genitive, or as subject and predicate? The answer to the question considerably affects the interpretation of the names.

So far as mere form goes אבי in אבימלך, to take a single instance, may be either the construct case or the nominative with the suffix of the first person or the simple nominative, the yod being in this last case a binding vowel as in *e.g.* אסרי לגפן, Gen. xlix. 11.[2]

[1] ברקר, בלשן, בבהל, mentioned only as follows:—2 K. ix. 25; Ezr. ii. 2 = Neh. vii. 7; 1 Chr. vii. 33.

[2] Not indeed a very decisive instance, since אסרי might be regarded as a cstr. before the preposition. But with the exception of cases such as these the "binding vowel" occurs only in the construct (Stade, *Hebr. Gram.* § 343). Still it may reasonably be assumed that if the old case ending tended to be preserved

Gesenius in the *Thesaurus* treated the first element as a construct, and did not hesitate to interpret Abiah as meaning "father of Yah," or the name of the *woman* Ahinoam as "brother of pleasantness." This interpretation is still approved by Nöldeke.[1] The Dutch scholar De Jong, author of a careful and elaborate examination of these names,[2] treats the names from the same *grammatical* standpoint, but regards the second element in the words with אב, etc., prefixed as being, except in the cases mentioned below (pp. 81 ff.),

by the close association of cstr. and gen., it would tend still more to be preserved by the yet closer association of a compound word.

[1] *ZDMG*, 1888, 480, 484. Similarly Robertson Smith in the second edition of *Rel. Sem.* (p. 45, n. 2), who appears to have abandoned the view advocated in the first edition (Abi-baal = my father is Baal) on a reconsideration of the Phoenician *woman's* name אמאשמן; in the first edition he accepted the suggestion (see Bloch's *Glossar*, *s.v.* אמעשתרת) that this might be an abbreviation for אמת אשמן = handmaid of (the god) Eshmun, and not therefore = mother (אם) of E. The difficulty presented by this Phoenician name must be admitted; but it appears to me slight as compared with those arising if we assume that in these names generally the prefix is construct. Robertson Smith's explanation is based on the assumption (shown above to be unjustifiable) that names were hereditary in the *early* history of the Semitic peoples. Moore (*Judges*, p. 236) also accepts the interpretation Abimelech = Father of (the god) Melech.

[2] *Over de met* ab ach *enz. zamengestelde Hebr. Eigennamen* in the *Versl. en Mededeelingen der Kon. Akad. van Wettenschappen*; 2de Reeks, 10de Deel, pp. 54-68 (Amsterdam, 1880).

the name of the actual kinsman. Ewald[1] assumes the same origin for אב in these compounds, but supposes that subsequently it was prefixed to any name as a kind of honorific title for a firstborn or favourite child. Then for the mere purpose of multiplying names other prefixes were employed, such as aḥi-, ḥamu-, ish-.

There are certain objections to taking אבי, etc., as constructs in these names, at least in all of them, which hold therefore against all the explanations mentioned in the last paragraph. There are other objections peculiar to one or more explanations in question. I will deal with the common objections first.

The words אב, אח, עם, דוד, חם, all denote a *male* relative, but the proper names compounded with them are used indifferently of men and women; on the other hand nouns with בן (son) prefixed are used exclusively of men, in the corresponding names of women the corresponding feminine word בת (daughter) replaces בן. The natural inference is that in the case of בן (בת) names, the particle connotative of kindred refers to the person bearing the name, and that in the names compounded with אב, etc., it does not; in other words בן (בת) is construct in such names as בן־חסד = "son of mercy," בת־שבע = "daughter of an oath," but אבי, etc., are not; and, *e.g.*, אביגיל does *not* mean "father of joy." Unless strong reasons to the contrary can be brought forward, the above inference should be held conclusive. As a matter of fact the reasons for accept-

[1] *Hebr. Sprache*, 273 *b*.

ing אבי, etc., as constructs are not strong. Nöldeke claims that the Phoenician אחתמלך is decisive in favour of the genitive relation in the Hebrew names אחימלך, אחיה, etc., and inferentially also in אבימלך, etc. As a matter of fact the Phoenician name in question is decisive only for Phoenician names in אחי and אחת, while a fuller examination of all the related classes of Phoenician names only strengthens the argument stated above. For in Phoenician we find that in names with אח or אחת prefixed, names of women *always*[1] contain the feminine, names of men *always* the masculine term of relation; on the other hand compounds with אב in Phoenician, as in Hebrew, are used indifferently of men and women.[2] The right conclusion here also is that in the former case the term of relation (אח or אחת) is construct, and consequently refers to the bearer of the name, that in the latter the term of relation (אב) is in the nominative and does not refer to the bearer

[1] The statement is based on an examination of the names in Bloch's *Phoen. Glossar.* The following complete list of names in אח, abbreviated ח, are all names of *men*—חיתם, חמלך (very frequent, *e.g. CIS*, i. 602 f., 691, in addition to Bloch's references), חמלכת (even more frequent than preceding; additional references, *e.g. CIS*, i. 489, 492, 496, 504 f.), חמלר (?), חמנכת (?), and חרם. The following complete list of names in אחת, abbreviated חת, are *all* names of *women*—אחתמלך, חתמלך, חתמלכת (add *CIS*, i. 677), חתמלקרת, חתנת, חתלת (add *CIS*, i. 646). If really a compound with אח, חיתמת (cited above, p. 41 n. 3), the name of a woman would be an exception. But its isolation in this respect is rather an additional reason for treating it as a derivative name.

[2] אבבעל is frequently the name of a woman.

of the name. The case is clear enough without pressing the evidence of the Phoenician name אבנבעל = our father is Baal; this would be very conclusive if we could be sure of the name, but the editors of the Corpus consider it a lapidary error for the common אדנבעל.[1]

A further common objection to all explanations which treat אבי, etc., as construct is suggested by the converse names אליאב, יואח, etc. Gesenius, it is true, does suggest that אליאב = *Deus patris*, but gives as an alternative meaning (*cui*) *Deus pater;* under יואח he gives only an interpretation parallel to the latter (*cuius*) *frater Jehova* (*est*). Surely אליאב stands to אביאל as אליה to יואל; in the latter case the genitive relation is out of the question, inferentially it is equally so in the former. Even apart from the parallel with אליה and יואל, it is surely most reasonable to treat the two names אליאב and אביאל as similarly constructed, unless there are good grounds for the contrary.

Another serious difficulty in the interpretation of Gesenius, ratified by Nöldeke, is the use of Abu-, Aḫi-, etc., that is presupposed by it. The use of Abu- with a noun denoting a quality to describe one who possesses the quality is a pure Arabism, as Gesenius admits;[2] he rejects the only Hebrew instance apart from the proper names which had been suggested, viz. אבי־עד in Is. ix. 5. Such a marked Arabism ought not to be lightly admitted; it would, if real, be all the more

[1] *CIS*, i. 476. [2] *Thesaurus*, s.v. אב, § 7.

remarkable because, of the two words which serve similar idiomatic functions in Hebrew, בן combines with very few words to form proper names denoting the possessor of a quality, and בעל with none.

The meaning thus obtained in a word like אביה (father of Yah) is unlikely; for it can scarcely be weakened down as Gesenius suggests into "*vir divinus, ut videtur, e.g.* איש אלהים." But on this I lay little stress; we ought from the proper names to learn Hebrew or Semitic methods of thought rather than to argue against certain interpretations from what we suppose those thoughts to have been. Still it is worth while to bear in mind such parallel forms as מלכיה, מלכיצדק, אליה; if the relation in these is not genitival, why should it be so in אביה, etc.?

In spite, therefore, of the weighty authority in favour of interpretations such as Abiah = father of Yah, Abinoam = father of pleasantness, I have no hesitation in rejecting them. Nor is the view that these names contain the name of the actual kinsman more acceptable; it is indeed free from the idiomatic objection discussed above, but is equally open to the other objections, which are quite sufficient in themselves to invalidate it. But De Jong's careful discussion deserves an equally careful reply. I therefore draw attention to one or two further points.

It is easy to over-estimate the importance of the fact which both De Jong and Ewald make their starting-point, viz. that in many cases the second element in these names occurs independently as a proper name —*e.g.* Ram, Nadab. For out of thirty-eight words to which either Ab or Aḥ is prefixed to form proper names, only thirteen[1] occur independently as names of persons, and of these several are compounded with יה or אל as well as with אב or אח, and yet no one surely would suggest that we are on that account to interpret the names Eliezer, Jonadab, as meaning "the God of Ezer," "Yah of Nadab," and so forth. But have we then any sound reason left for considering the elements in Abiezer, Abinadab to be genitively related, while in Eliezer, Jonadab they are predicatively related?

The real test of a theory that would explain all the names in אב, אח, etc., as consisting of a construct and a genitive is afforded by the names of women, and those which contain a divine name. In both cases De Jong is driven to resources of despair. Women received such names as Ahinoam = "brother of pleasantness," because, though at first these names had been conferred on *male* relatives only, they had long become hereditary and consequently meaningless. This involves several hypotheses; and the hypothesis that among the early Hebrews names were frequently

[1] It is scarcely necessary to enumerate. I have included נֹעַם, though independently we have only names differently pronounced, *e.g.* נַעַם, and ישַׁי, though the second part of אבישַׁי may quite as probably be שַׁי, which does not occur as a proper name.

hereditary, is not only groundless but against the evidence.[1] The explanation offered—very tentatively, it is only right to say—of אביה and the like is that as the need for new names increased the divine names were added to Ab, Aḥ simply to constitute fresh names, and without it being intended that the names should convey any particular meaning.[2] It is unnecessary to argue against this at length; two remarks may suffice. There is nothing to show that the names Abiel, Abijah were the latest formations of the class, and it is strange that the divine names should have been used to create mere meaningless symbols when such a wealth of names of men was left unused. It is a curious but not unimportant fact that very few names popular in early times are found as the second element in these early compound names.

In the great majority of cases some or all of the foregoing objections hold against the construct relation

[1] De Jong speaks (p. 63) of "de bekende erfelijkheid der namen in de Semietische familien"; but I have shown above (pp. 4 ff.) that this inheritance of names was, at least among the Hebrews, probably also among other Semitic peoples, a comparatively late custom—a custom that only came into existence after names in Ab and Aḥ had ceased to be used.

[2] I think I have correctly represented De Jong's view of the case; but I give the more important sentences in his own words: "Om nu in de behoefte aan nieuwe nomina propria te voorzien, werden, naar mijne vorstelling, deze elementen [viz. אל, יה] tot naamsvorming gebezijd" (p. 67). "Dat bij eene dergelijke zamenstelling geene beteekenis in deze eigennamen gezocht moet worden, spreekt van zelf" (p. 68).

in compounds with אב, etc.; in the names in בן and בת, on the other hand, the relation is invariably construct. The only exceptions among the names in אב, etc., are אחאב, אבי, and perhaps אחבן and אחיאם. The first of these names probably means "brother of a father," *i.e.* "uncle"; the second "my father"; the third and fourth, if pointed, אֶחִיבָן, אֶחִיאָם may mean respectively "brother" and "maternal uncle,"[1] just as דָוִד (David, originally דוד, cf. Renan, *REJ*, v. 168) and דודו may mean respectively "paternal uncle" and "his paternal uncle." Unlikely as these meanings must at first sight seem, they are supported by very considerable Semitic analogy. In a Nabataean inscription (B.C. 31) a person is called בנית, *i.e.* "little daughter"; אחא = "the brother" was a very frequent name among both Jews and Christians in the early centuries A.D.; another common Aramaic name is Abba = "the father." In Palmyrene we find both the terms for uncle—דדא and חלא—used as proper names.[2]

[1] Cf. the textually uncertain אַחְיָן = "fraternal."

[2] The above examples are taken from Nöldeke's article in *WZKM*, 1892, pp. 306 ff., where many others will be found to which still more might be added (see *ZDMG*, 1895, p. 720); cf. also Robertson Smith, *Kinship*, p. 157; Halévy in *REJ*, x. 6 f.; and Wellhausen in *Gött. Gelehrte Nach.* 1893, p. 447 (חנה *perhaps* = "wife"). The name אחילוד is a further Hebrew example, if it means "child's brother," an interpretation cited in the new *Oxf. Lex.* from the *Thesaurus* with the addition of a well-advised query. The explanation of אחבן ("brother of an intelligent one") should at least have been queried also: if the

The separation from the whole classes of this little group of names united to one another, but distinguished from the rest in point both of formation and general significance, somewhat strengthens the argument for the early obsolescence of other compound names in אב, אח, etc.; אבי and אחאב were two of the small number of names which could not be traced up to Davidic times, and the latter was one of those still used by the later Jews.[1]

In all the other names the relation between the two parts is that of subject and predicate, the predicate most generally being a noun. This noun is in several cases an abstract noun, but the construction so arising is perfectly idiomatic; thus אבשלום (the father is peace) is a sentence exactly parallel to אני־שלום in Ps. cxx. 7.[2]

The only general ambiguity which still remains and which has divided interpreters is the force of the yod which occurs in most of the forms: Is it the first person singular suffix,[3] or is it merely an old ending retained[4]

Massoretic pointing be correct, it means rather "the brother has given heed" (for form cf. אחיקם, and for meaning אבירע).

[1] P. 32.

[2] See further, Driver, *Tenses*, § 189, 2.

[3] So Olshausen, *Hebr. Sprache*, § 277 *e*, *h*; cf. also König, *Hebr. Sprache*, ii. 418, who considers the yod in some names the personal suffix, in others the old genitive ending—the word in the latter case being construct.

[4] So in some cases Nestle, *Eigennamen*, p. 182; Baethgen, *Beiträge*, p. 156.

—as so often in the construct case—in consequence of the close connection, due in this case to word composition, with the next word?

Several points favour the latter alternative, viz. the forms where the yod does not occur, *e.g.* אברם, אבשלום, which are found alongside of אבירם and אבישלום, the forms in which the old ending ו occur (*e.g.* אבוגיל, 1 S. xxv. 18, Kt.), the parallel names in which the two elements change places, such as אביאל and אליאב. To these linguistic reasons we may add another of a different kind, at least in the case of names like אביה, אחיאל; in these names the analogy of names such as ירמיה, יחזקיה suggests an utterance respecting Yah or El as he is towards all his worshippers rather than a merely personal utterance.[1] But if in these particular cases the *yod* is not suffixal, there is no reason for supposing it to be so in others, especially if it be admitted[2] that in the other names God is referred to under the title Ab, etc.

In favour of the yod being the first personal suffix is the fact that except in proper names the old genitive ending only occurs in the construct and not the absolute case. I have already indicated my reasons for not treating this as cogent. The only other reason that I am aware of might be found in the analogy of the Phoenician אבנבעל (= "our father is Baal"), which is however an isolated instance, and perhaps merely an error.[3] The balance thus inclines in favour of

[1] For this last reason I have to thank Prof. Cheyne.

[2] Cf. below, p. 254. [3] P. 79.

interpreting the names—The, or a, father is God, a light, generous, etc.

I have now determined the chronological distribution of these classes of names, their interrelations, and their general significance; other interesting questions connected with them can only be satisfactorily discussed in connection with the history of groups still to be considered.

II

Animal Names

The exact number of names included in this class, it is difficult to state; for in several cases etymological uncertainty still reigns. But if different forms of the same animal name, *e.g.* דישון and דִּישָׁן, be reckoned as single instances, the number amounts to about fifty, and the different persons, towns, etc., called by one of this class of names to about a hundred.

Simon in his *Onomasticon* devotes a section to the discussion "de nominibus animalium quae nomina propria faciunt." His list, while far from complete, includes names which have no good claim to be there. This is not surprising in a work written a century and a half ago. Fortunately attention has been drawn afresh to this subject by the late Prof. Robertson Smith in his article "Animal Worship and Animal Tribes among the Arabs and in the Old Testament,"[1] and more in-

[1] *J. Ph.* ix. pp. 75-100.

cidentally in his later works.[1] By adding to the genuine instances cited by Simon those which Robertson Smith has established, and some other real instances,[2] I hope I have succeeded in obtaining a comparatively complete and accurate list; but where some uncertainty is inevitable, it is important that it should be clearly realised. Before proceeding to argue with regard to these names, I give the list with brief indications of the justification for the inclusion of the several names in it, and of their diverse applications.

I classify in the first instance all those proper names which are identical with, or closely related in form to, words actually occurring in the O.T. to designate animals. I will then add those the inclusion of which is justified by the evidence of the cognate languages. On the basis of these the argument will rest; and then, finally, some doubtful instances which have been cited by various writers will be discussed in their bearing on the conclusions reached.

[1] *Kinship and Marriage in Early Arabia* (1885), and *The Religion of the Semites* (1st ed. 1889, 2nd ed. 1894).

[2] Though I have found it necessary to differ from him in some respects, I have throughout this section been much indebted to Nöldeke's important review of Robertson Smith's *Kinship* in *ZDMG*, 1886, pp. 148-187. A careful criticism of the article on "Animal and Plant Names" will be found in Jacobs' *Studies in Biblical Archaeology* (1894). It has been a great satisfaction to me to find myself in several points in agreement with Mr. Jacobs, though I may add that my conclusions were reached before becoming acquainted with Mr. Jacobs' essay.

Where the appellative is identical in form with the proper name I simply give the word once and its English equivalent; where the appellative differs, I cite it before the English equivalent. The names are the following:—

1. אַיָּה, vulture.
   - *a.* Horite, Gen. xxxvi. 24.
   - *b.* (Rizpah bath) Aiah, 2 S. xxi. 7

2. אַיָּלוֹן ; cf. אַיָּל, stag.
   - *a.* Amorite town, Judg. i. 35.[1]
   - *b.* Town in Zebulon,[2] Judg. xii. 12.

3. הָאַרְיֵה ; cf. אַרְיֵה, lion.
   A man of the eighth century, 2 K. xv. 25.[3]

4. בֶּכֶר (*a*, *b*) and בִּכְרִי (*c*); cf. בִּכְרֵי (cstr. pl.), young camels, Is. lx. 6.
   - *a.* Ephraimite family, Num. xxvi. 35 (P).
   - *b.* "Son" of Benjamin, Gen. xlvi. 21 (P).
   - *c.* Sheba ben Bichri, 2 S. xx. 1.

5. גְּמַלִּי ; cf. גָּמָל, pl. גְּמַלִּים, camel.
   Ammiel ben Gemalli, Num. xiii. 12 (P).

[1] The place here mentioned is probably identical with that mentioned in Jos. x. 12; 1 Chr. vi. 54, viii. 13; cf. Riehm's *Handwörterbuch*, and *New Oxf. Lex.*, *s.v.*; otherwise Jacobs (p. 101), who gives in all four towns of this name.

[2] Doubtful, for the LXX. (B and Luc. Αἰλώμ, A Αἰλών) suggests אֵילֹן, *i.e.* the name of the town is identical with that of the judge; cf. Moore, *Judges*, p. 311.

[3] The name occurs only here, and here the text is doubtful; cf. Kautzsch, *Die Heilige Schrift des A. T.* p. 410, and *New Oxf. Lex.*, *s.v.*

6. גְּדִי—עֵין גֶּדִי, kid.
Place on Dead Sea, Ezek. xlvii. 10.

7. דְּבוֹרָה, bee.
a. Rachel's nurse, Gen. xxxv. 8 (JE).
b. Prophetess, thirteenth to twelfth century, Judg. v. 15.

8. דִּישׁוֹן (*a*, *b*) and דִּישָׁן (*c*), a clean animal (Dt. xiv. 5), perhaps the mountain goat.
a. Horite, Gen. xxxvi. 20.
b. Horite, Gen. xxxvi. 25.
c. Horite, Gen. xxxvi. 20.

9. בֵּית דָּגוֹן; cf. דָּג, fish.[1]
a. Place in Judah, Jos. xv. 41 (P).
b. Place in Asher, Jos. xix. 27 (P).

10. זְאֵב, wolf.
Midianite prince, Judg. vii. 25.

11. זִמְרָן (*a*) and זִמְרִי (*b-f*); cf. זֶמֶר (Pausal), mountain sheep, Dt. xiv. 5.
a. "Son" of Keturah, Gen. xxv. 2 (J).
b. Captain, tenth century, 1 K. xvi. 9.
c. Simeonite, Num. xxv. 14 (P).
d. "Son" of Zerah, 1 Chr. ii. 6.[2]
e. Descendant of Saul, 1 Chr. viii. 36.
f. Nation, Jer. xxv. 25.

12. חָגָב, חֲגָבָה, חֲגָבָא, locust.

[1] The connection of דגון with דג, fish, is questionable: see the literature cited in *New Oxf. Lex.*, *s.v.* דָּגוֹן.

[2] In the parallel passage Josh. vii. 1 *MT* reads זַבְדִּי; but LXX. (except Luc. in Jos.) in both Jos. and Chr., reading Ζαμβρεί, supports זִמְרִי.

Family (or families) of Nethinim, Ezra ii. 45 f.; Neh. vii. 48.

13. חֵזִיר;[1] cf. חֲזִיר, swine.
a. Levite family, 1 Chr. xxiv. 15.
b. "Chief of the people," Neh. x. 21.

14. חֻלְדָּה; cf. חֹלֶד,[2] weasel.
Prophetess, in seventh century, 2 K. xxii. 14.

15. חֲמוֹר, ass.
Father of Shechem, Gen. xxxiii. 19 (JE); cf. Judg. ix. 28.

16. חֻמְטָה; cf. חֹמֶט,[3] a kind of lizard, Lev. xi. 30.
Town in Judah, Jos. xv. 54 (P).

17. טְלָאִים, lambs.
Town,[4] 1 S. xv. 4.

18. יוֹנָה, dove.
Prophet, eighth century, 2 K. xiv. 25.

19. יָעֵל (*a*), יַעֲלָה (*b*), יַעְלָם[5] (*c*); cf. יְעֵלִים m. pl. and יַעֲלַת cstr. s. f., mountain goat.

[1] For this punctuation, *vide* Stade, *Hebr. Gram.* 210 *b*, 1; or for another explanation, Nöldeke, *ZDMG*, 1886, p. 162.

[2] The feminine form is appellative in Mishna; *vide* Buxtorf's *Chaldee Lexicon*, *s.v.* חלדא.

[3] Cf. Trg. חֻמְטָא, and cf. Buxtorf, *s.v.*

[4] If טֶלֶם (Jos. xv. 24) be identical with טלאים—so Kimchi, cf. Ges., *s.v.*, Driver on 1 S. xv. 4, and most—then Telaim lies in the Negeb of Judah. A porter of the time of Ezra (Ezra x. 24) has the name of טֶלֶם; but this, like טַלְמֹן, also the name of post-Exilic individuals, is more probably connected with Aram. טלם = "to oppress."

[5] Possibly not connected with יעל (in which case strike out *c* above), for יָעֵל corresponds to Ar. وعل, cf. LXX. Ἰαήλ; but

a. Kenite woman, Judg. iv. 17.
b. Family of "Solomon's servants," Ezra ii. 56.
?*c.* Edomite, Gen. xxxvi. 5.

20. בֵּית כַּר and כְּרָן; cf. כַּר, lamb.
a. Philistine town, 1 S. vii. 11.
b. Horite, Gen. xxxvi. 26.

21. כָּלֵב;[1] cf. כֶּלֶב, dog.
a. Spy, Num. xiii. 30 (JE).
b. "Son" of Hezron, 1 Chr. ii. 18 (cp. and ct. ii. 50).

22. לְבָאוֹת (בֵּית);[2] cf. לָבִיא, lion.
Simeonite town, Jos. xv. 32 (P).

23. לַיִשׁ, lion.
a. Palti ben Laish, 1 S. xxv. 44.
b. Town in N. Israel, Judg. xviii. 27.
c. Town N. of Jerusalem, Is. x. 30.

24. נָחָשׁ (*a-c*) and נַחְשׁוֹן (*d*), serpent.
a. Ammonite king, 1 S. xi. 1.
b. Ammonite, Shobi ben Nahash, 2 S. xvii. 27.
c. Ir-Nahash, city in Judah, 1 Chr. iv. 12.
d.[3] Prince of Judah, Num. i. 7 (cf. Ruth iv. 20).

the LXX. 'Ιεγλόμ suggests that the ע in יעלם is = Ar. غ. This favours the reference of יַעְלָם in Ges. *Thesaurus*, *s.v.* יעל to the root עלם = غلم.

[1] The identity of the forms כָּלֵב and כְּלֻב is defended by W. Robertson Smith (*J. Ph.* ix. 89). Nöldeke's criticism (*ZDMG*, 1886, 164, n. 1) renders the identification precarious though not impossible. Cf. No. 25 with note.

[2] The form with בית occurs in Jos. xix. 6, for which 1 Chr. iv. 31 reads בית בראי.

[3] We have not another real Nahash in 2 S. xvii. 25, for the phrase בת נחש is a textual corruption; *vide* Wellhausen, *ad loc.*

25. בית נִמְרָה ; cf. נָמֵר,[1] leopard.
Place in Gad, Num. xxxii. 36 (JE).

26. חצר סוּסָה [2] and סוּסִי (*b*); cf. סוּס, f. cstr. סוּסָתִי, horse.

a. Place in Simeon, Jos. xix. 5 (P).
b. Manassite family, Num. xiii. 11[3] (P).

27. עֶגְלָה (*a*), עֶגְלוֹן (*b* and *d*), עֵין עֶגְלַיִם (*c*); cf. עֵגֶל, עֶגְלָה, calf.

a. Wife of David, 2 S. iii. 5.
b. King of Moab, Judg. iii. 12.
c. Place on Dead Sea, Ezek. xlvii. 10.
d. Town in Shephelah, Jos. xv. 39 (P).

28. עֵפֶר (*a-c*), עָפְרָה (*d-f*), עֶפְרוֹן (*g-i*);[4] cf. עֹפֶר,[5] young gazelle.

a. Midianite, Gen. xxv. 4 (J).
b. Judahite, 1 Chr. iv. 17.

Against the identity of *a* and *b*, *vide* Thenius on 2 S. xvii. 27. Perhaps we should add to proper names meaning serpent that of נחשתא, a queen-mother of the seventh century, 2 K. xxiv. 8.

[1] Arabic has in the sense of "leopard" both نَمِر = נָמֵר and نِمْر = נֶמֶר, the regular feminine of which would be נִמְרָה; cf. also Syr. ܢܶܡܪܳܐ.

[2] In 1 Chr. iv. 31 חצר סוסים, the form supported by the LXX. in Jos. xix. 5 also.

[3] In this passage, where alone the name occurs, the name is textually suspicious; cf. Nestle, *Eigennamen*, p. 203.

[4] If the text in Mic. i. 10 is correct (which is doubtful, *vide* Stade and Siegfried, *Wörterbuch*, *s.v.*), we must add בֵּית לְעַפְרָה, a town in the south; on the etymology, cf. G. A. Smith, *The Twelve Prophets*, p. 384.

[5] Cf. also Ar. غُفْر = עֹפֶר.

c. Manassite, 1 Chr. v. 24.
d. Town in Manasseh, Judg. vi. 11.
e. Town in Benjamin, Jos. xviii. 23 (P).
f. Judahite, 1 Chr. iv. 14.
g. Hittite, Gen. xxiii. 8 (P).
h. Mountain in Judah, Jos. xv. 9 (P).
i.[1] Place, 2 Chr. xiii. 19.

29. עַכְבּוֹר ; cf. עַכְבָּר, mouse.
a. Edomite, Gen. xxxvi. 38.
b. Contemporary of Josiah,[2] 2 K. xxii. 12.

30. עֹרֵב, raven.
Midianite prince, Judg. vii. 25.

31. עֲרָד ; cf. עָרוֹד, pl. Aram. עֲרָדַיָּא (Dan. v. 21), wild ass.
a. Town in the Negeb, Judg. i. 16.
b.[3] Benjamite, 1 Chr. viii. 15.

32. עֵיטָם ; cf. עַיִט, bird of prey.
a. Town in Judah, 2 Chr. xi. 6.
b.[4] Town in Simeon, 1 Chr. iv. 32.

33. עַקְרַבִּים, scorpions.
Mountains near Dead Sea, Num. xxxiv. 4 (P).

34. הַפָּרָה, cow.
Town in Benjamin, Jos. xviii. 23 (P).

[1] According to Bertheau on 2 Chr. xiii. 19, *h* = *i*; or Siegf.-Stade perhaps = *d*.

[2] Riehm's *Handwörterbuch* identifies this person with the father of Elnathan (Jer. xxxvi. 12). Jacobs distinguishes them.

[3] Jacobs also connects עירד (Gen. iv. 18) with ערוד. Cf. Dillmann on the passage.

[4] Bertheau on 1 Chr. iv. 32 makes *a* = *b*; Ges.-Buhl, on the other hand, distinguishes three places of the name—in addition to the two given above, also the rock Etam (Judg. xv. 8).

35. צִבְיָה (*a*) and צִבְיָא (*b*); cf. צְבִי, f. צְבִיָּה,[1] gazelle.
a. Queen-mother, ninth century, 2 K. xii. 2.
b. Benjamite, 1 Chr. viii. 9.

36. צִפּוֹר (*a*) and צִפֹּרָה (*b*), sparrow.
a. Moabite, Balak ben Zippor, Num. xxii. 2 (E).
b. Midianite wife of Moses, Ex. ii. 21 (E).

37. צָרְעָה; cf. צִרְעָה, hornet.
Town in Shephelah, Judg. xiii. 2.

38. פִּרְאָם; cf. פֶּרֶא, wild ass.
Canaanite king, Jos. x. 3 (JE).

39. פַּרְעֹשׁ, flea.
Post-Exilic family, Neh. x. 15.

40. רָחֵל, ewe.
Wife of Jacob, Gen. xxix. 6 (J).

41. הַשְּׂעִירָתָה; cf. שְׂעִירָה,[2] goat.
Place E. of Jordan (?), Judg. iii. 26.

42. שׁוּעָל (*a*), חֲצַר שׁ׳ (*b*), and ארץ שׁ׳ (*c*), fox.
a. Asherite, 1 Chr. vii. 36.
b. Town in Simeon, Jos. xv. 28 (P).
c. District in Benjamin, 1 S. xiii. 17.

43. שָׁפָן, rock-badger.
a. Contemporary of Josiah, 2 K. xxii. 3.
b.[3] Jaazaniah ben Shaphan, Ezek. viii. 11.

[1] On the relation of the forms צִבְיָה and צְבִיָּה to one another, *vide* Stade, *Hebr. Gram.* 192 *b*.

[2] The ground form as seen in the Masc. is שָׂעִיר; in spite of the variation in punctuation, שֵׂעִיר, the Horite (Gen. xxxvi.), and Mt. Seir (Jos. xv. 10, not identical with Judg. iii. 26) should probably be interpreted "goat."

[3] Siegf.-Stade suggest that *b* = *a*; Ges.-Buhl distinguish at least two persons of the name.

44. שְׁפוּפָן;[1] cf. שְׁפִיפֹן, a kind of serpent.
Benjamite, 1 Chr. viii. 5.

45. שָׂרָף, a kind of serpent.
Judahite, 1 Chr. iv. 22.

46. שַׁחֲצִימָה;[2] cf. בְּנֵי שַׁחַץ, lions (?).
Place in Issachar, Jos. xix. 22 (P).

47. תּוֹלָע, worm.
a. "Son" of Issachar, Gen. xlvi. 13 (P).
b.[3] Judge, Judg. x. 1.

48. תַּחַשׁ, porpoise.
"Son" of Nahor, Gen. xxii. 24 (J).

Of animal names which are supported not directly by the vocabulary of O.T., but by that of the cognate languages, the following seem fairly certain :—

49. צִבְעוֹן (*a*) and צְבֹעִים (*b*); cf. ضَبُع and ضِبْعان, hyena.[4]
a. Horite, Gen. xxxvi. 20.
b. Benjamite town, 1 S. xiii. 18; Neh. xi. 34.

[1] In Num. xxvi. 39 שפופם. Jacobs also includes in his list שפים, a Benjamite (1 Chr. vii. 12), and a Levite (1 Chr. xxvi. 16): in the latter case the name results from a textual error. *Vide* Bertheau, *ad loc.*

[2] An uncertain instance; for בני שחץ may be merely a descriptive epithet of great beasts of prey. Textually also the name is a little uncertain. The above is the reading of the K'ri, which is supported by Vg. Trg. Syr. Arab., the K'tib is שחצומה, LXX. ἐπὶ Σαλεὶμ (A, Σασειμὰθ) κατὰ θάλασσαν.

[3] On the relation of *a* to *b*, *vide* Moore, *Judges*, pp. 270 f.

[4] Ges. *Thesaurus*, *s.v.*; *J. Ph.* ix. 90; Nöldeke, *ZDMG*, 1886, p. 168; Graf. on Jer. xii. 9; Lagarde, *Nominalbildung*, pp. 35 f.

50. שַׁעַלְבִים; cf. ثَعْلَب, fox.[1]

Town in the south, Judg. i. 35.

51. לֵאָה and (*b*) לֵוִי; cf. لَأًى, wild cow.[2]

a. Wife of Jacob, Gen. xxix. 16 (E).
b. Tribe, Gen. xxxiv. 25 (J).

52. נוּן; cf. Syr. ܢܘܢ, fish.

Joshua ben Nun, Ex. xxxiii. 11 (E).

53. חָגְלָה and (*b*) בֵּית ח׳; cf. حَجَل, ܚܓܠܐ, partridge.[3]

a. "Daughter" of Zelophehad, Num. xxvi. 33 (P).
b. Town in Judah, Jos. xv. 6 (P).

A glance through the above list will show that (1) many of the names are those of places; (2) many occur in the tribal-genealogical lists in P (Gen. xxxvi., xlvi.; Num. xxvi.) and Chronicles (1 Chr. i.-ix.), or are otherwise presumably names of families; and (3) a considerable number are really or apparently names of individuals. But it will be well to bring out this distribution of the names more exactly. For that purpose I add a

[1] *J. Ph.* ix. 92.

[2] Nöldeke, *ZDMG*, 1886, p. 167 (Lea, *vielleicht* "Wildkuh"); Friedr. Delitzsch, *Prolegomena*, p. 80.

[3] The short ŏ of the first syllable in the Hebrew proper name is not well supported. The LXX., in agreement with the vocalisation of the appellative in Ar. and Syr., indicates an *a* vowel; cf. Ἐγλά, B and Luc., Αἰγλά (AF) in Num. xxvi. f., xxxvi., Βαιθαγλά (Is. xv. 6, Luc.). The *a* also appears in Jerome's form *Bethagla* (*Onom. Sacra*, ed. Lagarde, p. 103, cf. p. 236), and the modern *Hajla* (Robinson, *Bibl. Researches*, ii. 268).

synopsis, showing also the chronological distribution of the personal names. As in particular cases there is room for a difference of opinion as to the right of a name to be included in this class, or as to its family or personal character, I shall give in the footnotes index numbers to the foregoing list for each class of names.

Of the foregoing names—

33 are names of places.[1]
34 „ clans, etc., viz. 23 Hebrew and 11 Foreign.[2]
33 „ individuals, viz. 22 Hebrew and 11 Foreign.[3]

The Hebrew individuals bearing names of this kind are distributed as follows:—

[1] See Nos. 2 *a b*, 6, 9 *a b*, 16, 17, 20 *a*, 22, 23 *b c*, 24 *c*, 25, 26 *a*, 27 *c d*, 28 *d e h i*, 31 *a*, 32 *a b*, 33, 34, 37, 41, 42 *b c*, 46, 49 *b*, 50, 53 *b*.

[2] Hebrew families—4 *a b*, 5, 11 *d e*, 12, 13 *a b*, 19 *b*, 21 *b*, 26 *b*, 28 *b c f*, 31 *b*, 35 *b*, 39, 42 *a*, 44, 45, 47, 51 *b*, 53 *a*; foreign families—1 *a*, 8 *a b c*, 11 *a f*, 19 *c*, 20 *b*, 28 *a*, 29 *a*, 49 *a*. The one exception to the probably tribal character of the names in 1 Chr. ii.-ix. is זמרי (11 *e*) 1 Chr. viii. 36, a personal descendant of Saul mentioned in a section subsequently (p. 241) shown to be ancient.

[3] For Hebrew individuals, see the following notes. The foreign individuals are 10, 15, 19 *a*, 24 *a b*, 27 *b*, 28 *g*, 30, 36 *a b*, 38.

4 are directly connected with the patriarchal stories.[1]
4 „ „ stories of the wandering.[2]
2 lived in the times of the Judges.[3]
4 „ „ of Saul and David.[4]
4 „ „ between David and Josiah.[5]
4 „ „ of Josiah.[6]

Names of this class, then, were certainly common to Israel and other nations. Probably in Israel they were prevalent in the earliest periods, continued through the period of the later kings, apparently becoming more frequent again in the time of Josiah, but disappeared after the Exile.

Consequently, if names of this class are due to a common cause, we should expect to find it a cause equally operative among the Hebrews and their neighbours, and more effective in the earlier periods than later. We should further expect to find it one the effect of which had spent itself before the Exile.

Now two theories of the origin of these names may be said to hold the field; the one finds it in the

[1] 7 *a*, 40, 48, 51 *a*.

[2] 21 *a*, 52 (JE); 11 *c*, 24 *d* (P).

[3] 7 *b*, 47 *b*; on 47 *b* see note.

[4] 1 *b*, 4 *c*, 23 *a*, 27 *a*, all in books of Samuel.

[5] 3 (see note), 11 *b*, 18, 35 *a*, all in books of Kings. Add 11 *e*; see p. 97, note 2.

[6] 14, 29 *b*, 43 *a b*, in Kings or Ezekiel.

existence of a totem stage in the development of the peoples in question,[1] the other in a kind of natural poetry.[2] According to the first, the names are primarily tribal or divine, and incidentally personal; according to the second, primarily personal and derivatively tribal. No direct evidence as to the original use of these names exists, but the much greater proportion in this than in other classes of clan and town names seems to point to the conclusion that most, or even all, of the clan and town names were not originally personal. In estimating this proportion it ought, moreover, to be borne in mind that many even of the names classified above as personal may be simply tribal, *e.g.* Rachel and Leah.[3]

But before attaching importance to this large proportion of clan names it will be well to consider how far the two theories can respectively explain the phenomena presented by the personal names. Nöldeke states the case for the "natural poetry" origin thus—"It is indeed very natural that the Beduin living in the open air should readily name their children after the beasts of the field. For this purpose

[1] The theory especially of Robertson Smith.

[2] So, at least in part, Nöldeke (see below), apparently also Friedr. Delitzsch (*Prolegomena*, p. 202); cf. also Siegfried's review of Jacobs' Essay in *Theol. Lit. Zeitung*, Sept. 14, 1895.

[3] Cf. *e.g.* Stade, *ZATW*, i. 112 ff., and *Geschichte*, i. 145-147; questioned, however, by Meyer, *Geschichte des Alterthums*, i 354. Cf. further, Robertson Smith, *Kinship*, p. 219; *Rel. Sem.*[2] 311.

they chose not simply the strong and noble, but the child was also named after all manner of disgusting creatures . . . in part out of mere uncomplimentary comparison of the small and ugly baby (des kleinen unschönen Kerls) with those insects, in part indeed also in order to express the hope that he might become thoroughly unwelcome to his foes."[1] It must be added that Nöldeke is here speaking with direct reference only to the Arabic animal proper names, and is indeed by no means blind to the possibility of a totem origin for some of the names of this class.[2]

In some respects this theory promises a satisfactory explanation of the facts; for the majority of the names in question belong to the period of unsettled life, or else to the time of David when the influence of the freer open-air life of earlier times, though on the wane, might have been felt. But yet the question arises—Why with a changed mode of life did the custom tend to *perish* instead of simply changing? For settled life does not involve loss of acquaintance with animals, but, at most, a difference in the animals seen and held and valued. It might, indeed, be expected that, as civilisation increased, comparison of the "ugly baby" with some undesirable animal would cease; it might equally be expected that pleasanter comparisons with animals attractive through form or character would take their place. Yet this was seldom the case,[3] while

[1] *ZDMG*, 1886, p. 160. [2] *Ib.* p. 167.

[3] Cf., however, Zibiah (35 *a*), and the compliment conveyed

among the comparatively few instances of later names of this class more than one suggest an unpleasant comparison.[1] This theory is therefore insufficient because it fails to show why, if the custom of thus naming children once prevailed so extensively as, on the hypothesis that all town and clan names are derivative from personal names, it must have done, it subsequently grew infrequent and finally disappeared, *although comparisons of men and women with animals always remained popular;*[2] and also because, in particular, it gives no reason for the revival of these names in the time of Josiah.

I turn next to the totem theory. As I have already said, this deals with personal names only indirectly, and can, therefore, only be expected indirectly to explain them. Indirectly, however, the theory seems to me to explain the personal names thus: with the break-up of the totem clan system, the clan names became in certain cases personal, instances of which we perhaps find in Eglah (27 *a*), the name of David's wife, the two Deborahs (7) and other names of early individuals, though we have, it is true, no direct evidence that these were ever tribal. But the strictly personal character of many of the early names classified in the synopsis is open to doubt. Leah and Rachel I

by a comparison to the same animal (the gazelle) in Cant. ii. 9, 17; and ? 2 S. i. 19.

[1] *E.g.* Huldah (14), the weasel, Achbor (20), the mouse.

[2] For instances, cf. p. 100, n. 3, and below (p. 113, n. 1).

have already referred to; the *personal* existence, moreover, of Caleb (21 *a*), Tahash (48), and Tola (47 *b*) can be with more or less reason called in question. It is certainly curious that so many of the early and apparently individual names turn out on closer inspection possibly or even probably tribal. Of the four names of this kind found in the time of David, Eglah alone is certainly personal; the rest occur *only* as the names of the fathers of individuals; but in such cases, owing to the ambiguity of Hebrew idiom, we cannot be sure whether *e.g.* Palti ben *Laish* (23 *a*) means that Palti's actual father was named Laish, or merely that he belonged to a clan named Laish.[1] The same ambiguity exists in the case of Sheba ben *Bichri* (4 *a*) and Rizpah bath *Aiah* (1 *b*), and the pre-Davidic name Joshua ben *Nun* (52). The view that the names Laish, Bichri, Aiah, and Nun in the foregoing cases are clan names, is favoured by the fact that none of them occurs elsewhere as the name of an individual, but most of them do appear elsewhere as town or clan names.[2] I draw

[1] This use of בן (בת) is certainly common. It is rarer in the sing., but several tolerably clear instances occur in Neh. iii.; cf. the closely analogous בן־נביא, בן־הרקחים = a member of (the guild of) the perfumers. Cf. also Num. iii. 30 with v. 27.

[2] That Bichri in Sheba ben Bichri is a clan name is rendered very probable by a comparison with 2 S. xx. 14, where instead of "Berites" the true reading is Bichrites; see Driver, *ad loc.* In 1 S. xxv. 44, we read "Palti ben Laish, which was of Gallim"; in Is. x. 30, a town Laish (לַיְשָׁה) is referred to. As the context shows, it lay near Gallim. May it be that in the Samuel narrative

attention to these uncertainties to show that the occurrence of these names as applied to individuals, in any case little more than sporadic, may be quite exceptional. Such a sporadic or exceptional usage is more probably the result of transition than due to a deep-seated custom such as is implied in the theory of natural poetry. This latter theory, moreover, gives no satisfactory account of the subsequent disappearance of these individual names; but if they were due to transition, their disappearance was inevitable.

The totem theory, again, explains without any violent assumptions what the theory of "natural poetry" cannot—the occurrence of three or four of these names in the time of Josiah, each of the names being that of an *unclean* animal. Robertson Smith deals only with the case of Jaazaniah ben Shaphan, and sees in Shaphan the name of a *still existing* totem clan. This is an assumption that has met with little acceptance; even if admitted, it only explains the clan name Shaphan, and leaves us still in need of an explanation of unquestionably personal names of the same period, viz. Huldah (weasel), Achbor (mouse), and Shaphan itself in 2 Kings xxii. 3.[1] So far as the evidence of the names goes the occurrence at this time of three names at least which are certainly personal, and but one

Laish is the name of a clan then resident in Gallim, which in the course of the three centuries between David and Isaiah gave its name to a place in the neighbourhood?

[1] Perhaps we should add Nehushta; cf. p. 91, n. 3.

at most of which is tribal, does not favour the view that totem *clans* were then in existence. On the other hand, Ezek. viii. 11 testifies to the worship of unclean animals at about this period; and in this Robertson Smith saw, not without good reason, the survival—perhaps rather the revival—of superstitious practices originally derived from totem belief and totem organisation. It is reasonable enough to suppose that the revival of these practices goes back to the time of Manasseh—a period which, though very few details concerning it have come down to us, we know to have been one of religious syncretism. Granted this, these curious and hitherto unexplained names will have been due to parents giving their children names of animals unclean according to the ordinary code, but sacred according to these ancient and then rejuvenescent superstitions. The mouse, which gives its name to one of the persons in question, certainly played a part in unlawful cults somewhat later;[1] so also did the swine, the name of a post-Exilic family. If very ancient, this "swine" family may originally have been a totem unit; otherwise we may suppose its eponymous ancestor lived at the time of the superstitious revival. The post-Exilic family Parosh (flea) may have originated in the same way. Apart from some such assumption, it is certainly difficult to account for these post-Exilic family names. On the whole, then, the phenomena presented by even the personal names can be most

[1] Is. lxvi. 17.

easily explained as the indirect results of a preceding totem stage.

Clan names and, if derivative from them, town names are immediately explained by the totem theory; the only question is whether other explanations are not equally satisfactory. But the attempts made by Gesenius and Nöldeke to explain town names of this type on the supposition that the names as place names are primary, are scarcely happy, and have been well criticised by Robertson Smith. If, however, they are secondary, it necessarily throws back the existence of the eponymous clans to a very early and quite probably a pre-Hebraic period.

The most striking feature of the town names is their geographical distribution; by far the greater number of them occur in the south of the country, broadly speaking in the territory of Judah. The sites of the towns have not been in every case identified, but sufficiently for present purposes they can be inferred from the contexts in which they are referred to.

In detail these towns are situated as follows:—

Out of a total of thirty-three,[1] four *at most* lie north of Shechem. These are the Danite Laish,[2] Aijalon in

[1] Perhaps rather fewer; cf. the notes on some uncertain instances accompanying the list, and the remarks above. Perhaps, on the other hand, one or two other places should be added, viz. Beth-le-Aphrah (Mic. i. 10) and a third Etam, both these places being in the south; cf. Nos. 28 and 32, with notes.

[2] On lion worship in the district of Laish, cf. Robertson Smith, *Rel. Sem.*[1] pp. 185 ff.

Zebulon, Beth Dagon in Asher, and Shaḥazumah in Issachar. But of these the first only is certain; Aijalon is almost certainly a false reading for Elon, which is not an animal name, and it is etymologically uncertain whether the other two names denote animals. In addition to these the Abiezrite Ophrah[1] (28 *d*), and perhaps, if distinct from it, Ephron (28 *i*) probably lay near Shechem.

The remaining twenty-seven names are those of towns which clearly lay south of Shechem. Many of these are contained in the list of tribal cities, etc., where they are distributed thus—

In Judah, eight.

Mentioned in Joshua xv.—Ḥumtah, Beth-Dagon, En-Gedi, Eglon, Mt. Ephron, Ascent of Aḳrabbim, Mt. Seir; in 1 Chr. iv. 12, Ir-Naḥash.

In Simeon, four.

Mentioned in Jos. xix. 2-6—Ḥazar-Shual, Ḥazar-Susah, Beth-Lebaoth; in 1 Chr. iv. 32, Etam.

In southern territory of Dan, three.

Mentioned in Jos. xix. 41, 42—Zorah, Shaalabbim, Aijalon.

In Benjamin, three.

Mentioned in Jos. xviii. 21-23—Beth-Ḥoglah, Parah, Ophrah.

The remaining nine places are not tribally defined,

[1] Cf. Moore, *Judges*, p. 184.

but clearly lay to the south of Shechem. They are Telaim, probably in the Negeb of Judah; Beth Car, perhaps to be identified with 'Ain Karim,[1] south-west of Jerusalem; Laish(ch), which, as the context in Is. x. 30 shows, lay near Anathoth a few miles north of Jerusalem; Beth-Nimrah, east of Jordan, in the territory of Gad; En-Eglaim on the Dead Sea; Arad in the Negeb; Seirah, Ehud's goal after killing Eglon; Zeboim and the land of Shual, both mentioned in 1 S. xiii. 17, 18.

Now whatever the origin of these animal names may have been, this striking preponderance of towns so named in the south is worthy of notice; and if we trace them to totem organisation, the inference can scarcely be wrong that this organisation was more prevalent or lasted longer in the south than in the north. In themselves the town names admit of no safe conclusion as to totem organisation among the early *Hebrew* tribes; this, if it is to be drawn at all, must be drawn from the names of Hebrew clans.

The proportion of tribal names identical with those of animals out of the whole number of tribal names mentioned in O.T. is, as Mr. Jacobs has pointed out, far from striking. But in connection with the geographical distribution of town names discussed above, the geographical distribution of certain of the family names is significant. Out of eleven of these names found in

[1] G. A. Smith, *Historical Geography of the Holy Land*, p. 224, n. 2.

1 Chr. ii.-ix., nine are found among either the Judahites or Benjamites,[1] one of the others is a Manassite on the east of Jordan, and the other an Asherite. Of the remaining names five are mentioned only in P, viz. an Ephraimite (4 *a*), Benjamite (4 *b*), Danite (5), Issacharite (47), and two Manassites (26 *b* and 53 *a*), one is that of the tribe Levi, and five (12, 13 *a b*, 19 *b*, 39) are clearly post-Exilic families. Of these last five I have already referred to Ḥezir and Parosh; Ḥagab is the name of a family of Nethinim, and Jael of a family of "Solomon's servants," two classes of obscure origin.[2]

Before finally summarising the results of the preceding analysis, some few uncertain instances of these names must be briefly examined:—

1. אֲרָן, an Edomite family (Gen. xxxvi. 28), is claimed by Robertson Smith[3] as the equivalent of أُزَّن, wild goat; Nöldeke's[4] objection that "nun" must be servile in ארן as in the other names in the passage is not decisive; but since even the Syriac word is a ἅπ. λεγ., the instance is most uncertain.

2. ימימה (daughter of Job), connected by Gesenius

[1] See Nos. 11 *d*, 21 *b*, 28 *b f*, 45—Judahites; and 11 *e*, 31 *b*, 35 *b*, 44—Benjamites. Note further, Sheba ben Bichri was a Benjamite, Palti ben Laish lived near Jerusalem.

[2] Cf. Jacobs, *Studies in Biblical Archaeology*, pp. 104 ff.

[3] *J. Ph.* ix. 90.

[4] *ZDMG*, 1886, p. 168.

in the *Thesaurus* with يمامة (=dove); but the vowel change î and â is improbable.

3. חוה, Eve, may mean serpent.[1]

4. יְעוּשׁ. Robertson Smith's suggestion that this is the Hebrew equivalent of يَغُوث (the Arabic lion god) has been rejected by Lagarde though accepted by Nöldeke and Wellhausen.[2] It is the name of a Horite clan, one or two Benjamite families (1 Chr. vii. 10, viii. 39), and, according to the Chronicler, of a son of Rehoboam and of a Levite contemporary with David.

5. שׁוֹבָל, the name of a Horite and of a Judahite, is considered by Robertson Smith to be a diminutive of شِبْل (=young lion). But this involves the not very probable theory that in the same connection (Gen. xxxvi. 20) we have one name which is the North Semitic equivalent of an Arabic name (צבעון = ضبع), and another which is a pure Arabic name; for, as Nöldeke points out, phonetic laws prevent שבל being the North Semitic equivalent of شِبْل.

[1] Nöldeke, *ZDMG*, 1888, p. 487; *New Oxf. Lex.*, *s.v.*

[2] Robertson Smith, *Religion of the Semites*[2], p. 42, n. 4; Lagarde, *Bildung der Nomina*, p. 133 (LXX. Ιεους points to ع not غ in the Arabic); Nöldeke, *ZDMG*, 1886, p. 168; Wellhausen, *Reste*, pp. 19, 171. Nöldeke, however, rightly questions the originality of the animal reference: the word means "to protect."

6. עֲנָה, also a Horite, is not clearly the same as عانة, and in any case the regular meaning of the Arabic word is "herd," and the meaning "wild ass" given to it in the Ḳâmûs is very probably an error.[1]

7. תֶּרַח, the name of Abraham's father, and of a station in the wilderness. Robertson Smith gives this name the meaning "wild goat," comparing ܬܪܚܐ; Friedr. Delitzsch[2] compares the Assyrian turâḫu with the same meaning; but both the Syriac and the Assyrian words appear to be from a פ״א root (cf. أرخ = antelope); it is therefore quite questionable whether the Hebrew is a real parallel.[3]

8. גַּעַל, apparently a Shechemite. According to Wellhausen[4] = beetle; cf. Ar. جُعَل.

9. חֹבָב, a Midianite, Num. x. 29 (JE). Wellhausen[5] compares حُبَاب, serpent. The correspondence is exact; for the retention in Hebrew of the originally long *ā*, though rare, occurs and may here be due to the desire for dissimilation.[6]

[1] Nöldeke, *ZDMG*, 1886, p. 168.

[2] *Prolegomena*, p. 80.

[3] Cf. *ZDMG*, 1886, pp. 167 f.; Lagarde, *Bildung der Nomina*, p. 131; Hommel, *Saügethiere*, p. 264.

[4] *Israel. und jüd. Geschichte*, p. 26.

[5] *Reste*, pp. 171, 217.

[6] It will be sufficient to refer still more briefly to one or two other names in a note. Jacobs includes in his list ארד,

Even if these derivations be considered satisfactory, the striking features presented by the first list become more rather than less accentuated by the inclusion of these instances; for among these also the foreign or family names preponderate. Out of some fourteen names thus added, one is that of an Edomite, three of Horite families, one (or two) of a Benjamite, and another of a Judahite family; the really personal character of the names Eve and Terah will scarcely be insisted on; in any case they are very ancient. The only clearly personal names are Jeush, according to the Chronicler, Rehoboam's son, and Jemima, Job's daughter. The former,

ארוד, ארדן. On these Gesenius (*Thesaurus*) says, "forsan, *i.e.* ערוד, onager"; from a pure guess of this kind it is hazardous to argue. *Oxf. Lex.* omits the suggestion. Jacobs also includes קֹרֵא, עַתַּי, and עתניאל; the first of these certainly can mean "partridge," but I see no reason for supposing that this rare meaning of the word attached to the proper names (1 Chr. xxvi. 1, ix. 19; 2 Chr. xxxi. 14). For עתי and עתניאל Gesenius (*Thesaurus*) compares عُتون = lion; but I can find no trace of this meaning in the *Lisân al ʿarab*. The connection of עִירָא, עִירוּ, עִירָם with עיר = a young ass, suggested, though in a different connection from the present, by Renan (*REJ*, v. 170), is less unlikely; the names are, as we should expect on this view of them and in the light of the usage of other animal names, early or tribal. Thus they belong to three contemporaries of David (2 S. xx. 26, xxiii. 26, 38), an Edomite (Gen. xxxvi. 43), and a Judahite (1 Chr. iv. 15). The connection of the Edomite name עירם with עֵיר (Ar. عَيْر) is rendered additionally probable by Lucian's transliteration in 1 Chr. i. 54, which preserves the diphthong—Αιραμ.

if genuine, is of the tenth century; the latter appears only in a late work, but may itself be early.[1]

The significant features of the animal names are these—

1. Town and tribal names form two-thirds of the whole—sixty-seven out of a hundred in the original list and about the same proportion in the supplementary list. The proportion may be greater; for several names provisionally classed as those of individuals were seen to be possibly those of clans.
2. Non-Hebrew tribal and individual names form a considerable proportion of the whole, viz. 11 + 11 = 22 out of 100. If to these we add, as we probably should do, most or all of the thirty-three town names, then more than half the names of this class in the O.T. are foreign, an extraordinary proportion compared with that obtaining in the other classes analysed, and in view of the fact that the O.T. contains far more Hebrew than foreign names.
3. A very large proportion of the town and tribal names belong to the south of the country—*at least* forty-seven[2] out of sixty-seven.

[1] Cf. Nöldeke, *ZDMG*, 1888, p. 479, "Doch dürfte auch בלדד . . . viel älter sein als das Buch Hiob selbst."

[2] Viz. twenty-seven town names (p. 106); and the following families:—nine Judahite and Benjamite mentioned in 1 Chr. ii.-ix., and one Benjamite mentioned in P (p. 108), six Horite, two

4. Only about one-fifth of the names at most are those of Hebrew individuals. Among these several may be tribal. In detail: no instance occurs among post-Exilic individuals mentioned in O.T.; but three and perhaps four or five contemporaries of Josiah have names of this class, in each the name being that of an *unclean* animal. Still working upwards we find three or four instances[1] between Josiah and David; in the Davidic period one and possibly three or four instances; in Period I. the two Deborahs are certain instances. Several others are open to doubt as occurring only in P and being possibly tribal.

These phenomena do not appear to me to receive a satisfactory explanation from the fact or hypothesis that children of nomads readily receive animal names.

Edomite, one Midianite (28 *a*), and one "son" of Keturah (11 *a*). Several of the remainder are not clearly northern; and, moreover, the total (sixty-seven) includes some uncertain instances (pp. 105 f.).

[1] None of these is of an animal distinctly specified as unclean. On the other hand, יחמר (whence יחמי) and צבי (whence צביא) are particularly mentioned as clean (Dt. xiv. 5). Again, יונה was much used in legitimate sacrifice. Further, three are actually used in O.T. as terms of endearment or in complimentary comparisons. These are יונה; cf. Cant. ii. 14, v. 2, vi. 9 (of the women) and v. 12 (of the man); צבי Cant. ii. 9 and possibly 2 S. i. 19 (of men); cf. also Cant. iv. 5 in reference to the women; אריה Gen. xlix. 9, 2 S. xvii. 10. The remaining name, יחמר, occurs only in Dt. xiv. 5.

On the other hand, in themselves they do not prove a totem stage in the development of Israel; but it so far favours a totem theory that they receive from it a reasonable explanation. Thus—

1. The preponderance of clan over personal names finds its explanation in the fact that, according to the hypothesis, the names were primarily clan names.
2. The existence of a small number of personal names was due to the transition from a totem tribal to a national organisation of society.
3. The use of the names of "unclean" animals is due to the sacred character of these animals in totem worship.
4. The occurrence of these names in the time of Josiah finds a natural if indirect explanation in the survival of ancient superstitious practices. Half consciously the characteristic belief of totemism, that men are of the same stock with the divine animal, may have survived and led to the conferring of the divine name.
5. The virtual cessation of these names after the Exile is explained by the final extinction of the superstitious survivals.

It will be seen that none of these phenomena demand the supposition that totem organisation lasted in Israel down into historic times—rather the reverse; and if the convergence of evidence requires the assumption of totemism among the Semites, the evidence of the O.T. names would suggest stating the case, so far as the Hebrews are concerned, thus — Before the amalgamation of the Hebrew tribes into a nation, totem worship and totem organisation existed among some of the peoples of Canaan and some of the Hebrew tribes, especially those dwelling in the south. Among the Hebrews, at any rate, this manner of worship and organisation was on the wane before the Davidic period, but left behind it certain superstitious ideas and practices which at times asserted themselves in the subsequent centuries.

III

Names containing an Element denoting Dominion

These names are comparatively few, but very important; their religious character is scarcely open to question, but their precise religious import has been differently regarded. They, therefore, require a somewhat detailed examination. They naturally fall into three sub-classes accordingly as they are compounded with מלך, בעל, or אדן.

1.

Names compounded with מלך

Three simple names may be noticed first: of these Hammolecheth and Milcah do not appear to be those of individuals. Hammolecheth is clearly tribal; in the only passage[1] where the name occurs it appears as that of the sister of Gilead and mother of Abiezer—Gideon's *family* name—and Maḥlah one of Zelophe-ḥad's "daughters." Kuenen[2] has conjectured that Zelopheḥad's "daughters" are towns; and this is tolerably clear in the case of Tirzah, certainly the name of a town, and Ḥoglah, which is probably a mere abbreviation[3] for Beth Ḥoglah. If this be so, Milcah is a town name in Num. xxvi. 33, etc., and as such perhaps an abbreviated form of Beth Milcah if, as would appear probable, Milcah is a divine name or title. In Gen. xi. 29 Milcah is wife of Nahor and daughter of Haran, and, according to Nöldeke,[4] is, "in such a mythical context, scarcely anything else than מלכת, who was worshipped by the Phoenicians." In any case these simple names originate in early times, and they are probably tribal rather than individual. The third of these uncompounded names—Melech[5] (1 Chr. viii. 35, ix. 41)—is, however, the name of an individual, as the context sufficiently indicates.

The compound names in מלך—Hebrew, unlike Phoenician, has none in מלכת—number fourteen; but of these two are names of Assyrian gods Anammelech and Adrammelech (2 K. xvii. 31), the latter being also

[1] 1 Chr. vii. 18.

[2] Cf. Dillmann on Num. xxvi. 33.

[3] On parallel abbreviations, see below (p. 127).

[4] *ZDMG*, 1888, p. 484.

[5] Cf. Nabataean מלכו, the name of several kings in first century B.C. to first century A.D.

the name of an Assyrian individual (2 K. xix. 37). Another is the name of a Canaanite[1] and another of an Ethiopian;[2] but in the last case the name עבדמלך, since it cannot be Ethiopian, may be Hebrew, although its bearer is unquestionably foreign. I shall have occasion to return to it again. The evidence of the other foreign names that this class of names was not peculiar to the Hebrews is abundantly confirmed from extra-biblical sources. As Canaanite names of the fifteenth to the fourteenth century B.C. we find in the Tel-el-amarna (Brit. Mus.) tablets A-bi-mil-ki, Abdi-milki, I-lu-mil-ki, Mil-ki-lu. Malik-rammu was king of *Edom* in the eighth century, *Phoenician* princes of the seventh century are Abimilki and Aḥimilki in Arados, and Milki-asaph in Gebal. The Assyrian eponym for the year 886 B.C. is Ilu-milki.[3] Assyrian names of this type are very numerous; so also are the Phoenician,[4] though these latter can be chiefly illustrated from the somewhat later periods from which the Phoenician inscriptions date.

Yet another O.T. name is that of a town, אַלַּמֶּלֶךְ,[5]

[1] מלכי־צדק, king of Salem (Gen. xiv. 18).

[2] Jer. xxxviii. 7, etc.

[3] These particular instances are taken from *KAT*², 105, 150, 185; *RP*², ii. 113. Cf. further, Nestle, *Eigennamen*, p. 176 f.; and Bloch's *Phoen. Gloss.*, *s.v.* מלך.

[4] Bloch (*Phoen. Gloss.*) cites six or seven beginning with מלך and (*s.v.* מלך) fifteen ending in מלך.

[5] The etymological problem involved in this word remains unsolved; the LXX. Ἐλειμέλεχ (Luc. Ἐλμέλεχ) is too easy and

and is therefore quite probably not Hebraic. Another, רגם-מלך, is certainly the name of a Hebrew, but apparently of foreign origin.[1]

This leaves only eight names at once Hebrew and belonging to Hebrew individuals. One only of these, מלכיה, occurs of more than one Hebrew person or family, but this one is the name of ten or eleven different people.

The seven names which are found each designating one Hebrew person appear as follows:—

אבימלך and אלימלך in Period I.
אחימלך and מלכישוע in Period II.
נתנמלך [and עבדמלך] in seventh century.
מלכירם[2] in seventh or sixth century (beginning).
מלכיאל is the name of a family mentioned in Gen. xlvi. 17, Num. xxvi. 45, 1 Chr. vii. 31.[3]

From this we should infer that these names, always sporadic, finally disappeared before the return from the

at the same time improbable as the name of a *town*. Gesenius's suggestion that it is אל (= אלה = oak) and מלך gives a suitable name for a town, but it is etymologically hazardous.

[1] As that of his companion שראצר unquestionably is, Zech. vii. 2.

[2] References for the above names, Judg. viii. 31 (cf. also note in App. II. 1, No. 14); Ruth i. 2; 1 S. xxi. 2, xiv. 49; 2 K. xxiii. 11; 1 Chr. iii. 18. In every case, except the last, and, perhaps, the second, we have the evidence of the early writings; and there is no reason to question the accuracy of the particular list in which מלכירם occurs in Chronicles.

[3] The Hebrew authorities here are late (P and Chr.), but the *name* (among the Tyrians) is ancient, occurring in the Tel-el-Amarna letters.

Exile; and this inference is substantially correct in spite of the history of the name מלכיה. This name occurs as follows:—of two contemporaries of Jeremiah (Jer. xxi. 1, xxxviii. 6), of five post-Exilic individuals (Ezra x. 25, 31; Neh. iii. 14, 31, viii. 4), and one post-Exilic family (Neh. x. 4). By the Chronicler it is referred to a pre-Davidic individual (1 Chr. vi. 25) and a Davidic family (1 Chr. xxiv. 9); in both cases, however, in lists which are of very questionable historical value.[1] Very probably, therefore, מלכיה was first coined in the seventh century. In any case its usage is mainly late.

The usage of מלכיה thus stands in marked contrast to that of the other Hebrew names containing מלך; it is frequent, they are rare; it is most frequent after the Exile,[2] they disappear before the Exile. We shall scarcely be wrong, then, in inferring that the connection between מלכיה and the other names in מלך is accidental; it affirms something not of מלך but of יה. This, therefore, at least may be safely said—the formation of names in order to affirm something of מלך—always sporadic among the Hebrews—ceased entirely after the Exile. The discussion of the significance of מלך in these names I postpone to the end of the main section.

If I am right in my contention that מלכיה is only

[1] See below, pp. 172, 228.

[2] The name also appears in the list of the Amoraim and Tannaim.

accidentally connected with the other names containing the same element, and also in the suggestion that the name was first coined in the seventh century, it throws an interesting light on the vigour of the theocratic idea at that time: the two earliest persons to bear the name were born and named while the Deuteronomic reformation was ripening. In any case the frequency of the name after the Exile is significant; it was conferred with the same zest with which Psalmists opened their songs, triumphantly declaring Yahweh has become king, *e.g.* Ps. xcvii. 1; xcix. 1. The idea thus expressed that the (national) deity is king was, it is true, in no way peculiar to the Hebrews;[1] but its strength among the later Hebrews and the tendency among all classes to express it in the names of their children may have been partly due to a revolt against the claim made in names with which they must have been frequently meeting, such as Nabu-malik; to the claim of Babylon, "Nebo is king," "Assur is king," the Jew proudly replied also in the names of his children, "Not so, but Yahweh is king."

2.

Names Compounded with בעל

The personal (or family) names compounded with בעל, with the exception of one or two occurring in

[1] Nestle, *Eigennamen*, p. 176.

1 Chr. ii.-ix., are all found in or before the time of David. Especially in the books of Samuel, these names have been corrected by the scribes in such a way as to remove the element בעל which, in consequence of prophetic protests, became an offence to a later generation.[1] Fortunately the correction has been so made that it is in most cases possible to restore the original form with certainty. The Hebrew names of this class with their original forms restored are—

ירבעל, the name of the judge, Judg. viii. 35.

אשבעל, a son of Saul, 1 Chr. viii. 33 = אישבשת in Samuel generally, אשיו in 1 S. xiv. 49.[2]

„ one of David's mighty men, 2 S. xxiii. 8 (ישבבשבת) = 1 Chr. xi. 11 (ישבעם).

מרי-בעל, son of Jonathan = מריבעל, 1 Chr. ix. 40*b* = מריבבעל, 1 Chr. ix. 40*a* (LXX. Μαρειβάαλ),

[1] This is now so generally accepted as a fact that it is unnecessary to argue the point again; it will be sufficient to refer to some of the literature: see Geiger in *ZDMG*, 1862, pp. 728 ff.; Wellhausen, *Bücher Samuelis*, pp. xii. ff., 30 f., and on the passages cited above; Baudissin, *Studien*, i. 108 f.; Dillmann in *Sitzungsberichte der Akad. der Wissenschaften zu Berlin*, 1881, pp. 601 ff.; Driver, *Samuel*, pp. 186, 195 f., 279. Jastrow (*J. B. Lit.* 1894, pp. 19 ff.) argues that the forms בשת (= Bast, a divine name) may have been from the first parallel forms, yet admits that the forms with בעל were concurrently in use.

[2] Cf. Wellhausen, *Bücher Samuelis*, p. 95, and Kittel on 1 Chr. ii. 31; cf. further note on ישבאב above, p. 24.

1 Chr. viii. 34 = מפיבשת, 2 S. iv. 4 (Luc. Μεμφιβάαλ).

/מרי־בעל, son of Rizpah, mentioned only in 2 S. xxi. 8 (מפבשת).

בעלידע, son of David, 1 Chr. xiv. 7 = 2 S. v. 16 (אלידע).

בעליה, one of David's helpers, 1 Chr. xii. 5.

בעלחנן, a Gederite,[1] mentioned only in 1 Chr. xxvii. 28.

To these eight certain cases some add two that are less certain, viz.:—

אביבעל, restored[2] by Wellhausen in 2 S. xxiii. 31, as the name of one of David's heroes.

יובעל, restored by Kuenen in Judg. ix. 26.[3]

The simple name בעל[4] is that of a Reubenite (1 Chr. v. 5) and a Benjamite (1 Chr. viii. 30).

Besides these Hebrews we find two foreigners with names of this type, בעלחנן an Edomite, and אתבעל a Phoenician, Gen. xxxvi. 38; 1 K. xvi. 31. Among

[1] Possibly a foreigner, *vide* Baethgen, *Beiträge*, p. 142.

[2] Against the restoration, see p. 25.

[3] *Rel. Israel* (E.T.), i. 404; against the restoration, Nestle, *Eigennamen*, p. 122, n., and Moore, *Judges*, p. 256.

[4] On the question whether this represents an original עבר בעל or a similar compound, cf. Nestle, *Eigennamen*, pp. 114 f., 215, with the literature there cited, to which add Wellhausen, *Die Reste des arab. Heidenthums*, pp. 2 ff., and the literature cited in the footnotes. The simple name מלך (see above, p. 116) is similar.

the Phoenicians these names were very common; early names from the Assyrian inscriptions are Aziba'al, Abiba'al, Aduniba'al, Sapaṭi-ba'al, Pudiba'al, Ba'alja-šupu, Ba'alḫanunu and Ba'almaluku;[1] in the Phoenician inscriptions (later) they are very numerous.[2] Among the Assyrians names compounded with the etymologically identical word Bil (Hebr. בל) are frequent, and may be exemplified by Bil-ṣar-uṣur written in O.T. בלשאצר; in Assyrian this word (Bil) is the proper name of a deity;[3] we have yet to determine whether this is the case with בעל in Hebrew personal names. Meantime it must be pointed out that the form בל probably appears in two or three O.T. names—one (אשבל) being the name of a Benjamite tribe. The word בלדד can scarcely be explained except on the supposition that it is compound, the first element being בל; אשבל also is most probably compounded of איש and בל; but בלעם is very ambiguous. Of these names the first and the last are in any case foreign; while אשבל is a clan name and of uncertain origin. Moreover, there is no good reason for treating these names as precisely parallel with names in בעל; the Assyrian inscriptions sharply distinguish between the Canaanite names in בעל and the native names in Bilu.[4] More probably where Hebrew or Canaanite names offer this abbrevi-

[1] Cited from Schrader, *KAT*, 105.

[2] See Bloch, *Phoen. Gloss.*, *s.v.* בעל, and the following names beginning with בעל: about seventy different names are cited.

[3] *KAT*, 174. [4] *Ib.* 173.

ated form בל, we are to trace Assyrian (or Babylonian) influence, and the worship of the Assyrio-Babylonian deity Bel.[1] In this case the absence of the abbreviated form from Hebrew personal names, and its presence in the one[2] tribal name אשבל, are alike noticeable.

The broad fact, then, with regard to the Hebrew personal names is that they are not altogether infrequent in and before the Davidic period, but that they entirely disappear afterwards; a significant and not unimportant detail is the connection of several of these names with the families of Saul and David.

In the present case the place names are more than usually valuable in suggestion. Including a few simple forms these place names are as follows:—

בעל, also called בעלת באר,[3] in Simeon.

בעלה, *a.* A town on the west border of Judah, also

[1] Winckler, *Geschichte Israels*, p. 120; *A.T. Untersuchungen*, 117 f. In addition to the names cited above, Winckler suggests the presence of Bel in עיבל (LXX. Γαιβηλ) in Gen. xxxvi. 23. I have suggested that this is also the case with Mt. Ebal (עיבל) and that the name should be explained as a compound of עי (cf. העי) and בל = The . . . of Bel; see the *Academy* for June 20th, 1895 (p. 510), and also Prof. Cheyne's Letters, *ib.* pp. 531 f. and (4th July) p. 16. He also suggests that הרבלה (LXX. Αρβηλα) in Num. xxxiv. 11 = mountain of Bel.

[2] Or two, if Reuben is actually connected with Bel; but this is most uncertain, see p. 65.

[3] The place is mentioned only in Jos. xix. 8 (in the fuller form), and in the dependent passage 1 Chr. iv. 33 (in the shorter form). These appear to be other names for ראמת־נגב, Jos. xix. 8; so Dillmann on Jos. xv. 24.

called בעל יהודה ,בעל ,קרית, and קרית יערים.[1]

b. A town in the south of Judah, Jos. xv. 29.

c. הר הבעלה, a mountain on the west of Judah, Jos. xv. 11.

בעלת, a town in Dan (south).[2]

בעלות, *a.* A town in the south of Judah.

b. Apparently a more northern town.[3]

בעלת באר; see בעל.

בעל גד, in the valley of Lebanon, Jos. xi. 17.

ב׳ המון, site uncertain: mentioned only in Cant. viii. 11.

ב׳ חצור, probably[4] in Benjamin, 2 S. xiii. 23.

ב׳ חרמון, exact site disputed, but near Lebanon, Judg. iii. 3.

ב׳ יהודה, see בעלה.

[1] Jos. xv. 9 f., 1 Chr. xiii. 6 (locative, בַּעֲלָתָה); Jos. xv. 60; xviii. 14; 2 S. vi. 2. On the identifications and the reading in 2 S. vi. 2, see *ZDMG*, 1862, pp. 731 f.; Driver, *Samuel*, p. 203; G. A. Smith, *Hist. Geog. of Holy Land*, pp. 225 f. See also Wellhausen, *Bücher Sam.*, 166 f.; Stade, *Geschichte*, i. 272, n.; Winckler, *Gesch. Isr.* 70 f., all three of whom, however, question the identification with Kiriath jearim.

[2] Jos. xix. 44; Dillmann writes, "Ob einerlei mit dem xv. 11 genannten הַבַּעֲלָה?"

[3] For the first of these places, cf. Jos. xv. 24; Dillmann thinks perhaps they are the same. But if, as the context ("in Asher and Bealoth") appears to require, the town mentioned in 1 K. iv. 16 is northern, they cannot be identical.

[4] For the probabilities in this and other cases, see Riehm's *Handwörterbuch*.

ב׳ מעון, a Reubenite town, Numb. xxxii. 38.
ב׳ פעור, a Moabite town, Hos. ix. 10.
ב׳ פרצים, probably near the valley of Rephaim, 2 S. v. 20.
ב׳ צפון, near the Red Sea, Ex. xiv. 2, etc.
ב׳ שלשה, near Gilgal, 2 K. iv. 42.
ב׳ תמר, perhaps near the Benjamite Gibeah, Judg. xx. 33.
במות בעל, in Moab, Num. xxii. 41 : called also במות, Num. xxi. 19.
קרית בעל ; see בעלה *a*.
גור בעל, 2 Chr. xxvi. 7.[1]

Places with names of this class are, it will be seen, situated in all parts of the country—in the extreme north as well as the far south, in the east and in the west; whatever significance may be found to attach to these names holds good for all parts of the country occupied by the Hebrews.

With the exception of the last three, the foregoing names do not appear to be *primarily* place names. Parallel forms in the case of some of the names confirm the truth of this appearance. Thus, assuming that מעון is correctly conjectured for בען in Num. xxxii. 3,[2] we have these four forms of the name of one town:—

[1] The text is almost certainly corrupt ; cf. LXX. The בעל part of the name should be struck out ; see Winckler, *Gesch. Israels*, p. 46.

[2] *MT*, supported by VV, reads בען ; but it appears to me

בית בעל מען, Jos. xiii. 17, cf. Mesha Inscr. line 30, בת בעלמען.
בעל מען, Num. xxxii. 38; 1 Chr. v. 8; Ez. xxv. 9; cf. Mesha line 9, בעל מען.
בית מען, Jer. xlviii. 23.
מען (?), Num. xxxii. 3; cf. the modern Mâ'in.

It is a natural inference that the only constant is also the only essential and fundamental part of the place name: *i.e.* מען itself was the name of a place. Further, the two forms with בית are also manifestly place names in the first instance; it is otherwise with בעלמען, which is primarily a personal name or title, and that undoubtedly of a god, who is thus described as "owner of Maon";[1] Baal Maon has then become a place name by the omission of Beth—a not infrequent occurrence; we have, *e.g.* Beth-Lebaoth, Jos. xix. 6 = Lebaoth, Jos. xv. 32; Beth-Azmaveth, Neh. vii. 28 = Azmaveth, Ezr. ii. 24; and Beth Reḥob,

most probable that this is an early transcriptional error for מען, ב and מ being letters that were frequently confused; cf. Driver, *Samuel*, p. lxviii. The other explanation of the text is less probable; בען is said to be an abbreviation for בית מען; for the possibility of the abbreviation of בית the case of בעשתרה is usually cited; cf. Ges. *Thesaurus*, 176 *b*; *New Oxf. Lex.* 110 *b*; Nestle, *Eigennamen*, 114; yet against admitting an abbreviation of בית even in this case, see Halévy, *REJ*, x. 2 f. In any case בעשתרה only gives a parallel for the abbreviation of בית; in בען we should, on this assumption, have an abbreviated בית prefixed to the second half of the other word.

[1] Cf. Robertson Smith, *Rel. Sem.*[2] 93 f., Baethgen, *Beiträge*, 19.

Judg. xviii. 28 = Reḥob, Num. xiii. 21. The variant forms on the Moabite stone in the present instance show that the longer and shorter forms were in some cases current at the same time.

Apparently then the forms are thus related to one another: Maon is the original name[1] of a place, Baal Maon is the specific title of the god or Baal of the people as worshipped there, Beth Baal Maon is primarily[2] the temple of this god, and secondarily a name of the whole place in virtue of the presence of this temple. Baal Maon and Beth Maon as names of the place are both abbreviations.

We have no other instance in which forms representing so many stages in the history of these names have survived; but several others help to confirm the history as just sketched, and the view that names of places beginning with Baal were, properly and originally, divine titles, and as place names presuppose at once a longer form with Beth prefixed, and a shorter consisting simply of the word following Baal.

[1] The purely general sense of the name is worth noting; it means "dwelling"; cf. the English "ham" which by itself and in compounds forms place names. It may like other general terms, such as Ramah, have been the name of several places: we know of one other—Maon in Judah (Jos. xv. 55). Beth Maon, therefore, which would have no good sense in itself, owes its origin purely to abbreviation, and, moreover, presupposes the form Beth Baal Maon.

[2] As a parallel term is accurately used in Judg. ix. 4, ויתנו לו שבעים כסף מבית בעל ברית.

A clear instance of the originally divine titular character of these names is seen in Baal Peor. This is clearly the title of a god in Num. xxv. 3 *b*, 5; Dt. iv. 3; Ps. cvi. 28; but it is as certainly the name of a place [1] in Hos. ix. 10, where the construction admits only of a place, and not of a personal name. But in this case also we have two parallel forms—the simple Peor and Beth Peor. By analogy with the last name (and others yet to be considered) we should infer that Peor was *originally* a place name; and as a matter of fact we read of ראש הפעור (Num. xxiii. 28), which implies a mountain of the name.[2] The simple term Peor is used also, it is true, as the name of the god in Num. xxv. 18, xxxi. 16, and possibly in Jos. xxii. 17; but this is easily explicable as due to abbreviation [3] (or even misunderstanding), especially since all these passages are by common agreement late.[4]

Again therefore the most natural explanation of the forms seems to be this: Peor was originally the

[1] *Vide* Hitzig, *ad loc.*, and the translations of Wellhausen and Kautzsch. Cf. also Dt. iv. 3 *a* with Driver's note thereon.

[2] Cf. τῷ ὄρει Φογώρ, Lagarde, *Onom. Sacra*, p. 292, cf. p. 103.

[3] To this we appear to have a parallel among the Babylonian Aramaeans; in *CIS*, ii. 20, we find the name מנוארבל, on which the editor writes, "id est 'quis sicut Arbela?' Arbela vero non alia ac Istar, Arbelae urbis dea. Cf. nomina biblica מיכיהו, מיכאל." Cf. also מקנארבאל, *ib.* 22, and ארבלר[בן], *ib.* 41.

[4] Dillmann attributes these passages to R (? Jos. xxii. 17), and presumably therefore regards them as late. They are generally recognised as belonging to P or R.

name of a district, Baal Peor the title of a god conceived as owning the district—in this case we think naturally of Chemosh, god of Moab; a temple erected in honour of the god worshipped under this local name gave rise to the name—primarily of the sanctuary, secondarily of the town surrounding it—Beth Baal Peor, which only survives in the abbreviated form Beth Peor.[1]

The above analysis and comparison render the assumption of Peor as an original divine name unnecessary and improbable: so far at least as the usage in extant literature goes, everything is explained by the analogy of the Baal names, if we start from the assumption[2]

[1] Dt. iii. 29, iv. 46. Cf. Βεθφογόρ, Lag. *Onom. Sacra*, pp. 233 and 103.

The documentary usage of the terms (which I give in full) is significant:—

הפעור place (mt.)	JE	Num. xxiii. 28 (cf. ὄρος Φογώρ, p. 129 n. 2).
בעל פעור god	JE, D, Psalm	Num. xxv. 3, 5; Dt. iv. 3 *b*; Ps. cvi. 28.
בעל פעור place	Hosea ix. 10.	
בית פעור place	JE? D, P	Dt. xxxiv. 6; iii. 29, iv. 46; Jos. xiii. 20.
פעור god	P or R	Num. xxv. 18, xxx. 16, and ? Jos. xxii. 17.

[2] Apart from the analogies above referred to, the primarily geographical character of the simple term פעור seems to me favoured by the existence of one or more places of the same name. A place Φαγὼρ (or Φογώρ) is mentioned in a passage preserved by the LXX. (Jos. xv. 59-60), on the genuineness of which see Dillmann *ad loc.* This lay near Bethlehem. Cf.

that the geographical term Peor is original; it would be exceedingly precarious to argue that the Moabites (or Midianites) worshipped a god with the proper name of Peor, and there is certainly nothing improbable in the supposition that the worship of Baal Peor was a local cult of Chemosh.[1]

In Baal Ḥermon we again have parallel forms though somewhat different in character; these are:—

הר חרמן, Dt. iii. 8 (cf. v. 9; iv. 48); several times in Jos. (D or Rd); 1 Chr. v. 23.

חרמן (meaning the mountain), Jos. xi. 3 (JE), Ps. lxxxix. 13, cxxxiii. 3, Cant. iv. 8.

בעל חרמן, 1 Chr. v. 23.

הר בעל חרמן, Judg. iii. 3.

The fundamental element (חרמן) is here again geographical, though, even by itself, it has a religious significance—the sacred enclosure—and perhaps reflects a stage in religion anterior to Baal worship. Baal Ḥermon was primarily a title of the god conceived as owning the mountain district of Ḥermon, though in the one passage where it occurs it is used geographically. The phrase הר בעל חרמן is peculiar: Is it pleonastic in the sense of the mountain belonging to

also *Onom. Sacra*, p. 300—ἔστι δὲ ἄλλη Φογὼρ κώμη πλήσιον Βηθλέεμ. Another place of the name is mentioned in Gen. xxxvi. 39, if the LXX. Φόγωρ be more original than *MT* פעו.

[1] Different or less decisive conclusions are drawn by Dillmann on Num. xxv. 3; Baudissin, *Studien*, ii. 232 f.; Baethgen, *Beiträge*, 14 f., 261.

Baal Ḥermon, or derivative from Baal Ḥermon in its geographical sense, and so equivalent to the mountain in the neighbourhood of this place? Bertheau's[1] explanation that it is an abbreviation for "Baal Gad under Mount Ḥermon" is improbable, especially since the passage in Joshua is later than that in Judges.

Corresponding to Baal Ḥazor we have the simple term Ḥazor as the name of several places, one of which, mentioned in Neh. xi. 33, is probably identical with Baal Ḥazor.

Baal Shalishah is to be connected with the "land of Shalishah" (1 S. ix. 4). In this case Baal Shalishah is the *town* or *village* surrounding the shrine where the god was worshipped as owner of the larger *district* around.

Of a place Hamon, implied by analogy in Baal Hamon, we have no independent evidence.

The name Baal-Tamar is not essentially different from the preceding names; but in this case the second element denoting the thing possessed refers to a natural (sacred) object—the palm-tree—instead of a place. To this we have a parallel in Baalath-Beer, originally the title of a goddess conceived as possessing this particular well.

In the names hitherto discussed we have no conclusive evidence that the *Hebrews* worshipped the Baals of the several places in question. They may

[1] *Commentary*, p. 54. Moore, so far as I can see, does not discuss this particular point.

have taken over from former inhabitants the names of the places without continuing the ancient cults. With regard to the following, the case is somewhat different. It is probable that, like the names already discussed, Baal Perazim (2 S. v. 20) implies the existence of a temple devoted to the local cult of a deity; Perazim, the original geographical term, was in this case a mountain (Is. xxviii. 21) just as in the cases of Baal Peor and Baal Ḥermon. If this be so, the explanation offered in 2 S. v. 20[1] will count as another of the many erroneous popular etymologies that are found in O.T. Even so, however, the passage appears to preserve a reminiscence of a time when the local Baal was identified by the Hebrews with Yahweh.[2]

But we are better justified in connecting the origin of some of these names with the Hebrews by the existence of בעל יהודה. We can hardly be wrong in concluding from it, that the early Hebrews not only took over place names containing Baal, but formed fresh ones; in this case a cult of a deity—presumably Yahweh—as owner of all Judah is implied.

Is Baal Gad to be similarly explained as meaning owner of the territory of Gad?[3] If not, the formation of the word may, in common with that of Baal-Zephon,

[1] Yet cf. Driver, *ad loc.*

[2] Cf. Oort, *The Worship of Baalim*, translated by Colenso (1865), p. 47.

[3] Cf. Stade, *Geschichte*, i. 272 n.; and for a similar suggestion with regard to Baal Zephon, Baudissin, *Studien*, i. 278.

be dissimilar to the rest, the second element in these two cases being itself the name of a god. In Baal-Zephon—a town situated on the Red Sea[1]—the second element (צְפוֹן) may be a god whose name is inferred from the Phoenician names בדצפן and עבדצפן, the former of which occurs in an inscription found at Abydos, the latter in one found at Carthage.[2] Gad is a tolerably well-known Syrian deity. If the interpretations just discussed be correct, these forms are difficult—especially, as Robertson Smith[3] sees, grammatically; since it is unsafe to assume the incorrectness of the interpretation, the effects of accepting it must be considered.

Now if we might assume that the towns Baal Gad and Baal Zephon were named after persons who founded or conquered them, the difficulty would disappear; as *personal* names they would be exactly paralleled by בעליה, the two elements being related as subject and predicate. But the small number of instances in which town names are identical with or even essentially similar to names of individuals, and the lack of evidence[4] that it was ever a common custom to name towns after individuals, make the

[1] A different place of the same name is apparently mentioned in the Assyrian Inscriptions, *KAT*, 154, 220.

[2] *CIS*, 108 and 265; cf. also צפנבעל (*CIS*, 207, 857), which is, however, quite as probably parallel to צפניה, צפן being a verb.

[3] *Rel. Sem.*[2] 94, n. 6.

[4] 2 Sam. xii. 28 is not to the point here: the "calling" is metaphorical: *vide* Driver, *ad loc.* Nor will narratives like Gen. iv. 17 be conclusive to many.

assumption hazardous. This, combined with the analogy of the other place names, makes it probable that the compounds Baal Gad, Baal Zephon were originally names (or titles) of gods. Then the double names are most naturally explained by the process which Baethgen[1] terms "Götteramalgamation," whereby two originally distinct deities are worshipped as one. But this implies that at a prior period Baal, like the Assyrian Bil, had become a proper name.[2] It is best, at any rate, to admit that in the neighbourhood of Baal Gad and Baal Zephon, Baal *may* have been a proper name; though it would be unwise to base much on a conclusion reached only by very hypothetical reasoning.

To sum up: save in the case of Baal Judah, possibly also of Baal Perazim, and, on one interpretation, of Baal Gad, there is no reason for tracing the creation of these place names to the Hebrews themselves rather than to their *Semitic* predecessors in the occupation of the country. But Baal Judah—certainly of Hebrew (Judaic) origin—is a name of the same formation and therefore of the same general significance as the other possibly pre-Hebraic names; consequently the conception and the cult of Baal implied in these

[1] *Beiträge*, 254.

[2] On the other hand the name במות בעל (Moab) need only imply that בעל in Moab was sometimes used as an *equivalent* term for the proper name of the deity, without itself becoming a proper name; cf. אל in Hebrew.

names were still current over the country when the Hebrews settled in it, and became current among them also. We may infer therefore that the Hebrews, in common with the people whom they dispossessed and with whom they shared the country, used Baal not as a proper name of a deity, but as a descriptive title of the god who was conceived as owning some particular town or district or natural object. This use of the word Baal and the connected local cults and shrines were distributed over the whole country. On the other hand, of the two places which *may* imply the currency of Baal as the proper name of a deity, one (Baal Gad) lay to the extreme north, the other (Baal Zephon) on the borders of Egypt; with neither of these districts were the bulk of the early Hebrews in any lasting contact, and in neither case—assuming the correctness of the interpretation in question—is there any reason for attributing the names, nor consequently the cults implied, to the Hebrews themselves.

3.

Names Compounded with אדן

Two of these are names of Canaanite kings—אדני צדק and אדני בזק,[1] Judg. i. 5; Jos. x. 1 (JE). Two are Hebrews of the Davidic period, one, אדניה, a son

[1] On the relation of these names to one another and their possible identity, see Moore, *Judges*, 14 ff.

of David (1 K. i. 8), and the other an officer, אדנירם.[1] According to the LXX. a name of this class was also borne by an officer of Rehoboam's time.[2]

These five are the only individuals mentioned in approximately contemporary writers. Among post-Exilic *families* two[3] bore names of this class—אדניה, Neh. x. 17, and אדניקם, Ezra ii. 13. The Chronicler mentions two persons with names of this class in the time of Jehoshaphat—אדניה and טוב אדניה, 2 Chr. xvii. 8.

Apparently therefore these names, never frequent among the Hebrews, early ceased to be formed, and ceased even to be used as personal names in or before the Exile.

Ethnographically the distribution is clear: O.T. shows that the formation was Canaanitish: the Assyrian Inscriptions[4] testify to the early currency of the Phoenician Aduniba'al; the Phoenician Inscriptions[5] to the frequency of this and similar compounds, *e.g.*

[1] 2 S. xx. 24, LXX. Ἀδωνειράμ: on the correctness of this reading, see Driver, *ad loc.* The person here named is probably identical with the Adoniram of the Hebrew text in 1 K. iv. 6.

[2] 1 K. xii. 18, LXX. A, Luc., Ἀδωνιράμ.

[3] Probably however the two are identical: אדניקם is read Ezra ii. 13; viii. 13; Neh. vii. 18; אדניה only at Neh. x. 17. Since אדניקם is at the same time the rarer name, it is textually to be preferred to אדניה in these passages (against Moore, *Judges*, p. 15, n. ff.).

[4] *KAT*, 105, 194.

[5] Bloch's *Glossar*, *s.v.* אדנאשמן and following words.

אדנאשמן, אדנשמש, at a later period. The formation is primarily and chiefly Phoenician: from the Phoenicians it passed to some of the peoples speaking closely similar dialects.

It is generally admitted that in all the names discussed in the present section the term denoting dominion or possession, whether it be בעל, מלך, or אדן, refers to a deity; but the question has arisen, mainly in the case of בעל, whether the deity referred to in Hebrew names of this type be Yahweh or a deity distinct from Yahweh. Great authorities can be cited for either view, though at present the former has a heavy balance of critical opinion in its favour.[1]

[1] The case for considering that בעל in these names is the name of a deity distinct from Yahweh was argued by Kuenen, 1869; see his *Rel. of Israel* (Eng. trans.), i. 304 f.; cf. 297 f., 403, 408. I am not aware that he ever seriously modified this view; from his criticism of Baethgen's *Beiträge* (in *Theologisch Tijdschrift*, 1888, pp. 571-588) it would seem he did not. For in reference to Baethgen's argument against the originality and "legitimacy" of polytheism in Israel he says, "Many details in this (argument) I cannot show to be unquestionably incorrect; he [*i.e.* Baethgen] *may* be correct . . . in striking out of the list some of the proper names from which the Israelite worship of the Baal or the Molech may be inferred" (*Ges. Abhandlungen*, translated by Budde, p. 462: cf. p. 458). For the other view—that Baal is a title of Yahweh—cf. among others, Oort, *Worship of the*

One unquestionable characteristic common to all three words is that they are used in Hebrew as appellatives—בעל in the sense of possessor, מלך of king, אדן of lord or master. The main question therefore resolves itself into this: In the proper names compounded with בעל, מלך, אדן, do these words retain their appellative force, so that the names, in so far as they refer to a deity, refer to him by a generic term applicable to more than one deity; or have the words in any or all the cases, previously to composition, become proper names of a specific deity?

It would take long to inquire fully how far the unquestionable appellatives בעל, אדן, מלך, became among certain Semitic peoples specific proper names; nor is it necessary. The argument may proceed on the assumption that these appellatives became in certain cases as much proper names as "God" is among ourselves. The question remains, was this the case with the Hebrews? and, even if so, were the names Baal, Melech, Adon, alternative proper names of Yahweh, or proper names of some deity distinct from Yahweh.

The argument may be simplified by first eliminating Adon. By the Hebrews it was certainly used as an appellative[1] with reference to Yahweh; no one has

Baalim (Colenso's trans.), pp. 25-63; Wellhausen, *Bücher Sam.* pp. xii. f.; Driver, *Samuel*, pp. 186, 195 f. (with lit. there cited).

[1] Cf. האדן י״י Ex. xxiii. 17; מלפני י״י מלפני אדן כל הארץ, Ps. xcvii. 5 (cf. Jos. iii. 11, etc.); מלפני אדן חולי ארץ, Ps. cxiv. 7.

ever yet argued, nor is likely to argue, that it was also used by them as the proper name of a deity distinct from Yahweh. It may be taken as agreed, therefore, that אדן in Hebrew proper names always retained its appellative force and never became itself a proper name. The names of this class mean "The[1] Lord is Yah" (Adonijah), "The Lord is exalted" (Adoniram),[2] "The Lord has arisen" (Adonikam), and in Hebrew "the Lord" referred to is clearly Yahweh, as the first of these names directly states;[3] but among other peoples

[1] Cf. for alternative views as to the significance of the ׳ in these forms the discussion on אבי, etc., above, pp. 84 ff.

[2] I do not understand Moore's statement, "In names compounded with *adōn*, the second part is uniformly the name of a god" (*Judges*, p. 15). If he means that the Hebrew word Adoniram signifies "the Lord is Ram," Ram being the proper name of a deity, this is against the analogy of יהורם where the latter part cannot be the name of a deity, and also inconsistent with his perfectly correct statement on p. 195, "in similar compounds of *el* and *adōn* [*i.e.* similar to Baaljada, Ishbaal], the unnamed deity is no other than Yahweh." We are hardly justified in inferring (from Is. lvii. 15) that רם *standing by itself* was ever a current title of Yahweh. The translation of Adoniram given in the text appears to me therefore the most probable, and Moore's objection to the form Adonikam groundless. On the other hand, his arguments against Adoni-bezek, at least in the sense Lord of Bezek, are strong: and the case for a deity of the name of בזק is made out. Cf. Moore, *Judges*, pp. 15 f.

[3] Cf. also טוב אדניה which occurs as a ἀπ. λεγ. in Chronicles. If the name is genuine it indicates that in some cases these compounds were differently construed: it can hardly mean anything but "Good is the Lord Yah."

it is used of other gods, as we see *e.g.* in the Canaanite (Biblical) name Adoniṣedek = The Lord is Ṣedeḳ, or the Phoenician name Adoneshmun = The Lord is Eshmun.

Like *adōn*, *melek* is unquestionably used appellatively of Yahweh; cf. *e.g.* Is vi. 5; Ps. v. 3, etc. But as to the use of *baal* there has been a difference of opinion; the *general* appellative use of the word is clear and undisputed, but its use as an appellative with reference to Yahweh has been questioned, yet, as it appears to me, without sufficient reasons. Independently of the proper names, the reasons for asserting that the Hebrews used to speak of Yahweh as Baal are these:—

1. The passage in Hosea ii. 16. This runs:—"And it shall come to pass in that day, saith Yahweh, thou shalt call (me) my ish (אישי) and thou shalt no more call me my baal (בעלי)." Kuenen[1] argues that this passage is sufficiently explained by the antithesis between *baal*, the technical term for husband, and the tenderer term *ish*; and, moreover, that, whatever the passage proves, it proves only for *baalī* = my baal, not for *baal* or *hab-baal*. As to the first contention, however plausible considered apart, considered in connection with its context the explanation is surely unsatisfactory. The passage continues, "For I will take away the names of the Baalim out of her mouth, and they shall no more be mentioned by name." As a continuation of a statement that, in the future, the

[1] Kuenen, *Rel. Isr.* i. 405.

Hebrews will address God in tenderer terms than in the past, this is pointless; but it is pointed enough if the whole thought is, the worship of local Baalim shall wholly cease; other deities who had been thus worshipped shall no longer be worshipped at all or even mentioned by name, and Yahweh, who will continue to be worshipped, will be worshipped no longer in this manner, nor spoken of by this title—"my baal." But if this be the meaning, surely the only natural inference is that the writer was conscious that Yahweh was still, or had at one time been, called Baal. *Baali* (my *baal*) is merely the specific personal usage corresponding to the general *baal* as אלהי (my God) to אלהים (God). And the more we question with Wellhausen[1] the probability of the Hebrews having actually employed the personal form—my *baal*—of Yahweh, the more must we assume the actuality of the usage of the general term. There must be some reason for the remark, and this is equally true whether it be Hosea's own or a scribal gloss;[2] the only effect of the latter assumption is to throw the usage of *baal* for Yahweh down to a later date. A scribe can only have written this gloss on the words "I will take away the names of the Baalim," if he was conscious that it had been, or still was, customary to call Yahweh *baal*.

2. The use of the corresponding verb with reference to Yahweh; cf. Is. lxii. 5; liv. 5.

[1] *Die Kleine Propheten*, p. 100.

[2] See Wellhausen, *l.c.*

These reasons—chiefly the former—seem to me by themselves decisive. There are, however, others which can be best considered in connection with the narrower question: In the compound proper names is Baal itself a proper name, or an appellative used with reference to Yahweh? My reasons for asserting the latter alternative are these:—

1. The lack of evidence for the existence of a definite deity having as its proper name the name Baal, among the Hebrews themselves or people with whom they were in contact at the time when names in בעל were current among them. Kuenen sees in such a name as Baal-jada a token of the worship of what he terms the "Canaanitish Baal." Now recent investigation has tended to show, and, in my opinion, has made out, that such a term is purely misleading. There were Canaanitish Baals; there was no Canaanitish Baal: the latter expression is not less inadmissible than such an expression as the Canaanitish El. Any deity might be termed El; any deity under certain circumstances might be termed Baal—the latter term taking its rise from the connection of the god in question with a definite place or object. In proof of this I must refer back to my analysis and discussion of the place names in Baal (pp. 127-136), and further to Robertson Smith's treatment of the subject, which was

there referred to. Here I have only to indicate the bearing of those names on the interpretation of the personal names. In the place names the use of Baal was clearly titular; most of them were probably of Canaanite origin; but at least one or two were formed by the Hebrews; in other words the Hebrews used the term baal as a *titular* term for a deity; what that deity was the place names by themselves leave in doubt.

2. But this doubt is solved by the personal name בעליה—Yah is baal. Now, if it be admitted that we may argue from the parallel name Adonijah that *Adon* in the *Hebrew* name Adoniram refers to Yahweh—and I am not aware that any one has disputed the probability of the inference,—surely we may argue from Baaliah that Baal in Baaljada, etc., refers to Yahweh. It would be unreasonable to insist that the first element of אליה and אדניה enters by itself into other compound names, and yet, in spite of its own general character, retains its reference to Yahweh, but that the first element of the precisely similar name בעליה cannot do so.

3. A further evidence in favour of treating בעל in these compounds as a title of Yahweh is the fact that unambiguous names of other deities than Yahweh are conspicuously absent

from Hebrew personal names. Some of the names that appear in the primeval traditions of the Hebrews probably have a divine character;[1] and possibly a few tribal names[2] contain those of deities distinct from Yahweh. But the instances cited among the names of individuals of any historical period are few, and these few are doubtful or capable of special explanation. Shamgar ben 'Anath, in which the last element is the name of the well-known goddess, is foreign, as we should perhaps be correct in considering the person himself to be.[3] The post-Exilic family names חנדד and עזגד, which probably contain the names of the deities Hadad and Gad respectively, may with probability be accounted for as due to worship of these gods in captivity. These three names practically exhaust the list.[4] Now if Baal denoted a god distinct from

[1] On this subject see especially Budde, *Urgeschichte.*

[2] But even Gad (also a personal name, 1 S. xxii. 5), one of the most likely instances, is capable of another explanation: see Baethgen, *Beiträge*, 160 f. On Ashbel and Reuben, *vide supra*, pp. 123 f.

[3] Cf. Moore, *Judges*, pp. 105, 143.

[4] On certain more hypothetical instances, see Barton's article in the volume of essays published by the Oriental Society of Philadelphia. His list certainly cannot be accepted entire: I criticise the inclusion of אליאל below. But even if most be admitted they hardly affect the above argument; for they are

Yahweh, it would be strange that several personal names originating in the worship of this god should have survived while none record the worship of gods with unambiguous names such as Astarte, Chemosh; and also that several names of the class occur in the families of Saul and David, both zealous worshippers of Yahweh, and neither, so far as our comparatively full and trustworthy information goes, addicted to the worship of a distinct and rival deity, Baal. While, on the other hand, no names of the class occur in the family of Ahab, who actually co-ordinated with the worship of Yahweh that of the (Phoenician) Baal.

I conclude therefore that the existence of proper names compounded with בעל is evidence not of the worship of other gods besides Yahweh, but of certain conceptions, which have already been sufficiently considered, concerning Yahweh.

The case of names in מלך differs very slightly. In מלכיה, the only name of the class in frequent use, מלך or מלכי is clearly a title of Yahweh. In the other names מלך or מלכי may be, so far as the forms go, either a titular or an appellative term or a proper name. Thus מלכישוע may be interpreted "*Melech* is opulence,"

isolated instances indicative at most of *sporadic* worship: the compounds with בעל are a group indicative of *prevalent* conceptions.

on the analogy of יהושוע = Yah is opulence; or the king is opulence, on the analogy of אבישוע, אלישוע = father, God is opulence. Similarly with אבימלך cf. אביה, but also אביאל; with אלימלך cf. אליהו, but also אליאב, אליעם; with אחימלך cf. אחיה, but also חיאל; with מלכירם cf. יהורם, but also אבירם, חירם. So much for the names in early use and the name of a descendant of David in the seventh century; failing independent proof of the worship of a god מלך distinct from Yahweh in these connections, we shall be on safest ground in adopting the titular interpretation.

The case differs in regard to the names נתנמלך and עבדמלך, both belonging to persons in the seventh century. We know that that was a time when Melech was becoming sharply distinguished from Yahweh, and was yet the object of persistent worship; in other words, we have proper names compounded with מלך from a period when, from evidence independent of these names, we know that מלך had (virtually) become the proper name of a deity distinct from Yahweh, and worshipped by the Hebrews. In the case of these two particular names, then, there is far better historical ground than in the case of Baal names for assuming that the ambiguous element is a proper name rather than a title. The forms also are noticeable; neither Nathan-melech (perfect *followed* by Melech) nor Ebed-melech have any analogy among the remaining names in Melech or among the names in Adon, Baal, Ab, or Aḥ. This is not decisive as to whether Melech in these compounds is a title or a proper name: for we have נתנאל (in late writings) as well as נתניה and עבדאל as well as עובדיה, but, on the whole, the latter alternative is more probable, especially in the case of עבד מלך. There appears to me therefore considerable probability that in the two names just considered we have survivals from Hebrew worship of another god than Yahweh, and that the names rightly interpreted mean "(the god) Melech has given," "Servant of (the god) Melech." Such survivals are so exceedingly rare that it is worth observing that in the present case there are good reasons for supposing that the names Nathan-Melech and Ebed-Melech were not given by Hebrew mothers to their children. In the latter case this is clear: Ebed-Melech is an Ethiopian, his name is probably enough Hebrew, but how he came by it we do not know. Nathan-Melech was a eunuch (2 K. xxiii. 11); eunuchs in Israel, as in other countries (cf. Dan. i. 3, 7; 2 K. xx. 18), were sometimes foreigners—*e.g.* Ebed-Melech, Jer. xxxviii. 7; further, the context in 2 K. xxiii. 11 implies that Nathan-Melech had been engaged in the establishment of the foreign god Melech, after whom he may have been appropriately named. Even these names then afford no satisfactory proof that other gods ever shared with Yahweh the feelings of gratitude and devotion which so frequently guided a Hebrew parent in the choice of his children's names.

IV

Names compounded with a Divine Name

1.

Names compounded with יה

The divine name יה is found in compounds either at the beginning of the word in one of the two forms יו or יְהוֹ or at the end in one of the two forms יָה or יָהוּ.[1] Compounds of this type number 156, a few more or a few less according to the view taken of certain doubtful forms discussed below. In a single instance יהו or יו stands in the middle of a name consisting of three elements.

Two theories, which would affect this class in an exactly contrary manner, the one enlarging, the other diminishing it, have been formulated. On the one hand it has been argued that in many cases, at the end of words, the divine name has survived in the termination ־ִי, and that for instance עַבְדִּי is a compound, meaning "Servant of Yah."[2] On the other

[1] On the philological reasons for connecting each of these four forms with יהוה, see Olshausen, *Lehrb. d. hebr. Sprache*, p. 611; Stade, *Hebr. Gram.* § 113; Driver, *Studia Biblica*, pp. 4-6.

[2] Cf. Delitzsch, *Wo lag das Paradies?* p. 159, who admits that ׳ = יה but denies that either = יהוה. The yod in these names is constantly interpreted Yahweh in Gesenius, *Thesaurus*

hand, Prof. Jastrow[1] has reduced this class to very modest limits. He also finds a close connection between names ending in simple י— and (many of) those ending in יה, but argues that neither termination is the divine name; he explains both "as one of the many afformatives in Semitic substantives that give emphatic force to the noun to which they are added." Prof. Jastrow's discussion is full of suggestion, and possibly in the case of some of the names in question his interpretation may prove to be correct, for there are a few which have hitherto remained without analogy or intelligible meaning on the assumption that the יה is a divine name. But he has reduced the compounds with the divine name to an improbably small number; were they no more than he admits, the Hebrews were singularly unlike their fellow Semites in the frequency with which they employed names of this type. Further, by far the greater number are, on the ordinary hypothesis, perfectly intelligible and in entire harmony with other Semitic compounds with a divine name, whereas in some cases,

(*e.g.* עבדי, ישמרי, מתני). Köhler (*Weissagungen Haggai's*, p. 1 f.) practically limits this interpretation to names of which the first (?) element is an impf.; even thus limited, the interpretation is improbable; the yod in most of these impfs. can be best explained as the third radical of ל״י roots. Cf. also Baudissin, *Studien*, i. p. 224. Philippi also discusses the question of י = יה in his essay "Ist יהוה Acadisch-Sumerischen Ursprung?" in *Zeitschr. f. Völkerpsychologie u. Sprachwissenschaft*, xl. (1883).

[1] *J. B. Lit.* xiii. (1894), pp. 101-127.

assuming that the יה is merely afformative, the meaning is not obviously apposite.[1]

Neither the view that forms such as עבדי contain a divine element, nor the view that forms such as אחיה lack it, appear to me well established; the names, therefore, on which the following discussion is based include, with exceptions to be discussed immediately, all names in יה, יהו, and exclude all ending merely in י. I will simply add here that the exclusion of the 63± names in which Prof. Jastrow regards יה as afformative would in some important respects strengthen my argument; to some of these I will draw attention below.

It will be convenient at this point just to draw attention to Renan's view[2] of the relation between

[1] My ignorance of Assyrian prevents me from criticising Jastrow's argument in full. But granting the legitimacy of explaining יה as afformative, the explanation of יה as the divine name still remains, as is of course admitted by Jastrow, an alternative. Two reasons for rejecting the latter in favour of the former interpretation which have weighed with Jastrow appear to me wholly lacking in force. There is no use in denying, on the ground of incompatibility with Semitic conceptions, that יה in אחיה, אביה, is a divine name, while we are left with indisputable instances like אביאל, אביבעל; not to mention חיאל, חמלך, חחלקיה, etc. And it is quite unreasonable to suspect all names in יה compounded with an element which does not happen to be also found compounded with a Hebrew name in אל. Phoenician compounds several times as many elements with בעל as with אל.

[2] In his essay "Des noms théophores apocopés," in *REJ*, v. 161 ff.; on p. 168 he directly denies that י in these names is a remnant of יה.

names in י and names in יה. He considers that names ending in one of the finals ה, א, י, ו, are generally speaking closely related, and that, "dans un grand nombre de cas, ces finales sont en réalité le pronom de la 3ᵉ personne, représentant d'une façon vague le nom de la divinité." But this view, apart from Renan's theory of Semitic monotheism which he finds indicated by this type of name, leaves names in י no more closely connected with those in יה than with those in אל; or, to put it otherwise, עבדי a name common to several languages would have had, to the different peoples who used it, meanings as different as names actually distinguished in form such as עבדיה, עבדאשמן.

The names and their usages with which the following discussion is concerned will be found classified in Appendix II. 3. As they stand there, they number 157.[1] Several are *ἅπαξ λεγόμενα*, and there is good reason for believing that in some cases these are merely differentiations from other names through

[1] I group together here some names which, superficially regarded, might be, but are not included in the list. Their exclusion does not, I think, require any lengthy justification, since, even if admitted, they scarcely affect my argument, and several have already been sufficiently discussed by others; see Baudissin, *Studien zur sem. Religionsgeschichte*, i. 224 f. The names in question are: בויותיה, a textual error for בְּנוֹתֶיהָ; ענתתיה; וניה; שכיה, a textually and etymologically uncertain ἅπ. λεγ. in 1 Chr. viii. 10; ארניה (= ארונה, etc.); יהוכל, derivative from יכל; חרחיה.

בעשיה will be found in App. II. 3 B, under מעשיה, No. 78; יוניה under יאוניה, No. 43.

textual corruption. The notes in the appendix will probably be found a sufficient index to the degree of certainty attaching to the textual tradition of these names. In dealing with the whole number this uncertainty—it is seldom more than a question between two forms, each of which would contain the name יה—rarely affects the argument to an appreciable extent. But there are other names, textually or etymologically ambiguous, which must be considered here, since throughout the argument it is important to bear in mind the extent of their ambiguity.

It is possible that some of the names beginning with -יו are simple and not compound. These are:—

1. יואב and יואח, which have been already discussed, p. 24, and found to be most probably compound.
2. יואל. This has generally been regarded as related to אליה as יואב to אביה; but it is, philologically, equally possible that יואל is the Hebrew equivalent of Arabic وَاَلَ, Himyaritic ואל, Nab. ואלו (cf. also ואלת). This latter view has been accepted by Nestle, W. Wright and Robertson Smith.[1] It is very questionable, therefore, whether יואל in 1 S. viii. 2, and in some of its tribal usages, should

[1] For the connection between יואל and وَاَلَ etc., see Osiander in *ZDMG*, 1856, p. 51; Nestle, *Eigennamen*, p. 86; Robertson Smith, *Kinship*, p. 301; *CIS*, i. 132 n.; ii. 198, 212, 214; and *Oxf. Lex.*, *s.v.* (where further literature is cited).

be regarded as a name in יה. But whatever the etymology, the later popularity of the name was most probably due to a popular interpretation of the name in the sense—Yah is God.[1]

3. יוֹאָשׁ, יוֹעָשׁ, יוֹתָם. So far as the form goes, these names might be kâtăl modifications of the roots יאש, יעש, and יתם respectively;[2] such forms actually occur in Hebrew proper names, cf. חותם. Of the roots in question the first and last (cf. יתום) occur in Hebrew; the second does not, but there is an Arabic وعس. The *possibility* therefore of these names being simple must be admitted. Perfectly suitable interpretations on this view may not be obvious, but that is not decisive; the meanings of uncompounded simple names is frequently obscure. Still it appears far more probable that at least יואש and יותם are compounds, since the form and meanings of the names are then well supported by analogy; both contain a perfect preceded by a divine name, cf. יהוחנן, בעלחנן,

[1] For the later tendency to find יה where it was not originally intended, cf. יהוסף Ps. lxxxi. 6 = יוסף, and see Goldziher, *Mythos bei den Hebräern*, p. 351.

[2] This appears to me far more probable than Jastrow's (*l.c.* p. 120) suggestion that יואש and יעש are Hifil forms. As Hifil forms he also explains, *inter alia*, יואח, יוקים, יורם; but of what roots?

etc.; יואש, if explained in connection with آس, means "Yah has bestowed"—one of the commonest ideas conveyed by names, and יותם—"Yah is perfect"—is sufficiently suitable. יועש presents a very probable meaning if we connect עש with غاث = "to come to the help of";[1] cf. the frequent compounds with עזר. Of the three names only יואש occurs also in the fuller form יהואש; the occurrence of this form probably indicates that יה was at an early period considered to form a part of the name; if this was not actually the case, the form יהואש must be explained on the analogy of יהוסף—cf. p. 154, n. 1. The form יהואש is used in naming the king of Israel and the king of Judah; otherwise the form יואש is employed.

4. יועד, יהועדה, הושמע; see App. II. 3 A, Nos. 17, 18, 26, with notes.

5. יהושוע. It has been questioned whether the Israelitish leader's name was really יהושוע. But the alternative form הושע is only recognised by P, and that only in Num. xiii. 8, 16; on Deut. xxxii. 44, see Driver. The parallel אבישוע and אלישוע favour the antiquity of the name and its compound character.[2] The text

[1] For آس and غاث and their Hebrew equivalents, *vide* Nöldeke in *ZDMG*, xl. 740, 168 f.

[2] For a suggestion that יהושע itself was not originally compound, but a Hifil, *vide* Stade, *Hebr. Gram.* p. 93.

of the name of a person mentioned only in 1 S. vi. 14 is open to question : see App. II. 3 A, No. 25*b*. The late name ישוע appears to be merely a modification of יהושע,[1] and I have therefore included all instances of both forms under one heading in the Appendix.

6. יוכבד. The view that this name is a compound with יה has been questioned, but remains the view least open to objection.[2] At the same time we may, I think, doubt whether the priestly writer who alone preserves the name, so understood it; the only other compound with יה found in his work is יהושע, and that he is careful to explain was first given after the Exodus, Num. xiii. 16.

The fourth group of names just discussed may be dismissed from consideration without materially affecting the argument. The remainder chiefly affect conclusions with regard to the earlier periods.

Of names ending in יה one only needs to be discussed here, viz. מִיכָיְהוּ, מִיכָיְהוּ; one of these forms and one or both of the forms מיכה, מיכא, are in some cases used of the same person. In later times they were perhaps virtually synonymous; but this is not

[1] On this point see *TSK*, 1892, pp. 177, 573 ; *WZKM*, iv. 332 f.

[2] The question is discussed by Nestle (*Eigennamen*, p. 77 ff.) who decides in favour of יו being the divine name. See also König, *Hauptprobleme*, p. 27.

to be assumed for early times. The shorter forms may well have had a purely secular reference, signifying—"who is like this child." But whatever the significance of the shorter forms, in themselves they have no more right to be included here than *e.g.* נָתָן. Consequently I have excluded from consideration the name of the person named in Judg. xvii.; the only properly attested form in this case is מיכה. *MT*, it is true, reads in verses 1, 4, מיכיהו; but it is supported only by LXX. B, which reads throughout the narrative Μειχαία. On the other hand LXX. A (Μιχά Μειχά), Vg., Syr., Ar. read מיכה in verses 1 and 4; Trg. reads so in verse 4, but מיכיה in verse 1. I have also excluded from the list of persons of this name the canonical prophet Micah, who is called מיכיה in Jer. xxvi. 18, Kt. only. The variants in other cases are not sufficiently serious to justify exclusion, but they raise a doubt as to the early existence of the name מיכיה; the literary history of such phrases as מי כמכה and the doubtful history of the parallel names מיכאל, מישאל (?) are worth observing in this connection. Merely on the ground of theological ideas involved no suspicion ought to rest on the early Hebrew usage of the forms; similar ideas are found in Assyrian (*e.g.* Mannu-ki-ilu-rabu).[1]

I now proceed to an historical analysis of the names of this class as collected in the Appendix.

[1] Cf. Schrader, *ZDMG*, 1872, p. 147; *CIS*, ii. 20, n.

Names compounded with Yah number 157.[1] All of these, with the one[2] exception of Bithiah, occur in connection with Hebrew persons or families. In 29 the divine name constitutes the first element, in 127 the last, and in a single name of three elements (אליהועיני) it occupies the middle position. I will use the symbol A for names in which the divine name stands at the beginning, B for names in which it stands at the end.[3]

From the foregoing statement it appears that B names are about four and a half times as numerous as A names. It will be important to discover whether this ratio was a constant one. For this purpose, and also with a view to indicate the growth and increasing popularity of these names, I append four tables. The first two tabulate the names (A and B being distin-

[1] This number depends on reckoning as single instances certain duplicate forms, viz., יהושע and ישוע; ברכיה and יברכיה; הודויה and הודיה; חזקיה and יחזקיה; יכניה and כניה; כונניה and כנניה; שלמיה and משלמיה; cf. the notes on these names in App. II. 3.

[2] Or two, if, on the ground of 2 Chr. xxiv. 26, we consider the only person of the name יוזכר a foreigner. In one or two cases names borne by Israelites are *also* borne by foreigners, *e.g.* Tobiah, Uriah.

[3] It is not assumed that all names ending (or beginning) with יה are homogeneous; but at the present point of the discussion different A and B formations cannot be distinguished without seriously complicating the following statistical presentation. The analysis of both A and B names into important subdivisions will be given below (pp. 175 ff.) and will then be found to accentuate certain marked differences which are brought to light by the first analysis.

guished) according to the periods in which they *first* occur; but, whereas Table 1 is based on approximately contemporary literature,[1] Table 2 is based on the whole of O.T. literature indifferently; yet, as a matter of fact,[2] the difference of the two tables practically consists simply in this—that in the first the evidence of Chronicles is disregarded, in the second it is admitted. The actual names will be found classified in Appendix III. In the tables I give in the right hand column the corresponding number of אל names; the comparison will, I hope, serve to bring out more fully the growth of the יה names.

TABLE 1.

The number of names first referred by approximately contemporary literature to

	A.	B.		Totals.	Names in אל.
Period I.[1]	(1 –)5	1	=	6 (at most)	15
,, II.	4	6	=	10	11
,, III. to cent. 8	8	18	=	26	6
,, ,, from cent. 7	4	27	=	31	9
,, IV.	1	42	=	43[3]	18
Totals	22	94	=	116	59

[1] For the sense in which this term is used, and for the Periods in the Tables, see above, pp. 20 f.

[2] The reason being that with one or two exceptions all the additional names with Yah are found only in Chronicles.

[3] Of the names first mentioned in reference to Period IV. several are certainly or possibly names of *families*. All of these, therefore, may have originated at an indefinitely earlier

TABLE 2.

The number of names first referred by any O.T. writer to

	A.	B.		Totals.	Names in אל.
Period I.	1(P)+(2−)6	14	=	21	44
,, II.	11	42	=	53	34
,, III. to cent. 8	4	13	=	17	9
,, ,, from cent. 7	4	17	=	21	7
,, IV. ,,	1	29	=	30[1]	7
Totals	27	115	=	142[2]	101

Strictly regarded the foregoing tables only indicate that a certain number of names occurred at least as early as Period I., certain others at least as early as Period II., and so forth; and in the case of any particular name it would certainly be unsafe to argue from

period; if we reject these as names of uncertain dates the final line in the two tables will stand thus:—

TABLE 1.

	A.	B.		Total.
Period IV.	0	25	=	25

TABLE 2.

	A.	B.		Total.
Period IV.	0	17	=	17

A further point to be noticed with regard to all the tables is that the name of Uriah the *Hittite* has been included (for the reasons, see below, p. 249). The exclusion of the name chiefly affects Tables 1 and 3; on 2 and 4 it has no appreciable effect.

[1] See previous page, note 3.

[2] Fourteen names occur only in connections which cannot be clearly determined; of these ten (A 1, B 9) occur in 1 Chr. ii.-ix. and four (A 1, B 3) in Neh. xi.

this that it was not in actual use at an even considerably earlier period than that to which it happens to be referred in extant literature. But where we are dealing with a considerable number, we may safely argue on the supposition that the *order* of reference in literature corresponds on the average to the order of occurrence in actual life; and also that the date to which they are first referred in literature represents approximately the date at which they actually first came into use. Thus, *e.g.*, of the forty-three names (see Table 1) first referred in the literature to Period IV., a certain number no doubt were actually in use in Period III., and a few may have been found earlier than some of the twenty-seven names referred to the later part of Period III.; but there can be no reasonable doubt that by far the greater number of the forty-three were actually formed at a later period than the twenty-seven. This explanation will, I hope, prevent any ambiguity in subsequent brevity of expression with reference to these tables.

The next two tables are less open to misunderstanding, and more directly bring into contrast the evidence of the approximately contemporary writings and Chronicles. The first tabulates the number of *persons* who bear names of this class, mentioned in the approximately contemporary writings; the second the number of persons mentioned *only* in Chronicles. The contrast extends only through Periods I.-III.; in Period IV. the documents coincide.

Table 3.

Hebrew persons bearing a יה name, and mentioned in approximately contemporary literature, number in

	A.	B.		Totals.	Persons bearing אל Names.
Period I.	1–5	1	=	6	16
,, II.	10	7	=	17	18
,, III. to cent. 8 . .	19	31	=	50	7
,, ,, from cent. 7 .	8	65	=	73	12
,, IV.	27	169	=	196	50
Totals	69	273	=	342	103

Table 4.

Hebrew persons bearing a יה name and mentioned *only* in Chronicles, number in

	A.	B.		Totals.	Persons bearing a Name in אל.
Period I.	2	13	=	15	3
,, II.	19	67	=	86	59
,, III. to cent. 8 . .	12	43	=	55	22
,, ,, from cent. 7 .	4	11	=	15	4
,, IV.	27	170	=	197[1]	50
Totals[2]	64	304	=	368	138

[1] The numbers for Period IV. in Tables 3 and 4 include the family as well as the purely personal references. Deducting cases where the reference is certainly or possibly to families, the statement runs—

	A.	B.		Totals.	אל Names.
Period IV. . .	20	123	=	143	43

[2] In addition to the above we find 84 (A 16, B 68) persons or families mentioned in uncertain chronological connections; in detail 62 (A 14, B 48) in 1 Chr. ii.-ix.; 22 (A 2, B 20) in Neh. xi.

Certain conclusions can be safely drawn at once, for Tables 2 and 4 agree with Tables 1 and 3 in pointing to them:—

1. Names compounded with יה were formed in all periods.
2. The A formations had become virtually extinct by Period IV.
3. Fresh B formations were still frequent in Period IV.
4. From Period III. onwards names compounded with יה were more popular than names compounded with אל.

Other conclusions, such *e.g.* as the gradually increasing predominance of B over A formations, an early preference for אל names giving way to a growing preference for יה names, are suggested by Tables 1 and 3, but derive no support from or are even directly discountenanced by Tables 2 and 4.

The further discussion of these points must be deferred to the next chapter.

2.

Names compounded with אל

These names will be found in Appendix II. 4.

In treating of this class, I use the symbols A and B as in the last section.

The O.T. contains 135[1] names compounded with

[1] The numbers depend on reckoning as single instances certain duplicate forms, viz. *e.g.* אלדד and אלידד · קבצאל and יקבצאל ;

אל: of these 39 are A and 97 B. Several names of this class also are ἅπαξ λεγόμενα, and some are textually uncertain; cf. the notes in Appendix II. 4. But etymologically very few are ambiguous so far as the element אל is concerned. There are, however, in addition to יואל (see p. 153) two or three which have been explained in such a way as to render them only apparent instances of the present formation. These are—

1. מחויאל: this has been interpreted by D. H. Müller[1] "(the god) יאל gives life." The peculiarity of the list in which the name occurs prevents us from confidently rejecting this etymology merely on the ground that the god יאל is otherwise unknown in the O.T. But the absence of any conclusive evidence in favour of the proposed etymology makes it safer to accept מחויאל provisionally as a name in אל.
2. מתושאל. This has received more than one interpretation on the supposition that it consists of two compounds only, מתו (man) and שאל (to ask): cf. Dillmann on Gen. iv. 18. The more usual view is that it contains three elements, מתו, ש, and אל, the whole being = "man of God." For such a meaning there is no lack of analogy, but for the use of ש there

שובאל and שבואל (originally identical). The total is 135 (not 136), since אליאל is included under both A and B.

[1] According to Gesenius-Buhl, *s.v.*

is no very satisfactory parallel.[1] The name must be regarded as a very doubtful instance of compounds with אל.

3. מישאל can with more confidence be accepted in the sense—"who is what God is?"; the use of ש is not open to objection, and the sense is parallel to מיכאל.

All names in the Old Testament compounded with יה, with one or perhaps two exceptions, occur as names of Hebrew persons or families. With names compounded with אל the case is different; fourteen (A 1, B 13) occur only as place names, seven (A 2, B 5) only as names of foreigners, and one (B) both as a place name and as the name of a foreign individual, but not as the name of a Hebrew family or individual.

There are thus 113 (A 36, B 78) Hebrew personal (or tribal) names in אל as against 157 in יה In both cases B names are the more numerous, but the proportion of B to A names among compounds with אל is much smaller (2⅙ : 1) than among compounds with יה (4½ : 1).

In one respect the analysis of these names is more complicated than that in the preceding section. Compounds with אל are frequent in P, as well as in the approximately contemporary literature and in Chronicles; several of the names are peculiar to P,

[1] Yet cf. W. Max Müller, *Asien u. Europa*, p. 193, who finds a parallel in the name of a Phoenician town conquered by Sety—Ba'-t'-ša-'-ra = בית־שאל.

and many persons bearing them are mentioned only by him; it will be convenient to distinguish these from names and persons mentioned in the other literature; naturally the analysis is affected by these names only in reference to Period I. Apart from the additional minuteness of the analysis thus rendered necessary, the following tables are precisely similar to those given in the last section, and what was said with reference to those applies *mutatis mutandis* with reference to these.

Tables illustrative of the origin and popularity of compounds with אל:—

TABLE 1.

The number of (personal or tribal) names first referred by approximately contemporary literature to

	A.	B.		Totals.
Period I.[1]	7	8	=	15
„ II.	7	4	=	11
„ III. to cent. 8 . .	4	2	=	6
„ „ from cent. 7 .	2	7	=	9
„ IV.[2]	1	17	=	18
Totals	21	38	=	59

[1] Of the seven A names in Period I. one (אלימלך) is attested only by Ruth, and another אליהוא is textually uncertain ; thus at lowest the number of A names would be five, and these are all clearly personal. Of the eight B names two only are at once certain and clearly personal. מחויאל, יואל, and מתושאל are etymologically uncertain (see above), ישראל and ירחמאל certainly, עתניאל probably, are tribal.

[2] Of the seventeen B names four are certainly or probably family names.

TABLE 2.

The number of names first referred by any O.T. writer to

	A.	B.	Totals.
Period I. . . .	11	33	= 44 (in P—A 4, B 25)
„ II. . . .	14	20	= 34
„ III. to cent. 8 .	6	3	= 9
„ „ from cent. 7	2	5	= 7
„ IV.	0	7	= 7
Totals	33	68	= 101

Thirteen other names occur in chronologically uncertain connections; of these twelve (A 3, B 9) occur in 1 Chr. ii.-ix. and one (B) in Prov. xxxi.

TABLE 3.

Hebrew persons (or tribes) bearing a name compounded with אל and mentioned in approximately contemporary literature number in

	A.	B.	Totals.
Period I.[1]	8	8	= 16
„ II. . .	13	5	= 18
„ III. to cent. 8 . .	4	3	= 7
„ „ from cent. 7 .	5	7	= 12
„ IV.[2]	22	28	= 50
Totals	52	51	= 103

[1] Of the eight A instances note that Elimelech is mentioned only in Ruth, and one of the Eliezers (Gen. xv. 2) may be foreign. This leaves six well-attested and certainly personal A instances. Of the B instances two only are well attested, unambiguous, and certainly personal. Cf. p. 166, n. 1.

[2] Of these A 2, B 5 are certainly or probably family names.

TABLE 4.

Hebrew persons (or tribes) bearing a name compounded with אל and mentioned *only* in Chronicles number in

	A.	B.	Totals.
Period I.	2	1	= 3
„ II.	19	40	= 59
„ III. to cent. 8	6	16	= 22
„ „ from cent. 7	0	4	= 4
„ IV.	22	28	= 50
Totals	49	89	= 138

Thirty-six persons mentioned only by P bear names compounded with אל; of these nine are A, twenty-seven B.

Forty-two persons (or tribes) are mentioned only in chronologically undefinable contexts; of these thirty-nine (A 12, B 27) are referred to only in 1 Chr. ii.-ix., two B in Neh. xi., one B in Prov. xxx. 1.

A close comparison of Tables 1 and 3 with Tables 2 and 4 will reveal some striking differences; still more striking is the divergent evidence of Tables 1 and 3 on the one hand, and of P on the other, to the popularity of names in אל in Period I., and to the ratio between A and B names at that time. To these differences I must return. Meantime I tabulate the very meagre conclusions to which all the evidence agrees in pointing:—

1. Names of both A and B formations were already current in the earliest period.

2. Fresh B names were still being formed in the post-Exilic period, but the A formations had all but, if not quite, exhausted themselves.

3.

Names compounded with שדי

These are at most but three in number, and are confined to a single list in P. They are צורישדי, Num. i. 6; שדיאור, which *MT* points שְׁדֵיאוּר, Num. i. 5; and עמישדי, Num. i. 12.

The further consideration of these names must be postponed to the next chapter.

CHAPTER III

THE HISTORICAL CHARACTER OF THE NAMES IN CHRONICLES AND P

In the last section of the preceding chapter it was found that the evidence both of Chronicles and of P differed in a marked manner from that of the unquestionably pre-Exilic literature in regard to the growth and popularity of names compounded with יה and אל. I propose in the present chapter to examine into the causes of these differences, and to determine, so far as may be possible, the historical character of the names and persons mentioned only in one or both of the books in question—Chronicles and P.

I turn first to the names in Chronicles. I hope to prove conclusively that *these names largely consist of those of the compiler's own time* (c. 300 B.C.), *that they are at least not genuine survivals from the days of David and the subsequent kings.* Such a conclusion would not indeed be surprising in respect of an author who "reflects faithfully the spirit of his age," when "a new mode of viewing the past history of his nation began to prevail," when "pre-Exilic Judah was pictured as already in possession of the institutions, and governed . . . by the ideas and principles, which were dominant at a later day."[1] I say it would not be surprising that such a writer should transfer to the past the names also of his own day, as well as its institutions, ideas, and principles, but it requires proof, for without proof it would be only natural to suppose that at least for his names the author relied on ancient sources; and it requires proof all the more, since the determination of the historical character of the Chronicler's names is crucial in estimating the evidence of the O.T. proper names as to the history of religious ideas in their growth and extension.

To begin with the most general aspects of the case. Of names compounded with יה, 143 are referable to definite periods; 27 are mentioned *only* in Chronicles; of the remaining 116, only 16 (or including יוכבד, the solitary instance in P, 17) are referred in pre-Exilic writings to the Davidic or pre-Davidic periods; the proportion of the whole is in this case *under one-seventh;* but, admitting the evidence of Chronicles, we find that out of 143, 74 (or, including יוכבד, 75) are Davidic or pre-Davidic; in this case the proportion is just over *one-half.*

Some of this difference in proportion might reasonably be explained by the fact that a great number of

[1] Driver, *Introduction*, p. 500.

the Chronicler's names belong to Period II., but this could not satisfactorily explain the full extent of the difference, and as a matter of fact the more detailed the investigation becomes, the clearer it grows that such is not at any rate the main cause. Thus, *e.g.*, though the Chronicler refers many names to the Davidic, he refers few that are not found also in earlier writings to the pre-Davidic period; in other words, the pre-Davidic persons mentioned *only* by the Chronicler are by no means so numerous as the persons mentioned in the pre-Exilic writings; yet among this comparatively small number of names of persons mentioned *only* by the Chronicler and referred to Period I., fourteen different names compounded with יה are found; the pre-Exilic writings refer to the same period only six (or, including יוכבד, seven). The genealogies (1 Chr. v., vi.), in which these fourteen compounds with יה, assigned by the Chronicler to Period I., occur, show other signs of not being genuine records of that early period, for (1) they repeat the same names in the same family. Now it has been already shown (pp. 4 ff.) that there is no early evidence for admitting, but that there are the strongest reasons for denying, that the custom of naming the child after the father, grandfather, etc., which would lead to such repetitions, was prevalent in earlier times; on the other hand, the custom was coming into vogue about the time of the Chronicler. (2) Of the fourteen names, nine are known to have been in use in the post-Exilic period, and some of them were then in very frequent use; מלכיה occurs six times, מעשיה nine times, in Period IV.

The real cause of the difference in the character of the Chronicler's names becomes clearer when we take into account the *forms* of the names. Of 22 (23)[1] A names found in approximately contemporary writings 9 (10), *i.e. between a third and a half*, occur in or before the Davidic period; of the 94 B names, only 7, *i.e. less than one-thirteenth*. The mere addition of the Chronicler's evidence changes these proportions thus: of 26 (27) A names, 17 (18), *i.e. two-thirds*, but of 115 B names, 56, *i.e. all but one half*, occur in or before the Davidic period; that is to say, by the admission of the Chronicler's evidence, the proportion of Davidic and pre-Davidic names to the whole number is in the case of A names *less than doubled*, but in the case of B names it is *increased more than sixfold*. This difference, which is far too striking to be merely accidental, is inexplicable if the Chronicler's names are all, or even for the most part, genuinely Davidic or pre-Davidic; but if they are names current in his own day, the difference is at once and completely accounted for; for in the post-Exilic period, whereas new A names had ceased to be formed, B names were still in constant process of formation; and although old A names continued to be used, B names were

[1] The numbers in brackets include יוכבד (P).

more than five times as frequent; see ch. ii. section 4, Tables 1-4.

Further, an examination of Table 1 (p. 159) indicates that the proportion between the newly created A and B names—or, to speak quite accurately, between A and B names, classified according to the first reference to them in literature—changes in regular progression throughout the first three periods, *i.e.* down to the time when new A names entirely cease to be formed, and in new compounds with יה the יה always stands at the end of the word; thus the proportions are in

Period I. .	A : B = 5 : 1	(or[1] 3 : 1, or 1 : 1).
„ II. . .	„ = 1 : $1\frac{1}{2}$	
„ III. to cent. 8	„ = 1 : $2\frac{1}{4}$	
„ „ from cent. 7	„ = 1 : $6\frac{3}{4}$	

The mere addition of the Chronicler's evidence changes this progression; the proportions[2] for the various periods then are in

Period I. . .	A : B = 1 : $2\frac{2}{3}$	(or[1] 1 : $3\frac{2}{3}$, or 1 : 7).
„ II. . .	„ = 1 : 4	
„ III. to cent. 8	„ = 1 : $3\frac{1}{4}$	
„ „ from cent. 7	„ = 1 : $4\frac{1}{4}$	

Without the Chronicler's evidence, then, we infer

[1] The alternatives are according to the view taken of (1) יואש and יותם; (2) יואל and יהושע.

[2] The following table is based on Table 2 (p. 160) exclusive of one A name in Period I.—viz. יוכבר (P).

that *the A formation was at first more frequent than the B formation, but from the Davidic period onward the B formation became increasingly more frequent than the A formation until in the post-Exilic period the latter became extinct;* admitting the Chronicler's evidence we should have to infer that B was always more numerous, but that from the earliest (or at least the Davidic) period the ratio between B and A was virtually constant, and that then suddenly A ceased while B continued. Once again the difference is immediately explained if the Chronicler's names are in large part late, but is otherwise inexplicable.

Hitherto I have discussed these names simply as classified according to the position in them of the divine name. They may with advantage be examined more grammatically and less externally: the differences already noticed will in that way become still more accentuated, and the cause of them still more clearly discernible.

Olshausen[1] divides compound names on philological grounds into seven classes; three concern us here, Nos. i., iv., vii.; these are :—

1. Names consisting of two nouns, a construct and a genitive, *e.g.* ידידיה.

2. Names consisting of two nouns, subject and predicate, *e.g.* יואב.

3. Names consisting of a verb (predicate) and noun (subject), *e.g.* יהונתן.

[1] *Lehrbuch der hebr. Sprache*, § 277, pp. 609 ff.

It is often doubtful whether the first part of a name is construct or subject (typical instance אֲבִיָּה); to distinguish between the first two classes in the case of the names with which we are dealing would therefore render the classification complex, and to some extent uncertain, without giving any equivalent advantage. But combining classes (1) and (2) we find that *in later times the combination of* יה *in proper names with a verb was more frequent than its combination with another noun.* Thus according to Table 1, out of 43 fresh instances (for which see App. III.) in Period IV., 31[1] certainly consist of combinations with a verb; according to Table 2, out of 30, certainly 22—in each case a little over *two-thirds.*[2] Now, according to Table 1, this proportion is less in the earlier periods: in Period I. 3 out of 6, *i.e. one half* in Period II. 5 out of 10 (9), also *one half.* With the addition of the Chronicler's evidence the numbers and proportions run in Period I. 11 out of 20, *over one half,* in Period II. 37 out of 52, *over two-thirds*—in the latter case the post-Exilic proportion.

A further detail, interesting in itself, is equally significant in the present connection. In later times the names of the verbal class mainly consist of a

[1] Exclusive for instance of הודויה which is uncertain though quite probably verbal: see App. II. 3 B, No. 24, n.

[2] This proportion is somewhat increased if we exclude family names; the numbers then are 19 verbals out of a total of 24 (Table I.) or 13 out of 18 (Table 2).

perfect tense followed by יה: thus of the 31 verbal names in Period IV. (Table 1), 24, or of the 22 (Table 2), 17 are so formed,[1] and of the remainder not a single one consists of a pf. *preceded* by יה; yet this latter formation was, it appears from the early writings, in early use, and down to the Davidic period was as frequent, if not more frequent, than the former; subsequently it gave way more and more to the newer formation. The following table will show this.

The first appearances in

	Pf. preceded by יה.	Pf. followed by יה.
Period I. consist of . . .	3	0
„ II. „ . . .	3	2
„ III. to cent. 8 consist of .	4	11
„ „ from cent. 7 „ .	2	13
„ IV. consist of. . .	0	24

Again the admission of the Chronicler's evidence entirely changes the complexion of things, by giving to the names of all periods the same general character, and that the general character of post-Exilic names. Thus of the names referred by him *alone* to Period I., eight are verbal compounds; in every case the verb is perfect, and in every case the verb precedes. This is exactly what we should expect in post-

[1] If the names in which Jastrow regards the יה as afformative be deducted the *proportion* of names (in Period IV.) in which pf. precedes יה to the whole number is scarcely affected; it then stands 17 : 26.

Exilic names, exactly the reverse of what we should expect in pre-Davidic names. In Period II. the addition of the Chronicler's evidence also greatly changes the proportion; it then stands thus: the pf. is preceded by יה in seven, followed by יה in twenty-one names; the evidence of Chronicles changes a proportion of 1 : $\frac{2}{3}$ into 1 : 3.

I have now in several instances shown that so long as we confine our attention to names recorded in approximately contemporary writings, certain well defined peculiarities—chiefly consisting of the different ratios observable at different periods between certain formations—clearly distinguish earlier from later names; but that as soon as we *also* take into account the names in Chronicles, these differences are wholly or largely obliterated, and the names of an early period are marked by the same characteristics that unquestionably mark the post-Exilic names. The line of argument hitherto followed might be carried further either by a similar examination of compounds with אל or by a still more detailed examination of the compounds with יה; but probably enough has been already adduced to illustrate the nature and cogency of this particular class of evidence.

I now proceed, in somewhat different ways, to bring even more sharply into relief the similarity of the names in Chronicles to post-Exilic names, and their dissimilarity to names referred by early writings to the corresponding periods.

As soon as we come to deal with persons we can directly contrast the complexion of the names as a whole in Chronicles with that of those in the early writings. The figures here may be left to speak for themselves; they are those of persons bearing names compounded with יה—at the beginning A, at the end B. In each case the numbers in the first line are those of persons bearing names of the class in question and mentioned in the early writings, in the second line those of persons in the same period but mentioned *only* in Chronicles, and in the third those of persons mentioned in the post-Exilic period.

	A.	B.	Proportion of A to B.
1. Period I.—Early writings	(1-)5	1	$1 : \frac{1}{5}$
„ „ Chronicles *only*	2	13	$1 : 6\frac{1}{2}$
„ IV.	27	169	$1 : 6\frac{1}{4}$
2. Period II.—Early writings	10	7	$1 : \frac{2}{3}$
„ „ Chronicles *only*	19	67	$1 : 3\frac{1}{2}$
„ IV.	27	169	$1 : 6\frac{1}{4}$

In Period I. the names of persons mentioned only by the Chronicler are practically identical in character with the names of post-Exilic persons, in Period II. they greatly approximate to the same character; in both periods they greatly differ from the names referred in early writings to the respective periods.

It is seldom safe to argue as to date from the mere presence or absence of any single *indi-*

vidual name; for, generally speaking, any particular name occurs comparatively seldom. But still there are certain names used so frequently at certain times as to be characteristic of those times, and this is particularly true of the post-Exilic period. Several of these characteristically post-Exilic names are frequently referred by the Chronicler, though seldom or never by the earlier writings, to pre-Exilic periods. Some of the more significant instances I give in the following table. Under each heading I give the number of different Hebrew persons bearing the name in question, but under Chronicles I of course include *only* the persons mentioned *only* in that book and referred by it to pre-Exilic periods. After the numbers in the post-Exilic period I give the number of families (certain or probable) *included* in the preceding number.

	Early Writings.	Chronicles.	Post-Exilic.
יהוזבד . .	1	6	2
יהוחנן . .	1[1]	8	6 (F. 1)
אמריה . .	1	5	2 (F. 1)
זבדיה . .	0	5	2
זכריה . .	3	12	9
חשביה . .	0	5	3 (F. 1)
ידעיה . .	0	1	3 (F. 2)

[1] Sixth century; with one exception all the persons mentioned in Chr. are referred to a century earlier than the seventh.

	Early Writings.	Chronicles.	Post-Exilic.
מעשיה . .	2 [1]	6	9 (F. 1)
מלכיה . .	2 [1]	2	6 (F. 1)
פתחיה . .	0	1	3
שכניה . .	0	2	6 (F. 2)
אליהועיני .	0	1	4
אלישיב . .	0	1	6
יחזיאל . .	0	4	1
יחיאל . .	0	7	3
יעיאל . .	0	6	2
מיכאל . .	0 [2]	4	2 (F. 1)
נתנאל . .	0 [2]	6	3

On the other hand it is to be observed that in a few cases names of persons mentioned only in Chronicles are found elsewhere only in pre-Exilic writings; the most noticeable instances will be found among the compounds with יה; see Appendix II. 3 A, Nos. 2, 3, 5, 23, 27. But the paucity of these heightens rather than diminishes the significance of the foregoing table; and it must be added that that table by no means presents all the striking phenomena in the usage of particular names; for instance, several names of frequent recurrence in the Chronicler's account of David and his earlier successors

[1] Both these names are first referred by the earlier writers to the close of the seventh century; with one exception, the eight occurrences in the Chronicler are in or before the eighth century.

[2] Both מיכאל and נתנאל occur in P.

are first referred in the earlier literature to the close of the seventh century.

The force of the immediately preceding observations will be increased by comparison with the following. In the narrative of the Davidic period in the books of Samuel thirteen[1] compounds with יה occur; two of these are borne by more than one person, viz. Jonathan by four, and Benaiah by two. Not more than six[1] of these are also borne by persons mentioned *only* by the Chronicler; Benaiah and Jonathan, according to Samuel the most popular names, are each the names of but one person mentioned only by the Chronicler. And yet there are other names of frequent recurrence among the persons mentioned only by the Chronicler; as against thirteen names distributed among seventeen people in Samuel, the Chronicler records fifty-eight names distributed among eighty-five persons mentioned *only* by himself. Five of these—Johanan, Zebadiah, Zechariah, Hashabiah, and Isshiah (App. II. 3 A, No. 10; B, Nos. 26, 27, 38, 69)—are distributed among seventeen people, a number equal to the total in Samuel; all of these names are unknown to the Books of Samuel. They are all current in the post-Exilic period, being borne by twenty-two persons; only one

[1] This number includes two *textually* uncertain instances, יואל and יהושע; cf. the notes in the Appendix. If rejected on this ground, there will be only four names (out of eleven) common to the narratives of Samuel and persons mentioned only by the Chronicler.

(Zechariah) can be traced up as far as the eighth century, only one other (Johanan) as far as the sixth, in the early writings. The remaining three are unknown before the Exile, apart from the evidence of the Chronicler. Other names recurrent in the Chronicler's account of the Davidic period are worthy of attention; but it must suffice to refer to the Appendix, see more especially A, No. 7; B, Nos. 67, 122. I will add only one further general observation here. Eighteen of the names are recurrent among the persons mentioned only by the Chronicler; three of these each occur as the name of one person in Samuel; fourteen are current and several frequent in the post-Exilic period; of the four not then current two (ישמכיה and עוזיה) are probably textual corruptions of names (סמכיה and עזיה) which were current, and one יהושפט is a name attested by Samuel as being Davidic. Briefly, names recurrent in Samuel are not recurrent in Chronicles; of names recurrent in Chronicles most never occur and none recur in Samuel, but almost all occur and most recur in the post-Exilic period.

I turn lastly to a consideration of the general complexion of the whole of the names in certain narratives, more especially with a view to illustrating the growth in the proportion of names compounded with יה or אל to all others. The narratives, etc., have been selected as being typical of particular periods or special classes, but in every case they include only Hebrew individuals. They are as follows:—

1. Names[1] in Judges ii. 6-xvi.
   A typical *pre-Davidic* list.
2. Names[1] in 2 S. ix.-xx.
   A typical *Davidic* (court) list.
3. Names[1] of Jeremiah's contemporaries.
   This list is an illustration of names in use at the *close of the seventh century.*
4. Names of "those of Israel" who had taken strange wives (Ezra x. 25-43).
   A typical list of *post-Exilic laity.*
5. Names of the priests who had married strange wives (Ezra x. 18-23).
   A typical *post-Exilic priestly* list.
6. Names of "those that sealed" (Neh. x. 1-27).
   These are post-Exilic *family* names, viz.—
   Verses 2-8, priestly families.
   Verses 9-13, Levitical families.
   „ 14-27, lay families.

[1] The names in Judges and Samuel (2 S. ix.-xx.) will be found classified in Appendix I. Especially in regard to the first of these lists some difference of opinion as to details is inevitable, particularly with reference to the tribal or personal character of certain names. But it is unnecessary to discuss the matter in full; the proportion of names compounded with אל or יה will in any case remain strikingly small. Shamgar and Anath I have excluded as being probably not Hebrew names; see Moore, *Judges*, pp. 105, 143. I have regarded the עבר of *MT* in Judg. vii. 26 a superior reading to the יובל of LXX.; see above, p. 122, n. 3. Jeremiah's contemporaries are classified in Nestle's *Eigennamen*, pp. 204 ff. My numbers are based on that list, except that I exclude Ebed-melech (Jer. xxxviii. 7) and Magormissabib (xx. 3).

Unfortunately no sufficiently long and typical list of names from the first part of Period III. can be obtained. Even those in Jeremiah are perhaps not quite typical, as will be seen later, but they are nearly enough so for comparison with the others.

I add two lists from Chronicles:

7. Of names occurring in 1 Chr. xxvi. 2-32, with the exception of names in ver. 28, which are taken from Samuel, the manifestly earlier names Ladan and Merari (vv. 19-24), and the corrupt name Ahijah in ver. 20 (see p. 36).
8. Of names occurring in 1 Chr. xxvii. 16-24.

The first of these two lists consists of Levites, the second of ordinary Israelites stated to have been contemporary with David.

The analysis of the several lists is as follows:—

Names in	Compounds with יה.	Compounds with אל.	All others.		Totals.
1. Judg. ii. 6-xvi.	2	1	25	=	28
2. 2 S. ix.-xx.	9[1]	2	34	=	45
3. Jeremiah	53	9	25	=	87
4. Ezra x. 25-43	31	12	45	=	86[2]

[1] This number includes Uriah the *Hittite*. Similarly the two compounds with אל include Eliam (2 S. xi. 4), who was also possibly a foreigner.

[2] So, not eighty-eight; for Joel and Elijah have each been counted twice—once under compounds with יה, once under compounds with אל.

Names in		Compounds with יה.	Compounds with אל.	All others.	Totals.
5. Ezra x. 18-22		10	5	2	= 17
6. Neh. x. (*a*) 2-8	Families	10	1	10	= 21
(*b*) 9-13	Families	8	1	8	= 17
(*c*) 16-27	Families	8	1	35	= 44
7. 1 Chr. xxvi. 2-32		20	10	13	= 43
8. 1 Chr. xxvii. 16-24		9	8	9	= 26

The most immediately markworthy feature of the above analysis is the proportion between compounds with either אל or יה, and all others. To make this still clearer I add a table of these (approximate) proportions. In—

1. Judg. ii. 6-xvi.		compounds with אל or יה	: others	$= 1 : 8\frac{1}{3}$
2. 2 Sam. ix.-xx.		„	„	$= 1 : 3$
3. Jeremiah		„	„	$= 2\frac{1}{2} : 1$
4. Ezra x. 25-43		„	„	$= 1 : 1$
5. 18-22		„	„	$= 7\frac{1}{2} : 1$
6. Neh. x. (*a*) 2-8	Families	„	„	$= 1 : 1$
(*b*) 9-13	Families	„	„	$= 1 : 1$
(*c*) 16-27	Families	„	„	$= 1 : 4$
7. 1 Chr. xxvi. 2-32		„	„	$= 2\frac{1}{3} : 1$
8. „ xxvii. 16-24		„	„	$= 2 : 1$

The first point to which I call special attention is this—the marked difference in proportion in the case of the two post-Exilic lists drawn from Ezra x. A similar difference exists between the proportion in the post-Exilic *family* names of Neh. x. 2-13 and Neh. x. 14-27. In each case where the proportion of compounds with אל and יה is greater, the names are those of priests, in each case where it is smaller the names are those of laymen. In these cases the cause of difference is difference of class. Now if we strike a mean between the two proportions of the post-Exilic priestly and post-Exilic lay list, we obtain $3\frac{3}{4} : 1$ as the proportion which would approximately exist between compounds with אל and יה in a mixed list;[1] the history in the growth of these names then appears thus—

In Period	I.	compounds with אל and יה	: others	$= 1 : 8\frac{1}{3}$
„	II.	„	„	$= 1 : 3$
„	III. (close)	„	„	$= 2\frac{1}{2} : 1$
„	IV.	„	„	$= 3\frac{3}{4} : 1$

and may be formulated thus. The proportion of compounds with אל and יה was consistently from first to last on the increase, yet down to the Davidic period these compounds were still greatly outnumbered by others, but by the post-Exilic period all others were as strikingly outnumbered by these compounds.

Once again, the Chronicler's Davidic names are seen to have a post-Exilic and not a Davidic complexion. In both lists from Chronicles analysed above the proportion of compounds with אל or יה is markedly different from that found in the names from Samuel,

[1] The proportion so obtained may, I think, be safely used in comparisons with the other mixed lists. It does not of course represent the actual proportion for all names then current, but unrecorded; for the laity greatly outnumbered the priests.

whereas it closely approaches the post-Exilic proportion.

One or two further points in connection with the names in 1 Chr. xxvi. 2-32 and xxvii. 16-24 are markworthy. Of thirteen names in the former list not compounded with אל or יה, *three* are names of post-Exilic families, viz. עילם, זכרי, שלומות. Of these two occur nowhere outside Chronicles except in reference to post-Exilic families or individuals; the third, זכרי, also occurs in Ex. vi. 21 (P). Of the rest *one* only, עבד אדם, occurs also in Samuel. One, עובד, occurs also in Ruth; the rest, as used of individuals, are confined to Chronicles.

Of nine names not compounded with אל or יה in 1 Chr. xxvii. 16-24, *four* occur also as members of post-Exilic families, viz. זכרי, הושע, עדו, ירחם, and one other as the name of a post-Exilic individual. Two, אבנר and צדק, are no doubt taken directly from Samuel.

Thus, even with these uncompounded names, it can be shown that they have on the whole a post-Exilic rather than a Davidic character.

With this I bring the present argument to an end. I have now shown that, whether tested by the mere number of compounds in יה first appearing in different periods, or by the number of persons bearing such names, or by the proportion existing in the several periods between different formations of the names, or again by the proportion existing between compounds with יה and אל and all other names, or by the usage of a number of individual names, the names in Chronicles approximate closely in character to those which unquestionably belong to the post-Exilic period and diverge widely, especially in respect of those it assigns to the Davidic or pre-Davidic periods, from those assigned to the same periods in admittedly earlier writings.

From all this the conclusion is inevitable. Distributed throughout the Chronicler's work are so many names of his own times that large sections of it bear, in respect of the names, the unmistakeable stamp of the post-Exilic period.

But are any of the names which, in themselves or as referred to particular persons, are peculiar to Chronicles ancient and genuine? Certain indications that this is the case have already appeared. Thus (1) certain names were found to be peculiar to Chronicles and the *pre-Exilic* sources; (2) the proportions based on the whole book *approximated* much more closely to the post-Exilic than to the early proportions based on the names in the early writings, yet they were not *identical* with the post-Exilic proportions.

This being the case, the more it can be shown that *certain* lists, such as the two recently analysed, *exactly* or *closely* correspond in character with post-Exilic lists, the more probable does it become that many of the residue of the names are not post-Exilic but, presumably, actual names of the period to which they are referred. Thus it appears probable that, although many names peculiar to Chronicles, either wholly or as assigned to certain persons, are not ancient, some others are so; in other words, that the Chronicler derived his names in part from those current in his own days, in part from ancient sources.

I will not attempt at the present point to discriminate between the ancient and modern names in Chronicles. In so far as this is possible at all, it can be more easily accomplished after the character of the names in P has been examined.

The names peculiar to P possess well-marked features. Even more striking is a certain negative characteristic of them; except for the one doubtful instance of Jochebed, compounds with יה are wholly absent. But this absence is capable of two equally satisfactory explanations. It may be due to the antiquity of the names; for as a study of the unquestionably early writings shows, compounds with יה were exceedingly rare in the earliest period. JE contains but one, the book of Judges only two or three. On the other hand the absence of compounds with יה from the names peculiar to P may be due to design; for the author was persuaded that up to the date of the revelation to Moses (Ex. vi. 2 ff.) the name יהוה was unknown to the Hebrews. If, therefore, his names be artificially formed or selected (the only alternative to their not being ancient, for they are not post-Exilic) he would naturally avoid constructing those which contained יה; it is noticeable that, in the case of the only name of the class common to his own and the prophetic narrative, he is careful to explain that it was given not at birth, but in manhood, and therefore after the revelation of the name Yahweh. Joshua's earlier name, according to P, was Hosea, without the element יה (Num. xiii. 16). Thus in considering the genuineness and antiquity of P's names, the absence of compounds with יה is indecisive. This being the case we are unfortunately deprived of the arguments which in the case of Chronicles were most convincing.

The second characteristic of P's names is the large number of compounds with אל, and among these the great proportion of those in which אל forms the last element. These facts tell, though perhaps at first sight not decisively, against the genuine antiquity of P's names.

In detail: the early narratives refer to Period I., in addition to certain foreign and place names, fifteen Hebrew compounds with אל—A 7, B 8; while of Hebrew names referred by P *alone* (or in a single instance, מיכאל, also by the Chronicler) to the same period, twenty-nine are compounds with אל, and of these only four are A, the remaining twenty-five are B. There is thus a very striking difference in proportion; among names of the early narratives A : B : : 1 : $1\frac{1}{7}$; among names peculiar (in the same period) to P, A : B : : 1 : 6; in the post-Exilic period the proportion is A : B : : 1 : 17 according to Table 1, : : 0 : 7 according to Table 2 on pp. 166 ff.

Further, there is some[1] evidence that, as in the case of compounds with יה, so also in the case of compounds with אל, the formation with the divine name *prefixed* to a perfect tense is earlier than that with the divine name post-fixed. Thus in

	אל Prefixed to Pf.	אל Post-fixed to Pf.
Period I.	2[2]	0
„ II.	2	1
„ III.	2[3]	2
„ IV.	0	2[4]

[1] Taken by themselves the above instances of compounds with אל would be too few to justify an inference of much weight. Taken in conjunction with the far more numerous names in יה, they are not insignificant. The general theory that the prefixing of the subject was earlier, is also supported by the analogy of compounds with אב and אח. These were shown to be ancient formations. In far the greater number of cases אב and אח are prefixed; a few clear instances exist of אב or אח *prefixed* to a pf., *e.g.* אביאסף, אחיסמך, אחיקם; in no case are they post-fixed. Note further בעלידע and אדנירם (both Period II.); in no Hebrew names are either בעל or אדן post-fixed to a pf. (contrast Phoenician); on the other hand in century seven we have נתנמלך.

[2] Three, if we include אלדד; but see p. 61.

[3] Three, if, as we probably should, we include אלישע.

[4] Three, if we consider בצלאל a compound with a pf.

The figures just given are based on names found in the approximately contemporary writings only; of names referred by P alone to Period I. there are—

With pf. prefixed, 2—with pf. post-fixed, 2 (or 3, including בצלאל). This difference is not very striking, nor could we expect it to be, for the *verbal* compounds with אל are in all periods comparatively few; but such as it is, it tells against the antiquity of some of P's names.

I will next illustrate the proportion of names containing a divine name to others from two specimen lists, viz. (1) Num. i. 5-16, and (2) Num. xxxiv. 19-28—in each case omitting the names of the tribes. In the first we find

Of names compounded with	(*a*) אל	9	
	(*b*) שדי	3	
			= 12
Of others			12

The proportion here is 1 : 1.

In list (2) we find

Of names compounded with אל	7
Of others	13

The proportion is 1 : 2; or, if we omit the names of the well-known persons Caleb and Jephunneh, in the residuum of names of persons known only through these lists, the proportion is 1 : 1½.

A comparison with the lists on pp. 187 f. will show that in both the foregoing lists the proportion of compounds with a divine name is much larger than among the names found in Judges or Samuel (2 S. ix.-xx.), and that in Num. i. the proportion is identical with that found in the list of post-Exilic laity, from which however the list in Numbers is sharply distinguished by this fact—in the names of Ezra x. the divine name compounded is generally יה, in Numbers exclusively אל or שדי.

Judged then by the proportion of compounds with a divine name P's names do not appear to be purely primitive.

The third striking characteristic of P's names are the compounds with צור and שדי. These are few in number, but they are very characteristic of, because entirely peculiar to, P.

The fact that names of this type occur nowhere outside the Priestly Code would be at once and entirely explained if they were artificial creations of its author; the other explanation that has been offered—viz. that these names were ancient and became obsolete at a very early date—is in itself less satisfactory; why do we find no instances in JE or Judges? Yet since we find only five in P, we need not press this absence from other sources too much. Still, admitting that it is inconclusive, we are left with two equally plausible explanations; if it is possible to determine between them, it will only be by a detailed examination of the names. In attempting this consideration we must consider the usage of the elements צור and שדי, the usage of the other elements in these names and the formations of the names.

1. The usage of צור and שדי.

צור is used of God (*a*) in *two*[1] *pre-Deuteronomic* passages, but in each of these cases it is defined by a genitive, thus צור מעוך, Is. xvii. 10; צור ישראל, Is. xxx. 29; many scholars would, of course, also regard the usages in 2 S. xxii. = Ps. xviii. and possibly in 1 S. ii. 2-10, which I discuss immediately, as pre-Deuteronomic: (*b*) in *numerous post-Deuteronomic*[2] passages, many of which are also post-Exilic. The usage in detail, which is of importance in the present connection, is as follows:—

(*a*) With the art., used absolutely of God—Dt. xxxii. 4.

(*β*) Without the art., used absolutely of God—Dt. xxxii. 18 (cf. xxxii. 37), Hab. i. 12.

(*γ*) Without the art., used generically of God—1 S. ii. 2; 2 S. xxii. 32 = Ps. xviii. 32; Is. xliv. 8 ("who is *a* rock," etc.).

[1] Or only one if Is. xxx. 29 be regarded as late; see Cheyne, *Introd. to Book of Isaiah*, 199 f. The *possibility* that צר in the place name ביתצור (Jos. xv. 58, P) is a divine name should also be considered.

[2] As to the date of the literature involved, see Kuenen's *Hexateuch*, 256 f.; on Deut. xxxii. cf. Driver, *Deuteronomy*, pp. 346 ff.; Cheyne, *Origin of Psalter*, 204 ff.; on 1 S. ii. 1-10, cf. Driver, *Introd.* p. 164, and Cheyne, *op. cit.* 57. I have myself argued for the post-Exilic origin of Ps. xviii.—*Jewish Quarterly Review*, vii. (1895), pp. 658 ff.

(δ) Defined by a following genitive—Dt. xxxii. 15; 2 S. xxiii. 3; Ps. lxii. 8, lxxiii. 26, lxxxix 27, xxxi. 3 = lxxi. 3, xciv. 22, xcv. 1; Is. xxvi. 4.

(ε) Defined by a personal suffix—Dt. xxxii. 30 f.; 2 S. xxii. 47 = Ps. xviii. 47; 2 S. xxii. 3 = Ps. xviii. 3; Ps. xix. 15, xxviii. 1, lxii. 3, 7, lxxviii. 35, xcii. 16, cxliv. 1.

In the names צוריאל, צורישדי, the צור is probably enough defined by the suffix; in אליצור it is presumably generic. The usage in these three names is therefore paralleled by the usage in *e.g.* Ps. xviii. But in פדהצור the צור is used absolutely (and presumably of God), and therefore has its analogy in literature only in Dt. xxxii. (cf. Hab. i. 12). The usage of צור in Hebrew literature thus gives no ground for supposing that it was an ancient name or epithet which could be used absolutely and undefined for God, nor that at an early date it was frequent even in comparisons; God is spoken of as a rock much more frequently in late than in early literature.

שדי is certainly an *ancient*[1] term for God, but in early times, to judge from its usage in literature, quite *infrequent;* its occurrence is certain in only three early (poetical) passages—Num. xxiv. 4, 16; Gen. xlix. 25—unless we add also Ruth i. 20 f.; in Gen. xliii. 14 the name appears to be redactional.[2] It

[1] According to Baethgen (*Beiträge*, p. 294) שדי is of Aramaic origin.

[2] So Dillmann, Kuenen, Cornill, Cheyne.

continued in use *later*, but except in P and Job was still quite *infrequent*, occurring only in Is. xiii. 6 = Joel i. 15 (in the alliterative phrase כְּשֹׁד מִשַּׁדַּי), Pss. lxviii. 15, xci. 1, and (if Ruth be late) Ruth i. 20 f. In Ezek. i. 24, x. 5, the word appears to be interpolated—see Cornill. Over against this infrequency in the ordinary usage of the word we have to set its *great frequency in Job* (thirty-one times) and its frequency in P (five times). P states the reason for his use of it; it was in his opinion the patriarchal name for God (Ex. vi. 3); he consequently employs it, to the exclusion of Yahweh, in his narrative of the pre-Mosaic times—Gen. xvii. 1; xxviii. 3; xxxv. 11; xlviii. 3. The author of Job is manifestly guided by a similar opinion; he also avoids the use of Yahweh and employs in its stead, as an archaism, the name Shaddai. Frequent as an archaism Shaddai is most infrequent at any time in ordinary usage, and in fact occurs only as a poetical epithet of God; from this we more easily infer that Ammishaddai, Zurishaddai and Shaddaiur are archaic artificial formations than that they were names actually current at any period.

The name צורישדי forms a link between the two classes, since it contains both elements. If all five names be artificial, we should therefore naturally attribute them all to a single mind. So far as Shaddai goes, the author of P seems likely enough to have been himself the creator of the names. But P never employs the word צור of God; should we infer from this that he did not create the names into which that term enters? If so, we must suppose that he drew these names from a source—a source which if the names be artificial and late must itself have been post-Deuteronomic. But perhaps the point should not be pressed; the style of P's narrative scarcely admits of the use of צור as an epithet of God.

2. The usage of the other elements in the names אליצור, צוריאל, צורישדי, פדהצור, שדיאור, and עמישדי.

אל or אלי is used in the composition of names of all periods. On עמי see above, pp. 44 ff.; except for certain names peculiar to P and Chronicles, compounds with עמי (= kinsman) appear to be ancient. The word אור occurs in אוריה—the name of a Hittite contemporary of David, a priestly contemporary of Ahaz, a prophetic contemporary of Jeremiah, and a priestly contemporary of Nehemiah, and in אוריאל—the name of two persons mentioned only by the Chronicler and, in post-biblical literature, of an angel. The simple name אורי is that of a contemporary of Solomon and a contemporary of Ezra; it is also the name of a Judahite mentioned only in P and Chronicles. In proper names the root פדה occurs as follows:—in (1) פדהאל, Num. xxxiv. 28 (P); (2) פדיה—the name of one person of the seventh century, *four* of the post-Exilic period, one referred by Chronicles to David's time, and another of uncertain date; (3) יפדיה, 1 Chr. viii. 25; and (4) פדון—a post-Exilic family.

Briefly—אל and אור occur in names of all periods; עמי occurs in a number of names peculiar to P and Chronicles (see pp. 45 ff.), but is otherwise confined to early names; פדה never occurs in early names (outside P and Chr.), but is frequent in names from the end of the seventh century onwards.

3. The formations.

With the exception of פדהצור all the names, so far as the formations go, might with equal probability be assigned to any period. But the analogies for פדהצור in which the perfect is *prefixed* are late; see above, pp. 177, 192.

The convergence of the preceding three lines of evidence appears to me to cast great doubt on the genuine antiquity of the names compounded with צור and שדי and to give much probability to the view that they are post-Deuteronomic and probably post-Exilic artificial creations. This convergence is clearest in the case of פדהצור; for the absolute use of צור as a name of God, for the occurrence of פדה in proper names, and for the prefixing of a perfect to its subject, we have no analogy in the earliest names recorded in the early writings, and but very little prior to the seventh century.

I will conclude this examination of the names in P by a detailed analysis of the two lists already referred to in Num. i. and xxxiv. respectively, and of the compounds with אל *peculiar* to P. The lists in question record the names of forty-four persons; twenty-four bear names peculiar to these lists, the remaining twenty names are found also elsewhere.

1. The twenty-four names peculiar to Num. i. and xxxiv.

Five of these are compounds with צור and שדי and have just been discussed.

Five others are compounded with אל, viz. שלומיאל, פגעיאל, דעואל, גמליאל, פדהאל. Are these names early or late? Apparently late, for in every case אל stands at the end of the name and in פדהאל after a perfect. The form of שְׁלֻמִיאֵל is noticeable; if the punctuation be correct, the name appears to be formed by a combination of אל with the passive kal *participle.* Now the occurrence of participles in compound proper names, though frequent enough in Assyrian, is exceedingly rare in Hebrew;[1] the few instances found in O.T. are, with the possible exception of מחויאל, late or confined to P and Chronicles. The early origin of the section Gen. iv. 18 ff. in which מחויאל occurs has been questioned,[2] and in any case the names found in that narrative are far from being typically Hebraic. The other instances[3]—certain or probable

[1] Cf. Driver, *Samuel*, pp. 14, 196; Nestle, *Marginalien*, pp. 7 f. On Assyrian participial compounds, Schrader, *ZDMG*, 1872, p. 119.

[2] By Nestle, *l.c.*

[3] שמואל is certainly not an instance; cf. Driver, *op. cit.* p. 14.

—of participles in compound names are משיזבאל, a post-Exilic family; מהיטבאל, the name of the grandfather (or ? family) of a contemporary of Nehemiah, and also of an Edomite (Gen. xxxvi. 39); (מ)שלמיה, the name of a Davidic Levite mentioned only by the Chronicler, otherwise only of several contemporaries of Jeremiah and several post-Exilic persons; מהללאל,[1] a post-Exilic family and also a descendant of Seth (P and Chr. only). We ought at least to compare also ידיעאל, the name of three persons mentioned only in Chronicles.

So much as to the forms of these names. As to the other constituent elements: פדה, it has been already seen, is frequent in late names but unknown in any that are unquestionably early (*i.e.* earlier than the seventh cent.) The use of the other four roots in proper names is without much significance; פגע occurs in none; גמל only in גמול, which occurs only

Zerubbabel should, however, be included, if really = זרוע בבל; so still König, *Hebr. Sprache*, ii. p. 481. Many also find another early instance in מרי־בעל, Nestle, *Eigennamen*, p. 120 f.; cf. Driver, *Samuel*, p. 196. But I regard מרי־בעל as the correct form of this name, the sense probably being "Hero of Baal" (cf. Imru al Ḳais). The form מרי־בעל receives no support from LXX., and from *MT* only in 1 Chr. viii. 34, ix. 40 *a* (but not *b*). The form מפי־בשת—which appears to me more probably a mere meaningless corruption (cf. Talm. אלקים for אלהים) than a significant one—also favours מרי־בעל.

[1] Notwithstanding *MT*, this should be punctuated מַהֲלַלְאֵל according to LXX. Μαλελεήλ; cf. Μετεβεήλ = מְהֵיטַבְאֵל; cf. further Nestle, *l.c.*

in 1 Chr. xxiv. 17, and גמלי, which occurs only in Num. xiii. 12 (P); שלם is common both in early and late uncompounded names; the only other verbal compound which it serves to make is שלמיה, which probably originated in the time of Jeremiah. The first element of דעואל is ambiguous; if from ידע, it also has analogies among names both early and late (cf. *e.g.* בעלידע, ידעיה, ידיעאל); but if from דעה (cf. دعا = to call), the only parallel is אלדעה—the name of a Midianite—Gen. xxv. 4 (J).

One other fact is to be noted: גמליאל though found nowhere else in O.T. is the name of several Rabbis mentioned in the Mishna.

Of the remaining fourteen names peculiar to the two lists, two, judged by the evidence of the approximately contemporary writings, must without hesitation be considered *ancient*, viz. אבידן, אחידע; see above, pp. 28, 38. The rest of the names are uncompounded, and with reference to them the data are scantier and less decisive. Yet there is probability that the following are of pre-Exilic origin—צוער, עכרן, גדעוני.

Thus the root of צוער is more frequent in early than in late writings and is never used by P; the other proper names from the root are all place and therefore presumably early names (ציער צער; perhaps צעיר, yet see Kautzsch on 2 K. viii. 21, and מצער (?), Ps. xlii. 7). The root of גדעוני is in use both early and late, but never occurs in P; the only other proper names from it are גדעון and the place name גדעם—both early. The root of עכרן is almost confined to pre-Exilic literature and is never used in P; the only post-Exilic occurrences are in 1 Chr. ii. 7, where עכר ישראל is clearly a reminiscence of the narrative in Joshua (vi. 18; vii. 25, JE), and Ps. xxxix. 3, unless we consider Prov. x.-xxii. post-Exilic, in which case we have four more post-Exilic occurrences—Prov. xi. 17, 29; xv. 6, 27; all the remaining (eight) occurrences occur in the early narratives of the Hexateuch, Judges, Samuel, and Kings. The only other name from the root is that of the valley of Achor (*e.g.* Hos. ii. 17).

In the nine names now left I find nothing suggestive, but note that three (עינן, ענן, שפטן) have the termination ָן (cf. עכרן above), and that פַּרְנַךְ is quite unique; יגלי, if it mean "led into exile," as the *Oxford Lexicon* suggests with a ?, would probably be late, but it may equally well signify "rendered conspicuous," or perhaps "exultant"[1]—meanings which may reflect any period. The other names are חלון, כסלון, אפד, שלומי.

2. Our lists contain, in addition to the twenty-four names peculiar to them, eighteen, borne by twenty persons, which occur elsewhere.

In the case of four of these not only the names,

[1] Cf. *CIS*, 692; the note on בעלגלא runs "Anne 'is quem Baal exsultare fecit?' Cf. *nomen hebraicum*, יגלי; Num. xxxiv. 22."

but also the persons are known to us from other sources; כלב can be traced to the earliest narratives, in which, however, it is probably the name of a tribe rather than an individual; יפנה with certainty only to D^2; in the earlier narratives it occurs only where it may reasonably be supposed to be redactional[1]—Num. xxxii. 12; Jos. xiv. 6, 13 f. Both נחשון and עמינדב are mentioned in a genealogy (Ruth iv. 18 ff.), the early origin of which I see no reason to question whatever view be taken with regard to Ruth as a whole. Possibly אלידד (Num. xxxiv. 21) is identical with the אלדד (a mere orthographical variation) of Num. xi. 26 (JE); the latter passage in any case proves the antiquity of the name.

The remaining thirteen names occur elsewhere, but only as the names of different persons.

Four of these—אליאב, אלישמע, שמואל, פלטיאל—are known to have been current in or before the Davidic period.[2]

Five others are probably of early origin, though we cannot trace them up to any very early period in extant early literature. These are (1) עמיהוד, the name of three persons in these lists; if the K'ri be

[1] Cf. *e.g.* Driver's analysis of the passages in question in his *Introduction.*

[2] It must be noted, however, that שמואל (Num. xxxiv. 20) is textually uncertain: LXX. (Σαλαμιήλ), Syr. = שלמיאל, a name peculiar to P. Further פלטיאל in P (Num. xxxiv. 26) is certain, but the Davidic name (2 S. iii. 15) is an uncertain variant for פלטי.

correct in 2 S. xiii. 37, we should have the name as that of a foreigner in the Davidic period. But in any case the existence of the parallels אביהוד, אחיהוד, favours interpreting עמי as kinsman, and consequently regarding the name as of early origin. (2) אחיהוד, אחיצור, are presumably early on the ground of their first element: see p. 38; with the latter cf. the unquestionably early names אביצור, אליצור. (3) אליצפן, though current after the Exile, can be traced up to the end of the seventh century; אליסף which occurs elsewhere only in another of P's lists is to be regarded on the ground of the formation (אל *prefixed* to pf.) as at least pre-Exilic.

Two others, חניאל and קמואל, are less decisive, though the latter occurs as the name of a foreigner in Gen. xxii. 21 (JE).

Only one name is more probably late than early, viz. נתנאל: on the form אל, *postfixed* to a pf., see p. 192. The name occurs elsewhere of two post-Exilic persons, a post-Exilic family, and six persons mentioned only in Chronicles: it is also frequent in the post-biblical period. In reference to בקי I note that it also occurs of a descendant of Aaron in 1 Chr. v. 31, and that בקיה is the name of two persons mentioned only by the Chronicler, 1 Chr. xxv. 4, xxv. 13. If the root be בקה, it is unknown to Hebrew except in these names; but cf. Aramaic בקא: if בקק, cf. further the post-Exilic names בקבק and בקביה.

Turning now to the compounds of אל recorded by

P, we find fifteen (A 3, B 12) absolutely peculiar to him; virtually peculiar, because found elsewhere only in the Chronicler's citations, are four others[1] all B, giving in all nineteen—A 3, B 16; the proportion between A and B is very significant.

Several of these names have already been discussed and their chronological character so far as possible determined; for אליסף, comparatively early, see p. 205; for פדהאל and נתנאל, comparatively late, see pp. 200 f., 205; for אליצור and צוריאל, probably artificial and late, see pp. 194 ff.; for שלומיאל, probably late, גמליאל, פגעיאל, דעואל, see pp. 200 ff. Three that have not yet been discussed deserve some attention: אלישבע is probably of pre-Exilic origin, for the divine name is prefixed; little more can be said of it, for the superficially similar name בתשבע of the Davidic period is differently formed and means "daughter *of* an oath," whereas אלישבע signifies "God *is* an oath"; מלכיאל, judged by the probable history of the similar name מלכיה, was perhaps not created or adopted by the Hebrews[2] earlier than the seventh century. But the most interesting of these names is לאל; it consists of a preposition + a divine name—a formation almost

[1] Thus מלכיאל 1 Chr. vii. 31 = Gen. xlvi. 17; אשריאל 1 Chr. vii. 14 = Num. xxvi. 31; יחציאל 1 Chr. vii. 13 = Num. xxvi. 48; נמואל 1 Chr. iv. 24 = Num. xxvi. 12.

[2] Though it is to be noted that it was in very early use (*cir.* 1500 B.C.) in Canaan, being found in the Tel-el-Amarna Tablets: see the Index to these, published by the British Museum (1892).

unique in O.T., למואל (Prov. xxxi. 1) being the only exact parallel; but we also find a few names consisting of a prepositional phrase + a divine name, *e.g.* בְּסֽוֹדְיָה and possibly בְּצַלְאֵל. In the absence of other O.T. names, our judgment as to the probable period in which לאל originated must be guided by other Semitic parallels and the growth of Semitic religious thought. On this point I am glad to be able to cite Professor Nöldeke:[1] speaking of names "which by means of a preposition express the thought that man belongs to or springs from the deity," he says, "this formation gives the impression of a later period: it appears to rest on a reflection which must have been foreign to the highest antiquity." Among other Semitic examples which he cites are the Palmyrene לשמש = "belonging to the sun," and the names of the two daughters of Abu 'l 'atâhiya, an Arabian poet of the latter half of the eighth century A.D., لله and بالله, and also several Ethiopic names which are, however, rather of the type בסדיה.

I will now summarise the conclusions which appear to me justified by the preceding discussions, indicating in each case the convergent lines of evidence.

1. The names in P are not as a whole pre-Davidic in character.

Proofs: (*a*) The large proportion, especially in certain

[1] In *WZKM*, 1892, p. 314. Cf., however, also on compounds with prepositions, Halévy in *REJ*, x. 1 f.

lists, of compounds with a divine name.

(*b*) The large proportion of names among compounds with אל, in which אל is the last element in the word.

(*c*) The presence of names in which the perfect is prefixed, פדהאל, פדהצור, נתנאל.

(*d*) The formations with a preposition (לאל) and a participle (שלמיאל). The compounds with צור and שדי are also to be noted.

2. The names—even those *peculiar* to P—are not similar in character to those current *in ordinary life* in the post-Exilic period.

Proofs: (*a*) Entire absence of compounds with יה.

(*b*) The occurrence of compounds with אבי and אחי; some also of the compounds with עמי, viz. עמינדב, עמיהוד, do not appear to be of late origin.

(*c*) The large proportion of compounds with אל in certain lists. Both in Num. i. and xxxiv. they are more than a third of the whole; in the post-Exilic priestly list they are less than a third, in post-Exilic lay list less than a seventh.

(*d*) The compounds with צור and שדי.

(*e*) Certain individual names, *e.g.* צוער, עכרן, גדעוני.

3. Some of the names are late artificial creations.

Proofs: (*a*) Compounds with צור and שדי.

(*b*) Compounds with a preposition (לאל) and a participle (שלמיאל); and perhaps

(*c*) Certain other names, *e.g.* פדהאל, נתנאל.

4. Some of the names peculiar to P do not appear to have been coined by the author, nor by any late writer, nor to have been current after the Exile.

Proofs: (*a*) Names compounded with אבי, אחי.

(*b*) Certain names from roots never used by P, and little, if at all, by any late writers, *e.g.* צוער.

(*c*) אליסף; and possibly, against the view that the words are artificial formations by P himself, we may add

(*d*) Compounds with צור, and therefore also compounds with שדי.

5. Some of the names borne by persons mentioned only in P, but also by other persons mentioned by other writers, are early in character and a few are not known to have been current late, *e.g.* אליאב.

Briefly, then, P's names consist in part of ordinary names that were current early, in part of ordinary names that only originated at a late period, and in part of artificial names that were never current in ordinary life at any time.

One or two inferences of some interest seem to follow. The systematic lists of tribal princes, etc., found in P are valueless as records of the Mosaic age:

the names are in part drawn from earlier sources (JE, D) still extant, in part (*e.g.* אליסף, עכרן) from earlier sources now lost; but these lost sources do not appear to have been considerable, since to complete the lists some and probably several names created *ad hoc* or chosen from current names had to be included. Both in the creation of artificial names and in the choice of late current names compounds were preferred, perhaps as being more suitably significant (*e.g.* פדהאל, צורישדי), but to the exclusion of all compounds with יה; hence the striking preponderance of compounds with אל. In the case of these last, it is impossible to determine with *certainty* the individual names which are late; but of the twenty-nine names (A 4, B 25) entirely peculiar to P, or by him alone referred to Mosaic times, the probability appears to me great that the following seventeen (A 1, B 16) are of late origin, and several also of artificial character— מהללאל, לאל, דעואל, גמליאל, גדיאל, גאואל, בצלאל, אליצור, פוטיאל, פדהאל, פגעיאל, עזיאל, נתנאל, מישאל, מיכאל, אוריאל, שלומיאל. These names have what appears to me an instructive parallel in the post-biblical angelic names; these it will scarcely be questioned are of post-Exilic origin, and in large part of artificial character; of twenty names of angels in the Greek text of Enoch vi., the following twelve are compounded with אל —Ἀρακιήλ, Χωβαβιήλ (probably = כוכביאל), Ῥαμιήλ, Ζακιήλ, Βαλκιήλ, Ἀμαριήλ, Θαυσαήλ, Σαμιήλ, Εὐμιήλ, Τυριήλ, Ἰουμιήλ, Σαριήλ. In comparing these with the seventeen probably post-Exilic names in P these points are noticeable: (1) in every name in Enoch the אל is the last element; with the exception of אליצור, the reverse of צוריאל, this is also true of the seventeen names from P; (2) the entire or almost entire absence of verbal compounds; contrast the pre-Exilic names, *infra*, pp. 212 f.; (3) the large number of forms containing the binding vowel י.[1]

We can now return to the names in Chronicles better prepared to determine the character of individual names, and by the help of the further results so obtained to consider the bearing of the proper names on the historical character of certain parts of the Books of Chronicles. There remain to be considered compounds with אל peculiar to the Chronicler, in general and in detail, and some details of the compounds with יה.

Firstly, the names in אל peculiar to the Chronicler. I will approach the discussion of these through a statistical presentation of the distribution over periods and in the different sources of all Hebrew personal (or tribal names) compounded with אל. Thus, of Hebrew personal (or tribal names) compounded with אל, there are—

[1] The presence of this is clear from the Greek forms; less clear in the Ethiopic which is alone extant for the list in chap. lxix. On the interpretation of the forms, and for a harmony of the Greek and Ethiopic texts in chap. vi. and the Ethiopic text in chap. lxix., see Dillmann, *Das Buch Henoch*, pp. 93-95.

		A.	B.		Total.
Found in the pre-Exilic sources		20	22	=	42
Confined to P		3	11	=	14
Confined to Chr.	1 Ch. i.-ix. A 3, B 7; Elsewhere A 8, B 12	11	19	=	30
Confined to P and Chr.		1	5[1]	=	6
" P and Period IV.		0	2	=	2
" Chr. and Period IV.		1	5	=	6
" P, Chr., and Period IV.		0	3	=	3
" Period IV.		0	6	=	6
		36	73	=	109

The following five names, all B, do not come under any of the above classes: למואל, only in Prov. xxxi.; מהללאל, except for Neh. xi. 4, confined to P; קמואל, the name of a foreigner in JE, otherwise confined to P and Chr.; רעואל, the name of foreigners in JE and P, otherwise confined to Chr.; פנואל, except as a place name only in 1 Chr. iv. 4.

In view of the conclusions already reached with regard to the names as a whole in P and Chr., safe conclusions as to the general character of pre-Exilic names can only be based on the pre-Exilic sources. Confining ourselves in the case of אל names to the pre-Exilic sources, we find that the certainly pre-Exilic names are thus composed:—

A number 20,

אלי being followed by a *noun* (or pronoun)		in	.	9 names.[2]
" " *verb*	(*a*) in impf. 2; (*b*) in pf. 6	"	.	8 names.[3]

[1] Yet cf. p. 206 n. 1.

[2] אלישוע, אליפלם, אליעם, אליעֶזֶר, אלימלך, אליחרף, אליהוא, אליה, אליאב.

[3] אלעשה, אלחנן, אלקנה, אלעזר, אלנתן אלישמע; אליחבא, אליקים.

In three cases the second constituent of the word is uncertain. אליקא is textually uncertain, and, if correct, etymologically obscure. אלישע is apparently a case of the pf. preceded by אלי—the verb in that case being either ישע (in which case the original pronunciation would have been אֱלִישַׁע) or more probably, since the LXX. (Ἐλισαῖε) already supports the present pointing, שוע; this is the view of Olshausen,[1] but the *Oxf. Lex.* appears to treat the second element as a noun, virtually identifying אלישע with אלישוע. In אלדד the ambiguity of the second element is greater; see p. 61.

B number 22,

אל being preceded by a *noun*		in	.	13 names.[2]
" "	*verb* (*a*) in impf. 4	"	.	7 names.[3]
	(*b*) in pf. 3			

The remaining names are פמנואל and דנ(י)אל; the latter was perhaps originally a verbal compound, "God has judged," and only later written with the yod as a substantival compound, "God is a judge."

Several details, *e.g.* the changing ratio in the different pre-Exilic periods between A and B and between

[1] *Hebr. Gram.* p. 619.

[2] אביאל, אריאל (in pre-Exilic sources only of a foreigner 2 S. xxiii. 20, and as a symbolic name Is. xxix. 1), חיאל (in *Oxf. Lex.* treated as verbal = יחיאל), יואל (*vide* p. 153), כרמאל (*vide* p. 164), עבדאל, עדיאל, עזריאל, עמיאל, עתניאל, פלטיאל (as pre-Exilic, doubtful, *vide* p. 204, n. 2), שמואל, פנואל (*vide* p. 164).

[3] יחזקאל, ישמעאל, ישראל, ירחמאל; עזראל, שאלתיאל, חננאל.

compounds in which the pf. precedes or follows אל, have already been discussed. One remains for examination here. From the foregoing analysis it appears that whereas, in pre-Exilic names, the pf. is prefixed twice or thrice as often as it is post-fixed, the impf. is prefixed only half as often as it is post-fixed to אל. But closer inspection shows that the compounds with a pf. or with an impf. *which is post-fixed* and the compounds with an impf. which is prefixed are not altogether homogeneous. All the former names are beyond question purely personal in character—they are the names of individuals; but three out of the four names in which the impf. is prefixed to אל are known to have been tribal (ישראל, ישמעאל, ירחמאל) and, apart from the tribal legends cast in personal forms, are not known to have been personal.

In *tribal* and *place names* this *prefixing* is paralleled in early times; we have

(1) Among the places (or tribes) of Oberrutenu, *i.e.* Palestine, mentioned by Thothmes III. *circa* 1500 B.C.

יעקבאל, יוספאל.

These forms compared with the well-known O.T. names יוסף and יעקב suggest that forms of tribal names such as יצחק are truncated.[1]

[1] See Meyer in *ZATW*, 1886, pp. 1-16; and the important discussion by W. Max Müller in *Asien u. Europa*, pp. 162-164, who shows that the equivalence of Y-ša-p-'a-ra = יספאל is open to less doubt than Meyer admitted, and that the names are of

(2) The O.T. place names

יורעאל, יקתאל, mentioned in the pre-Exilic sources.

יבנאל, יפתחאל, יקבצאל, ירפאל, mentioned only in uncertain or late sources, but as place names probably of early origin.

(3) The O.T. place names in which an impf. precedes פעם—יבלעם, יקדעם, יקמעם, יקנעם, ירקעם.

It is thus quite clear that the formation in which the impf. is followed by אל is early, but it is only proved customary with regard to tribal and place names.

That the formation was not in early use among the Hebrews for names of individuals appears to me tolerably certain from the following considerations:—

(1) The earliest and only pre-Exilic instances of impf. + אל are יחזקאל and ישמעאל (the latter previously tribal) at the end of the seventh century; but prior to the seventh century we have at least five compounds with the pf., and in the seventh century four more.

(2) The analogy of compounds with יה. Dis-

places (not tribes). The frequency of this (truncated ?) formation, both in Arabic and Hebrew place names, has been noted by Nöldeke (*ZDMG*, 1861, pp. 807 f.), who cites יפתח, יבנה, יגור, יפיע, يثيب، يبنى، يأجج، يثرب، ينبع and others, and notes that the absence of the Tanwin in Arabic indicates how keenly the verbal character of the forms was felt. He further discusses the parallel forms of 3rd f. impf., *e.g.* تنبغ , and perhaps תחמץ.

regarding Chr. we find in O.T. thirteen names of the type impf. + יה; two[1] only of these occur in the eighth century and *none earlier;* six others first occur at the close of the seventh century, the remaining five after the Exile. Contrast with this the occurrence in or before the eighth century of about twenty compounds with a pf.

(3) The comparative data. The formation in which an impf. precedes a divine name appears to have been rare in several other Semitic languages; in Phoenician we find יחומלך, and perhaps his father's name יחיבעל—fourth century B.C.;[2] in Aramaic יבחראל (sixth century or earlier), but the note in the Corpus on the last name runs—"haud multa sunt nomina cum imperfecto verbi composita."[3] Names of this type are rather more numerous in Assyrian;

[1] יחזקיה, יברכיה. Neither of these instances is quite certain. In the case of יְבֶרֶכְיָה (generally taken to be = יְבָרֶכְיָה: cf. *Ges.-K.* 27, 3), the initial yod is recognised by *MT* only in Is. viii. 2, by the LXX. (Βαραχίας; cf. Σαραβίας = שֵׁרֵבְיָה) and other VV. nowhere. The form יחזקיה is frequent in *MT*, yet the LXX. (Ἐζεκίας) never distinguishes it from the form חזקיה; contrast the distinctive transliteration of יחזקאל by Ἰεζεκιήλ. As the LXX. never recognises the yod in this latter name, although its occurrence in *MT* seems too frequent to be accidental, we ought perhaps to attach no great weight to its not supporting the י in the יברכיה of Is. viii. 2.

[2] *CIS*, i. 1.

[3] *CIS*, ii. 47.

> Schrader[1] quotes iḳ-bi-ilu, is-mi-da-kan, ir-ba-marduk, is-mi-bil, im-gur-bil, and several, which Professor Hommel considers to be of Arabian origin, have been found on early Babylonian contract tablets (*c.* 2000 B.C.).[2]

From this it follows that in determining the date and character of uncertain names, we must consider names in which the impf. precedes a divine name, if early, tribal and not personal, or, if personal, comparatively late—not earlier, let us say, than the eighth century.

I think we may go further and say that in the earliest Hebrew names of individuals the verbal element always stood in the perfect, for the total number of names in which an impf. *follows* a divine name are also very few and chiefly late; they appear as follows:—one in the Davidic period (אליחבא),[3] one in the eighth century (אליקים), two in the seventh (יהויכן and יהויקים), and two in the post-Exilic period (יויריב and אלישיב).

[1] *ZDMG*, 1872, p. 135.

[2] Hommel (*ZDMG*, 1895, p. 525) cites from Meissner's *Beiträge zum altbabylonischen Privatrecht*, Jarbi-ilu, Jamlik-ilu, Ya'zar-ilu; Sayce (*Contemp. Review*, Oct. 1895, p. 482), on the authority of Pinches, Jacob(-el) and Joseph(-el).

[3] This single instance in the Davidic period stands somewhat isolated; so far as the consonantal text goes it might be of the familiar early type אל and pf. (אֶלְיַחְבָּא); the LXX. ('Ελιαβά) is unfortunately indecisive as to the pronunciation of the name in the second century.

The early tribal or place names thus stand out in marked contrast with the early personal names, by reason of the occurrence of the imperfect and the position of the verb. Now it has usually been assumed that the imperfect in compound proper names has a simple imperfect sense, and this is certainly the case with the names in which the subject precedes and, in view of the parallel names containing the perfect, probable enough in the (late) personal names in which the subject follows. But may not the reason of the unusual tense and the unusual position of the verb in the tribal names be due to the fact that the verb is voluntative; in that case it would necessarily stand first? We should then interpret as follows:—יוספאל = Let El increase; ישראל = Let El strive; יבנאל = Let El build (the city); יזרעאל = Let El sow; יקנעם = Let the people (?) possess (?), etc. I agree with Meyer[1] that אל in the place names is the spirit of the place (*der locale Dämon*); if the voluntative interpretation of the verbal elements in these names be correct, these places probably received their names from invocations to the genius of the place by the first settlers. Are the tribal names derived from war cries?

Granted the correctness of the foregoing conclusions, another important inference may be drawn: tribal names, in many instances, are not derivative from personal names. In estimating the relation

[1] *ZATW*, 1886, p. 4.

between A and B in personal pre-Exilic names we ought, therefore, to deduct these tribal, non-personal names: then A just outnumbers B (20 : 19); a few other B names are questionable as personal instances; *e.g.* נתנאל, but the A names are unmistakably personal.

Turning to the names *peculiar* to Chronicles we find A : B = 11 : 19, a proportion different from that among pre-Exilic names, but approximating to that found among names still *current* in Period IV. (8 : 19). The inference is that some of these names are really post-Exilic, though referred by the Chronicler to pre-Exilic periods, and that some (since the proportion is not identical with the post-Exilic) are genuinely ancient names. In detail: names peculiar to Chronicles exclusive of those which are peculiar to 1 Chr. i.-ix. consist of eight A and twelve B names. The A names are—

אלידע (2 Chr. xvii. 17); pre-Exilic origin probable on account of the form, see pp. 192, 177; and also the second constituent, cf. יהוידע (Davidic). Among the neighbouring people of Syria the name was already current in the days of Solomon, 1 K. xi. 23; cf. the Midianite אבידע, Gen. xxv. 4 (JE). The name is not known to have been current among the Hebrews after the Exile.

אליאל. The name of *nine* different persons mentioned only by the Chronicler. If the name were really so popular as this indicates, why does it occur in no other source? It appears to me an artificial variant of יואל or אליה; cf. the parallel artificiality אלהים אלהי in the Elohistic Psalter.[1]

אֱלִיאָתָה. Form early; second constituent late, and, so far as I am aware, unknown in other proper names. The name occurs only in 1 Chr. xxv. 4, and thence in verse 27. The six names which follow it in verse 4 are, as has long[2] been recognised, the result of dividing a sentence into suitable lengths; should אליאתה be included and pointed אֵלִי אַתָּה? in any case the name seems artificial.

אליפלהו is in three respects unusual, for (1) it consists of three elements — vocative, verb, object; (2) the verbal constituent is imperative; and (3) the object of the verb is expressed. Analogies for each of these characteristics are, so far as they exist at all, entirely or mainly late. As to (1); compound names with three elements are common in Assyrian, but very

[1] Driver, *Introd.* p. 350. In view of the literary history of אליאל I cannot regard Barton's explanation of it as probable; he sees in the name a survival from the period when אל was the name of a special deity; he finds the same usage of אל in נתנאל, a name whose early origin is equally suspicious (cf. p. 205); Barton's argument will be found in the *Oriental Studies of the Oriental Club of Philadelphia*, Boston, 1894, pp. 97 f.

[2] Since Ewald; see his *Lehrbuch*, 274 *b*; cf. also Robertson Smith, *Old Test. in Jewish Church* (second ed.), p. 143.

rare in Hebrew, and in no other Hebrew name is one of the three elements clearly verbal. It has been suggested[1] that the *post-Exilic* חֲכַלְיָה should be treated as equal to חַכֵּהלְיָה (= Wait for Yah); this would give a name in two respects analogous to אליפלהי. The other instances of compounds with three elements are (*a*) אליהועיני, בסודיה, and perhaps בצלאל, all confined to the post-Exilic literature; (*b*) the allied forms מיכאל, מיכיהו, מישאל, of which the first and last are confined to the post-Exilic literature, and the second is not clearly found before the ninth century, see pp. 156 f.; (*c*) etymologically obscure, but possibly of this type are אבימאל and מתושאל (J), see p. 164; and ישבקשה (Chr.); and (*d*) the pronominal forms עמנואל (eighth century) and חפצי־בה (seventh century). Even if the yod in אליאב, etc., be suffixal, the foregoing examples remain rare examples, differing from the usual type אליאב, etc. As to (2) and (3) I note briefly that many instances of imperatives in proper names cited by Olshausen[2] are questionable, that most of the clearer instances, as *e.g.* שובאל, are confined to the post-Exilic literature, and that no certain early instance exists; clear cases of the occurrence of the

[1] Cheyne on Ps. xxxiii. 20; Siegfried-Stade, *s.v.*

[2] *Hebr. Gram.* 277 *g*, 3 *i*.

object are also late, שאלתיאל in the sixth century is the earliest, and some are apparently quite artificial, *e.g.* רממתיעזר. I infer, therefore, that אליפלהו is not a Davidic name, but a name either current in the fourth century or coined by the Chronicler.

אלישפט is presumably early; note (*a*) the form, see p. 192; (*b*) the second constituent, with which compare שפטיה and יהושפט (Davidic).

אלנעם. The form of the name and the root נעם are in early use.

אלעוזי ?

אלזבד. The form of the name and the early occurrence of the root זבד (Gen. xxx. 20, E) are in favour of regarding this as a genuine old name. It may be such; at the same time the affection shown by the Chronicler for names containing this root makes it questionable whether he was guided, in inserting אלזבד in his lists, by any ancient source.

In any case the history of זבד in Hebrew proper names is worth observing; names containing the root occur as follows:—

Name.	Persons mentioned in pre-Exilic books.	In Period IV.	In Chr. only.		Totals.
זבד		3	4	=	7
זבוד	1 (10th cent.)	1 (Ktb.)		=	1 or 2
זבידה	1 (text ?)			=	1 ?

Name.	Persons mentioned in pre-Exilic books.	In Period IV.	In Chr. only.		Totals.
זבדי		1	2	=	4 (P 1)
זבדיאל		1	1	=	2
זבדיה		2	7	=	9
יהוזבד	1 (9th cent.)	2	6	=	9
עמיזבד			1	=	1
אלזבד			2	=	2
	—	—	—		—
	3	10	23	=	36

The most significant features of the history are these: of the nine names only three occur in pre-Exilic literature and each as the name of but one pre-Exilic person; but seven of the names occur in Chronicles and most of them as the name of several persons. Again, of the nine names, one name only is common to pre-Exilic literature and Chronicles; but five are common to Period IV. and Chronicles.

The historical character, therefore, of persons bearing one of these names and mentioned only by the Chronicler appears to me suspicious. Did אלזבד and עמיזבד, the only names in Chronicles not also current in Period IV., arise by artificial variation from יהוזבד an early name still current in Period IV.? Compare the suggested case of אליאל as a variation of יואל.

One thing is certain, זבד in post-Exilic names is common; it is so also in Palmyrene names. Is this coincidence accidental? The comparison is in any case curious; Ledrain[1] cites זבד, 2; זבדא, 3; זבדבול, 14; זבדי, 1; זבדלא, 4; זבדנבו, 1; זבדעתה, 4; זבידא, 14; נבוזבד, 2; in all 45 persons.

The twelve B names peculiar to Chronicles (1 Chr. x.-2 Chr. xxxvi.) are:—

אוריאל, later the name of an angel, cf. p. 198. The parallel name אוריה is Davidic.

חזיאל. The affinities of this name are late or doubtful. Although the root חזה is found in all periods of Hebrew literature and occurs in the early Syrian names חזיון and חזאל, all the Hebrew names into which it enters are post-Exilic or referred to the pre-Exilic periods only by the late writers. The names are חזיה, יחזיה, יחזיאל, מחזיאת, כל-חזה.

ידיעאל;[2] form probably quite late, see p. 200.

יהללאל; form not early for personal names; see pp. 215 ff.; cf. also the parallel name מהללאל, which occurs only in P (Chr.) and Neh. xi. 4.

יעשיאל; form not early, see pp. 215 ff. Compounds with עשה occur in all periods from Period II., cf. עשהאל; but *some* are *very frequent late, e.g.* מעשיה.

יויאל, יעזיאל, יתניאל } In each of these names the initial yod which alone differentiates the last two from forms otherwise known is textually uncertain. If the yod be original, the names as personal

[1] *Op. cit.* (see p. 34, n. 7).

[2] Cf. Palmyrene ידיעבל.

are not early, see p. 217. Further, with regard to יעואל, note that the root עוז occurs only in late proper names.

עדיאל. The parallel names are יהועדן, eighth century; יהועדה and אלעדה confined to 1 Chr. i.-ix.; עדיה, seventh century, and still current in post-Exilic period.

רפאל is a post-biblical angel name; ירפאל is the name of a town; otherwise the root occurs only in late or uncertain names, viz. רפיה, רפא, and רפוא.

שובאל } שבואל } Form probably late, see p. 221. Affinities decidedly late; אלישיב[1] is the name of six post-Exilic persons and one mentioned only in Chr.; ישיב of one post-Exilic person and one mentioned only in P.

With regard to the ten names peculiar to 1 Chr. i.-ix., it is to be noted (1) that there is nothing in the second constituents of the three A names אלעד, אלעדה, אלפעל, to cast doubt on the comparatively early origin which their *form* suggests; (2) that three of the eight B names—יקותיאל, ישימיאל, יחדיאל—are tribal or comparatively late personal names (p. 217); that חמואל, if the first element signify father-in-law, is a name of early origin and of a formation that became obsolete before the Exile (p. 64). The remaining three names (אשראל, עבדיאל, יריאל) are inconclusive.

[1] Nestle, *Eigennamen*, 104.

With the help of the fuller data now at our command I return to the examination of the names peculiar to Chronicles, and to the attempt to determine the historical character of particular lists.

The post-Davidic character of the names in 1 Chr. xxvi. 2-32 was sufficiently evident from the proportion—closely approximating to that found among post-Exilic names—of compounds with a divine name to all others. I now note these additional features indicative of late date:—

1. The pf. *precedes* יה in thrice as many names as it follows יה—9 : 3; cf. pp. 176 f.
2. In the compounds with אל, B outnumbers A by seven to three.
3. The presence of participial compounds—משלמיה, ידיעאל; see p. 200.
4. The forms יחיאלי (cf. p. 217) and שבואל (cf. p. 221).

Certain points indicate that this list is one consisting in whole or in part of post-Exilic *family* names; thus the proportion between the compounds with divine names and others is not so great as that found in post-Exilic *personal* names, but greater than among the names of post-Exilic families (Neh. iii.); several of the names recur in other lists of priests, etc., mentioned by the Chronicler in connection with other reigns, *e.g.* זכריה (2 Chr. xx. 14; xxix. 13; xxxiv. 12), נתנאל (2 Chr. xxxv. 9), יואח (1 Chr. vi. 6; 2 Chr. xxix. 12); several actually occur elsewhere as (certainly or probably) family names, *e.g.* שפים (cf. שפופם Num. xxvi. 39), זכרי (cf. Neh. xi. 9), שלמית (cf. Ezra viii. 10), שמעיה (cf. Neh. xii. 36).

Granted that the list does largely consist of the names of post-Exilic families, an examination of the names throws some light on the date of the eponymous ancestors of the families—in other words of the origin of the priestly families. The list contains few antique features requiring a really early origin; on the other hand many features point to a period not earlier than the seventh century; note the proportion of divine names compared with that found among the contemporaries of Jeremiah, the proportion of אל B to אל A names, which is only equalled in and after the seventh century, the formations with a participle and with the imperf. preceding the divine name. One characteristic of the list indicates a still later origin for at least some of the names, viz. the relative numbers of compounds with אל and compounds with יה; the ratio is the same as that found in the names of post-Exilic individuals, but widely different from that in names of post-Exilic families, see p. 186. Note also that some of these names, though frequently recurring, are confined to post-Exilic persons (or families) and persons mentioned only in Chronicles, *e.g.* יחיאל, אליהועיני, חשביה, זבדיה.

The theory just proposed in explanation of the character and origin of the names in 1 Chr. xxvi. is confirmed by an examination of the twenty-four priestly names in 1 Chr. xxiv. 7-18; these, too, are clearly of post-Davidic origin, for the compounds with a divine name are all but half of the whole—eleven out of twenty-four; B compounds with יה are three and a half times as numerous as A (7: 2); none of the names are of the common early type in which a pf. *precedes* a divine name, but in four (שכניה, פתחיה, דליה, ידעיה) the pf. *follows* a divine name; in two the impf. follows and in one it precedes a divine name (אלישיב, יהויריב, יחזקאל).

On the other hand it is much clearer in the present case that the names are actually names of post-Exilic families; twelve of them occur as the names of post-Exilic *priestly* families, viz. Immer, Jeshua, Hakkoz, Malchijah, Mijamin, Maaziah, Jachin, Abijah, Bilgah, Joiarib, Jedaiah, and Harim (Ezra ii. 36 f., 61; Neh. x. 4, 8, 9, xi. 10, xii. 4 f., 6, 15); another, Hezir, is the name of a post-Exilic levitical family (Ezra ii. 36); further, the Delaiah and Shecaniah of the Chronicler's list should be compared with the families (?) of the same name in Neh. vii. 62, iii. 29 respectively.

It would be tedious to enter into a detailed examination of all the priestly and levitical lists; enough has already been said to show that an examination of the names confirms the conclusion arrived at on more general grounds by Graf [1] that, as an account of David's reign, 1 Chr. xxiii.-xxvii. is entirely void of historical

[1] *Die geschichtlichen Bücher des A.T.* 232 ff.

worth. I have already indicated that the character of the names suggests that the priestly and levitical families cannot have originated earlier than the eighth or seventh centuries B.C. For the history of early times the levitical genealogies of 1 Chr. v. 27-vi. 53 are equally worthless; names known to us from earlier sources are there, but the unknown names, taken as a whole, are clearly of later origin than the date to which they are assigned; several details in connection with them have already been discussed (p. 172; cf. pp. 177 f.).

Judged by the names of the brief levitical genealogy of 2 Chr. xx. 14 the accompanying incident, referred to Jehoshaphat's reign, must be considered of very questionable historical worth; the *formation* of the names יחזיאל and יחיאל is late (see p. 217); moreover both names though frequent in Chronicles are otherwise confined to the post-Exilic period; the remaining three names, though one is of early, another of comparatively early (eighth century) origin, are all frequent after the Exile.

I will now pass to names other than those of priests and levites; and firstly to certain Davidic lists.

In 2 S. xxiii. 24-39 we have a list of David's heroes; the same list is found in 1 Chr. xi. 26-41*a*, where the text of the names is on the whole better preserved; in Chr. moreover the list is continued so as to include twenty-two fresh names. Graf[1] infers

[1] *Op. cit.* p. 198.

that the Chronicler is here following not our present "Samuel" but a source common to both compilers: this may be so, and some of the additional names recorded in Chronicles may be genuine, but several are not; I note (1) the larger proportion of compounds with a divine name in these verses than in the preceding; (2) the *formation* (p. 217) and history (see App.) of (*a*) יחיאל, יושויה, יעשיאל, (*b*) ידיעאל; (3) אליאל, see p. 219; and (4) the history and affinities of עזיה, pp. 295, 309.

Possibly these additional names were in part derived from ancient, in part from late and worthless sources;[1] or the late names may have been inserted instead of certain names which had become obliterated in the early source.

The phenomena presented by chap. xii. are similar: some of the names in verses 1-22 are no doubt early, *e.g.* אחיעזר, יואש verse 3; בעליה verse 5. But the chapter does not appear to be based to any considerable extent on sources of historical worth; and certainly here also many of the names are post-Davidic, *e.g.* ישמעיה, ירמיה, יחזיאל verse 4; אליאל, verse 11; ידיעאל verse 20.

Of all the Davidic lists that which, judged by the proper names, has most appearance of being in large part a trustworthy record of David's reign occurs in 1 Chr. xxvii. 25-31. Of the sixteen names only five are compounds with a divine name, but two of these (עזיה, יחדיה) and one other, זבדי, are probably late

[1] For a similarly mixed origin of a section peculiar to Chronicles, cf. Graf, *op. cit.* 198 f.

names; removing these three we are left with three compounds and ten others—the ratio 1 : 3⅓ is practically identical with that found in the names of 2 S. ix.-xx. Further, the presence of בעלחנן in the list and the *formation* of two of the divine compounds (יונתן, יועש) favours an early origin for the rest of list; the other divine compound עדריאל, however, it must be admitted, is of more doubtful date. The name עזמות is ancient (2 S. xxiii. 31); it is significant that the only other person of the name mentioned by the Chronicler (1 Chr. viii. 36) is mentioned in a list which appears to be of good historical value, see p. 241.

The later we descend, the less conclusive does the critical argument from proper names become; but we need not hesitate to deny the historical character of Jehoshaphat's "princes," etc., 2 Chr. xvii. 7 f. Excluding Ben-hail, which is a mere textual error,[1] we have fifteen names; with one exception they are all compounds with a divine name: יה B outnumber יה A names by nine to two; the perfect precedes a divine name in six, follows in only three names. These features would not characterise a genuine list of the ninth century.

In 2 Chr. xxi. 2 the Chronicler records the names of six sons of Jehoshaphat otherwise unknown to us. I will in this case lay no stress on the fact that all the names are compounds with a divine name; perhaps this could be explained; but these points cast

[1] See above, p. 65.

doubt on the historicity of the record—(1) in all of the compounds with יה a pf. *precedes;* (2) the formation and history of יחיאל; (3) the history of מיכאל.

The historicity of a prophetic contemporary of Jehoshaphat—Eliezer, son of Dodavahu—mentioned only by the Chronicler (2 Chr. xx. 37) is more probable. It is true we have here only two names to guide us and one, אליעזר, is quite inconclusive; it is an early name, but it was also current late and occurs in other passages peculiar to the Chronicler. The remaining name is, however, very noticeable: if the reading דודיה and the interpretation suggested above (p. 62) be correct, the name is almost certainly of early origin, but we have no evidence that it continued current to a late period; its occurrence in Chronicles suggests, therefore, that it may have been derived by him from a good record of Jehoshaphat's reign.

The names in 1 Chr. i.-ix. remain to be considered. The data obtained in the preceding discussions appear to me to cast some light on these obscure chapters; they are available for determining, or helping to determine, whether the names in particular sections are tribal and family or personal, and in the latter case of fixing approximately the period in which the names originated. This however is to be remarked in general, that from a study of the names alone we can only determine, even approximately, the antiquity of the Chronicler's source when the names are clearly personal; if in these cases the names are late, the source must be late; on the other hand if the names are family names, even though they be shown to be of an early type, we cannot be certain that the source is early; the records may be of late periods in the history of the families in question. I will now summarise in a series of brief notes what the character of the names proves or suggests with regard to the Chronicler's sources for this part of his work.

Chap. i. 1.-ii. 17. Disregarding mere textual variations of the same name, all the persons, etc., mentioned here are with four exceptions mentioned elsewhere in O.T., *i.e.* the sources of the Chronicler are still extant.[1] The four persons whose names are known to us only through the Chronicler are עזריה (ii. 8), a name current in the tenth, eighth, and seventh centuries and after the Exile, and the three sons of Jesse, נתנאל, אצם, רדי. Whence did the Chronicler obtain these names? I find נתנאל suspicious, though not impossible, as a genuine early name; עשהאל (Period II.) is a parallel to the form, יהונתן (Period I.) to the use of נתן; but the form is rare in the early period, and the actual occurrences of the name in O.T. are confined to late writings (Period IV. 3; P 1; Chr. 6).

Chap. ii. 18-24. In the main this is clearly a geographical or tribal genealogy, for many of the names are

[1] For detailed references to the Chronicler's sources here and in similar cases, see Driver, *Introd.* pp. 487 ff., or Bertheau's Commentary.

well-known places, *e.g.* Hezron, Ephrath, Jair, Gilead, Tekoa; verse 20 is curiously interwoven into the context from P (Ex. xxxi. 2). In such a context the unknown names will presumably be also place or tribal; in any case there is nothing that indicates that they are late personal names; quite the reverse, for compounds with a divine name are entirely absent but for the well-known early name אביה.

Chap. ii. 25-33. The names are of comparatively early origin, for compounds with a divine name are all but entirely lacking; there are but two[1]—ירחמאל is an early tribal name (1 S. xxvii. 10), יהונתן an early personal name. This being the case the occurrence of the three names אבישור, אחבן, and אביהיל, the first two being unknown elsewhere, the third unknown in pre-Exilic writings, at once favours the antiquity of the names in general in this list, and strengthens the conclusions drawn above as to names in אבי and אחי. A large proportion of the names are otherwise unknown; but, in addition to the tribal name ירחמאל, the place name חצרון is to be noted; further, with עטרה (verse 26) compare the place names עטרות, עטרת אדר, עטרת שופן; with ימין (verse 27), the Simeonite family of the same name, Gen. xlvi. 10. In this section also we have to do with places, clans, and families, not individuals.

Chap. ii. 34-41. In contrast to the preceding and following sections, this section presents a continuous

[1] אחיה in verse 25 being a textual error.

genealogy in a single line; the descendants of an Egyptian, ירחע, by a daughter of ששן are given to the thirteenth generation. Presumably the names are those of individuals. The period at which Yarḥa' lived is not stated, but, assuming a date as early as 1000, the thirteenth generation takes us down approximately to 600. The character of the thirteen names presents nothing inconsistent with the genealogy being genuine. For only five of the names are compounds with a divine name, and these five consist of three compounds with יה—A 2, B 1; and two compounds with אל, אל in each case being *prefixed* to a perfect. Further, these compounds occur in the later parts of the genealogy, the late (personal) form יקמיה being the twelfth member (*circa* 630). In virtue of these facts this list stands in sharp contrast with others which appear to have been made up from names current in the Chronicler's own time. The only names which appear to me suspicious are זבד and, in a less degree, עתי.

Chap. ii. 42-55. Manifestly place names.

Chap. iii. The names in this line of David's descendants are, down to the Exile, derived from extant sources; the post-Exilic names even when otherwise unknown are of ordinary post-Exilic character.

Chap. iv. 1-23. Most of these Calebite names are those of towns, and many are familiar. In such a connection we are not surprised to find יהללאל (verse 16) and יקותיאל (verse 18), early tribal though late personal formations, see p. 217. The names ראיה (verse 2) and שריה (verse 13) are more questionable; they stand somewhat too isolated to prove the names in general late, and yet they are themselves of a formation not the most ancient (see pp. 176 f.). Is the text of ראיה correct? With iv. 2 contrast ii. 52, yet Kittel and Bertheau prefer the reading of iv. 2. And is the mention of שריה in 13 f. original? Othniel the Kenizzite is well known, but not so Seraiah; and when did the craftsmen live who gave their name to their valley? Further הודיה in verse 19 is suspicious; see the usage and textual traditions as stated in Appendix II. 3 B, No. 24. Is הודיה a corruption for יהודיה? Cf. LXX. and verse 18.

Chap. iv. 24-33. The *clan* names in verse 24 are derived from Num. xxvi. 12-14 (= Gen. xlvi. 10 = Ex. vi. 15) and the *place* names in verses 28-33 from Jos. xix. 2-8. The names in verses 25 f. are, as Simeonite, otherwise unknown. From the context we gather that they are not personal names. The absence of compounds with יה and the presence of מבשם and משמע—names which only recur as those of Ishmaelitish clans—favour the genuineness of these names. Still the names שלום, שמעי, and זכור, all of which frequently recur in Chronicles, and the last of which is unknown to the early writings, are markworthy.

Chap. iv. 34-41. Judged by the proper names this narrative must be considered thoroughly unhistorical in character. We have here twenty-two names purporting to be those of individuals living in or before the eighth century. These names consist of

Compounds with a divine name .	14
Others	8

Compounds with יה number 11—A 8, B 2, C 1: the three compounds with אל are all B. The perfect tense *precedes* יה in six names, follows it in none: the *impf. precedes* the divine name in two or three cases. The usage of אליועיני is specially noticeable; see Appendix II. 3 C.

Among the other names note זיזא; proper names from this root are confined to Chronicles; שמרי, the name of three other persons mentioned only in Chr.; and ימלך (form).

Chap. iv. 42 f. It is not clear that the Chronicler refers this incident to the same period as the preceding, though Bertheau (p. 49) so regards it. The four names (verse 42) are late; all are compounds with a divine name, and all are B. The usage and affinities of רפיה and עזיאל are, moreover, thoroughly late.

Chap. v. 4-6. The eight names in the genealogy of Beerah, a contemporary of Tiglath-pileser (eighth century), are not manifestly inconsistent with the implied date; still I have no confidence that the genealogy is genuine: note שמעיה, ראיה, שמעי, names frequently recurrent among persons mentioned only in Chr. Yet on the other hand note בעל.

Chap. v. 7 ff. As an early personal name יעיאל is improbable; if the record be genuine the names are of clans. But זכריה as a pre-Davidic (cf. v. 10) name is in any case suspicious, and יעיאל though so frequent in Chr.-Ezra never occurs elsewhere.

Chap. v. 11-17. These names appear to be largely old clan or place names (*e.g.* Gilead, verse 14) interspersed with more modern names—מיכאל, משלם.

Chap. v. 24. These names are late: note (1) the preponderance of compounds with a divine name; (2) אליאל; (3) יחדיאל, ירמיה, the former of these would indeed be quite intelligible as an early name, if tribal, the latter also so far as the formation is concerned; but did יה occur in early tribal names?

Chap. v. 27-vi. 66. These priestly and levitical genealogies have been already sufficiently discussed, see pp. 172, 177; and they have been found to be, when independent of old sources still extant, untrustworthy.

Chap. vii. In verses 1-29 most of the names are derived from sources still extant. In this first part of the chapter I only note that verse 3 contains a late group of names: note (1) that all are compounds with a divine name, and all are B; (2) the two names in which an impf. precedes יה—יזרחיה (?) and ישיה, the latter being a name frequent in Chr. (four persons) and Period IV. (one person) but otherwise unknown; (3) מיכאל. In verses 7 f. the names appear to be of different antiquity: עזיאל and אליועיני are recent, ענתת and עלמת are place names; perhaps ירמות is also a place name, and should be pointed יְרָמוֹת as in other cases where it is a geographical term; in that case אביה

would stand in the midst of a small group of place names of presumably early origin.

Chap. vii. 30-40. Of this section only verses 30, 31 (to מלכיאל) rest on known sources (Gen. xlvi. 17 = Num. xxvi. 44 ff.); of the thirty-five names which follow in verses 31*b*-40 about two-thirds occur nowhere else, and the remaining third do not occur in connection with Asher. The names in 30, 31*a* are, as the comparison with Numbers xxvi. 44 ff. shows, those of clans or families; presumably the names in the succeeding verses are the same: in any case they are not personal names of late formation, as the almost entire absence of compounds with a divine name (חניאל being the only instance) sufficiently proves. The presence of the four names of the impf. form (יפלט, ימנע, ימרה, יפנה) then becomes noticeable (cf. p. 214) and also the animal name שועל. Another indication that we have here to do with geographical or tribal names is the fact that several of the names not wholly peculiar to this list recur in other geographical or tribal usages: thus with יפלט (verse 32) cf. Jos. xvi. 3; בצר (verse 37) is the name of a Reubenite town, Dt. iv. 43; שועל (verse 36) the name of a district, 1 S. xiii. 17; יתרן (verse 37) the name of a Horite clan, Gen. xxxvi. 26; ארח the name of a family numbering 775 at the time of the Return, Ezra ii. 5. On the other hand, apart from חניאל, scarcely a single name is characteristically personal. Two explanations of this list of ancient names appear reasonable: either the Chronicler here embodies names of still existing but ancient Asherite families, or he had access, directly or indirectly, to an ancient record about the Asherites; the latter explanation appears to me more probable.

Chap. viii. 1-14. In the case of these Benjamites, as in the case of the Asherites of the preceding section, a few of the names (in verses 1-5) are common to Chronicles and other O.T. writings; but, as Benjamite, they are mentioned only here. This majority numbers twenty-eight and consists of ancient names, for only two are compounds with a divine name and each of these is of an early type—אלפעל in virtue of its formation, אחיה in virtue of the element אחי and its known history. Combined with this paucity of divine compounds we have the presence of three compounds with אבי (אבישור, אביהיד, אביטוב) and two compounds with אחי (אחיהד, אחיה), and an animal name (צביא). The explanations suggested at the close of the last paragraph are again applicable.

Chap. viii. 15-26. The thirty-nine additional names of these verses appear as a whole to be of much later origin than those in verses 1-14. Instead of only two out of twenty-eight, we find fifteen out of thirty-nine compounded with a divine name; and, moreover, these compounds are not of the early types: they consist of A (excluding אליאל, 2 and אליה, 1) 0; B (do.) 11; C 1, בצלאל; in seven cases a pf. precedes the divine name. Alongside of this greatly increased proportion of divine compounds, I note the entire disappearance of compounds with אבי and אחי. Note also זכרי (three times) and משלם. The difference in character between these names and those of verses 1-14 may be due to the fact that this section is based on a record of a much later period in Benjamite history, or that the Chronicler is here embodying the names of contemporary Benjamite families, or that he has here filled up mutilated passages of his source with favourite names of his own; or something may be due to all three causes: the presence of certain names that are by no means necessarily late (*e.g.* עדר, יובב, ישפן) favours the first, the double occurrence of אליאל and perhaps also the presence of זבדיה, זכרי and a few other names the last.

Chap. viii. 33-40 = ix. 39-44. These verses contain the genealogy of Saul to the twelfth generation downwards; the names are evidently meant to be personal. There appears to me every reason for concluding that the record is genuine. Thus of the twenty-three names in this genealogy not attested by the early writings only six (or seven[1]) are compounds with a divine name —by no means an undue proportion in names of people between *circa* 950 and 700 B.C.; further, of these three are A and three (or four[1]) B, and the B names belong on the whole to the later generations. Further, none of the names recur, which accords with our

[1] The alternative numbers are due to the variant reading רפה (viii. 37), רפיה (ix. 43).

conclusion that in early times names were not hereditary. A comparison, in the respect just indicated, of this genealogy with the genealogies of levites, etc., in chaps. v.-vi. is instructive and significant. The only name that in any degree arouses my suspicion is עזריקם (viii. 38), and this occurs in a place where we have reason for suspecting the text; possibly, therefore, עזריקם is an attempt on the part of the Chronicler or a scribe to fill up with an artificial name a name illegible in the MS. At the same time we cannot deny dogmatically the possibility of עזריקם being a real name of the eighth to the seventh century.

To summarise the bearing of the names on the question of the Chronicler's sources; to a certain extent, though a comparative small one, the Chronicler availed himself, directly or indirectly, of trustworthy sources of early periods now no longer extant: this is most conclusively shown by the personal genealogies of 1 Chr. ii. 34-41, viii. 33-40, less conclusively suggested by other passages, *e.g.* 1 Chr. xxvii. 25-31; but in many cases his sources were thoroughly unhistorical, *e.g.* in 1 Chr. iv. 34-41 and, if he is there dependent on a source at all, in 1 Chr. xxiv.-xxvii. (except xxvii. 25-31).

CHAPTER IV

GENERAL CONCLUSIONS

In the preceding chapter the general conclusion was reached that the names in both Chronicles and the Priestly Code were to a large extent not derived from ancient sources, many being of quite recent formation; but that some on the other hand were at any rate of ancient formation and origin, and must therefore have been derived by the authors of these late writings from ancient sources or have been the names of still-existing ancient clans or families (cf. Num. xxvi.). In some cases it was found possible to determine certain sections as consisting exclusively, or almost exclusively, of ancient names. Before proceeding further, it will be well to see how these results bear on certain provisional conclusions of the earlier chapters.

From an examination of all compounds with אב referred to clearly defined periods, the conclusion was drawn that the formation was obsolete before the Exile; this is now strengthened by observing that names of this class in 1 Chr. ii.-ix. occur in sections in which the rest of the names appear to be ancient when judged by other tests based on the early writings. Three of these compounds with אב are peculiar to the opening chapters of Chronicles: two (אביהוד, אביטוב) occur in 1 Chr. viii. 1-14 (cf. p. 240), and the other (אבישור) in 1 Chr. ii. 28 (cf. p. 234). Further, the name אביחיל could not be definitely traced earlier than Period IV. (p. 27); but since it occurs in 1 Chr. ii. 29 we may now feel confident that it also originated before the Exile, cf. p. 234. The evidence of these chapters also confirms the conclusion that, as personal names, compounds with אב ceased to be current after the Exile. In addition to the instances already noticed אביה occurs in two connections (1 Chr. ii. 24, vii. 8), אביחיל in 1 Chr. v. 14 as well as ii. 29, אבישוע in 1 Chr. viii. 4, and in יואב 1 Chr. iv. 14; in all these contexts some of the other names and in some of the contexts all the names are ancient, cf. pp. 233 ff. Under these circumstances we may conclude that the names of this class peculiar to P (אהליאב, אבידן, אביאסף) are ancient.

The conclusions with regard to compounds with אח are similarly confirmed. Three of the names peculiar to 1 Chr. i.-ix. occur among names free from signs of lateness, viz. אחומי 1 Chr. iv. 2, אחבן 1 Chr. ii. 29, and אחישחר 1 Chr. vii. 10; the remaining name, אֲחִי (1 Chr. vii. 34), occurs among late names, see p. 239; but it is not a compound, and is to be classed with those names denoting relationship which continued in use; see pp. 83 f. Names found elsewhere but also occurring in these chapters occur in sections containing exclusively ancient names, viz. three (אחיה, אחיהוד, אחירם) in 1 Chr. viii. 1-14 (cf. p. 240), and one (אחיו) in 1 Chr. viii. 31.

Subsequent discussions have not thrown much further light on the compounds with עם, except that עמישדי appeared to be artificial, and this being the case, other compounds with עם peculiar to P may be the same. At the same time nothing has arisen to weaken the conclusion that these names, so far as they are really parallel to compounds with אב and אח, are exclusively early in formation and currency.

I will now proceed to gather together the chief conclusions, philological and theological, which are justified by a critical treatment of the sources, and follow from a comparison of the results obtained in the separate discussions which have preceded.

Of all the classes of names which have been examined, two only—compounds with אל and compounds with יה—were still in process of enlargement for the purposes of ordinary life in the post-Exilic period; compounds with שדי and צור and possibly one or two with עמי were also created in this same period; but this was for literary and artificial purposes, not for actual current use. Names of all the other classes (compounds with אב, אח, דד, חם, בן and בת, מלך, אדן, בעל, and animal names) had ceased to be formed and in some cases entirely, in the rest almost entirely, ceased to be current as names of individuals at periods prior by a longer or shorter time to the Exile; as the names of clans and families which originated before, but continued to exist after, the Exile, several are naturally found in the later period also. Now if it be observed on the one hand that the increase in the number of compounds with יה or אל more than equals the decrease due to the almost entire disappearance of names of the other compound classes, and this may be seen by examining the several analyses in chap. ii., and on the other hand that with very few exceptions[1] all

[1] Several of these exceptions are names given to embody prophetic doctrine by prophets to their children: cf. the names of Isaiah's children (Is. vii. 3, viii. 3), and two of Hosea's, Lo-'ammi and Lo-ruḥamah (Hos. i. 6-9); the third Jezreel, Hos. i. 4, is of course included among the compounds with אל. The name אהליבה in Ezek. xxiii. 4 is purely figurative, though it has resemblance to a formation found in Phoenician (אהלבעל, אהלמלך: cf. *CIS*, 50 n.), Himyaritic (אהלאל, אהלעתתר), and Edomite (אהליבמה Gen. xxxvi. 2, 41), and also in one Hebrew name אהליאב (see App. II. 1, No. 27), unless in view of the generally foreign character of these names we may infer that Oholiab also was a foreigner—an artificer whose fame lingered long, but whose foreign origin was unknown to or suppressed by P. We find further two Hebrew compounds with 'אי, viz. איתמר and איכבוד (cf. Phoen. איזבל, 1 K. xvi. 31), though it is not clear that 'אי has the same sense in all these forms, nor is it quite clear what it means in any. That the *personal* name איתמר means "island of palms" (Ges. *Thes.* and with ? in *Oxf. Lex.*) is most improbable, the Phoenician names of islands (cf. *CIS*, i. 139 n.) being no true analogy for personal names. Though compound, therefore, these names are perhaps not

compound names of pre-Exilic Hebrew individuals have been included in the preceding discussions, a characteristic difference between earlier and later Hebrew personal names becomes clear; it can be stated thus: in early times the compound names are more varied in character, but less numerous in proportion to the simple uncompounded names, than in later times. Now the great majority of the compounded names are sentences; this is unmistakable in the case of the (later, mainly verbal) compounds with יה and אל, though it is, of course, not the case with the (earlier) names compounded with אב, אח, etc., if these elements be regarded as in the construct case to the following elements, and certainly not with the compounds (also early, but possibly foreign) with בן and בת where the two elements are clearly related to one another as construct and genitive. We may therefore state the difference in another form thus: the history of Hebrew personal names shows an increasing tendency (the increase being specially rapid in the seventh century) to confer on children names consisting of a sentence stating a fact or expressing a wish. One or two inferences are, not certainly warranted but, suggested by this: the

sentence-names. איעזר, it will be remembered, is an abbreviation of אביעזר. Two other early compound names, עזמות and מתושלח, are also probably not sentences. For one or two further instances cf. pp. 64 n. 2, 145, 221, 242; and among tribal names note ישׂשכר and אישהוד.

diminishing number of sentence-names as we ascend upwards suggests that such names represent a later stage in the development, and that if we had records of yet earlier periods we should find all the personal names to be simple; this slightly confirms the conclusion previously drawn that the early tribal names, ישראל, etc., are not derivative from personal names, and would consequently explain the fact that a large proportion of the names consisting of (apparently) a 3rd sing. impf. are place or tribal names; these also would be primarily tribal not personal names, and truncated from longer forms compounded with אל. If this be so we can only accept Renan's view that Hebrew names are abbreviated sentences (or expressions) having reference to the deity in a very limited degree. On the other hand we may with some reason infer that the process of truncation which affected early *tribal* sentence-names affected at a later date *personal* sentence-names, and that many of the post-Exilic names consisting (apparently) of a 3rd sing. pf. or impf. are in reality truncated forms.

Of the two classes which were still increasing after the Exile, and the names belonging to which were then in frequent use, one (the compounds with אל) had been in use from the very earliest times both in Israel and the surrounding nations, though possibly in the earliest (pre-biblical) times these names were only tribal and not yet formed to designate individuals. The other class (compounds with יה) was probably still quite recent in the oldest periods to which the O.T. carries us back, and in view of the disagreement among Assyriologists as to the significance of certain Assyrian names,[1] we may still consider it most probable that these names were originally, and continued to be, essentially peculiar to Israel; with this view the small number of foreigners bearing these names mentioned in the O.T. itself is certainly not inconsistent, for in each case the person in question probably owed his name directly to Hebrew influence.

These two classes which survived were essentially religious in character; so also were some, and perhaps all, of those that died out. But even if we add all instances of these classes to those compounded with אל and יה, it will be found that in the Davidic and pre-

[1] Nothing is to be gained by a fuller discussion here of this point, since I cannot criticise the Assyrian evidence independently. The literature is well known; cf. *e.g.* Driver's article in *Stud. Bibl.* i. pp. 1-20; Baudissin, *Studien*, i. 220-230; Delitzsch, *Wo lag das Paradies?* pp. 150 ff., and the literature there cited. Of recent literature I may refer to W. Max Müller, *Asien u. Europa*, p. 312 f., Mr. Pinches' note in *PSBA*, xv. 13 ff. (who cites several apparently striking Assyrian parallels to Hebrew compounds with יה), Prof. Jastrow's article already cited (p. 150, n. 3), and Dr. Jäger's essay (*Der Halbvokal* י *im Assyrischen*, pp. 26 ff.) in *Beiträge zur Assyriologie*, i. 443 ff.; the two former maintain, the two latter reject, the view that the final element in the Assyrian names is that of the deity Yah. If the case for an Assyrian Yah be considered established, the peculiarity of the Hebrew names will depend not on the name but the character of the god of whom they speak.

Davidic periods less than half the names have a distinctively religious character; whereas, just a half of the post-Exilic laity and all but the whole of the post-Exilic priests, mentioned in the lists analysed above, bear names compounded with אל or יה, not to mention a large number of others which probably consisted of simple verbal forms with יה or אל understood as subjects. This then is a further difference between early and late names. In later times a larger proportion of names possess a religious significance than in early times.[1]

Again, all the classes which became obsolete were common to the Hebrews and other Semitic peoples, among whom, as we have seen, several survived long after they had fallen into disuse with the Hebrews. Of the classes which survived compounds with אל as a whole, and many in particular which remained frequent, were also paralleled in most Semitic languages; but the fuller and deeper meaning which the teaching of the prophets had given to the con-

[1] This distinction may require to be somewhat differently stated, if it can be shown that a large number of the early simple names have a religious significance, and this is the drift of several of Grunwald's discussions; but I am far from convinced, to take a single example, that the names which betoken "all manner of imperfections, sicknesses, disgusting plants," were given to children "in order to place them under the guardianship of a hurtful demon, and so protect them against its hostility" (Grunwald, *Eigennamen*, p. 23). In any case a real difference is indicated in the text.

ception of אל, אלהים, may well have imparted a richness of significance to those names which among other peoples they did not possess; there was at any rate nothing to lead to the abandonment of this ancient type of name. But it is in particular the numerous compounds with יה which give to the later names their peculiar complexion; in the lists in Ezra x. more than a third of the laity, more than half the priests bear names of this class. These names also, it is true, are in many cases closely paralleled among other Semitic peoples, except that other divine names take the place of יה. But a most significant difference is this: among other peoples, Phoenicians, Palmyrenes, Nabataeans, etc., contemporary with the later Jews, several divine names were used at the same time, and often, as a hasty glance at the inscriptions wills how, in the same family. This multiplicity of gods honoured in proper names is also found at an early date among peoples who have left us any large number of names—the Assyrians and Babylonians to wit. We have too few names of the people more closely related to the early Hebrews—the Moabites, Edomites, etc.—to speak with confidence; but even if, as seems to me far from improbable, at an *early* date among them also the reference in their proper names was always to one national deity, whether mentioned by his proper name or some title such as בעל, the Hebrews of *later* times stood alone in making reference in their names to but one god and that by means only of his proper name

יה or the one appellative אל. We may therefore formulate a third difference between the early and the late names thus: in later times Hebrew proper names as a whole became more sharply distinguished from those of other contemporary Semites than had been the case in early times.

Such are some of the broad differences in the character of proper names brought about during the centuries that separate David and his contemporaries or predecessors from Ezra and his contemporaries. But other interesting features come to light, if we follow the stream of history more closely and consecutively. The history of proper names bears witness to the gradual decay and final disappearance, even from popular thought, of certain ancient and deeply-rooted ideas, to the gradual growth and permeation through all ranks of society of others. It will be convenient to review first, but quite briefly, the process of decay.

In the earliest times Israelite *families* bore *animal names*, and in this the Israelites were like their neighbours. To them or to those neighbours those town names, especially numerous in the south, were due which are identical with animal names. A few Israelite *individuals* bore names of the same class in the time of David, a few also later, especially in the reign of Josiah. Names containing a word denoting some form of kinship also go back to early times, and were also borne in common by Israelites and their neighbours; but the use of them probably began later than that of the animal names, and was certainly far more largely personal. Later still appear the names containing one of the words אדן, בעל, מלך, significant of dominion. These probably only came into use among the Hebrews after their entrance into Canaan. On their entrance they found *place names* also in all parts of the country compounded with בעל, and they themselves created at least a few additional place names of this type. All these classes fall into disuse (as personal names) after the Exile, having been long previously on the wane.

The conclusion was drawn at the end of the discussion on animal names that the application of these to *individuals*, as early at least as the Davidic period, pointed to a previous break-up of any totem organisation which may have existed. Have we a similar indication in the names containing at once an element denoting some form of kinship and the proper name of a deity? In other words, do such words as אביה, אחיה and, if compound, יואב indicate a transition from the totem conception of kindred with a divine or totem animal to a conception of kinship with a personal God? Are we to infer that the conception of God changed, but that the old idea of man's kinship with God survived in a modified form? Whether this be so or not, must depend on the extent to which the totem theory can be independently established; but, if it be so, it gives a satisfactory explanation of otherwise difficult names. Etymologically names like אביה are comparatively straightforward; theologically they are most difficult, and that whether we interpret them Father is Yah, or My father is Yah, or Father of Yah. For to attribute to אב in אביה a spiritual sense such as the term "father" as applied to God receives in the prophets, and more especially in the New Testament, is forbidden by the parallel אחיה ("Brother is Yah"), by the existence of the parallel names among other nations, but more especially by the fact that the name in question together with those related to it in form falls into disuse just when the deeper ideas of the fatherhood of God were developing.

But whatever be their ultimate explanation, the names אביה, יואב, אביאל, אליאב, אליעם, עמיאל, אחיה, יואח, חיאל, prove clearly that at an early period Yahweh, the god (אל) of the Hebrews, was called אב, אח, עם, just as the names אלימלך, אדניה, בעליה, prove that he was also designated מלך, בעל, אדן. And just as, at least in some cases, בעל, מלך, אדן, refer to Yahweh in such names as בעלידע, מלכירם, אדנירם, so also in such names as אבירם, אחיקם, עמינדב, the first part is naturally to be referred to God rather than the human relative. The history of the names appears to me to confirm the interpretation which is thus indicated by analogy. For if the custom once *extensively* prevailed of giving children names to perpetuate some characteristic of a relative, and that is what is involved on the supposition that אב, אח, etc., in these names refer to the human kinsman, there is no obvious reason why at a later date they fell *wholly* into disuse; whereas on the other hand if these names contained a tacit reference to Yahweh, they would inevitably tend to fall into disuse as the earlier idea of man's kinship with the gods faded away even from popular thought before the higher prophetic conceptions of man's unlikeness to Yahweh.

Passing next to the classes which survived, we shall find that within them there is the same process of waxing and waning, some sub-classes growing more numerous, others gradually ceasing to furnish fresh names. The first point to which I draw attention is the unequal growth in popularity of compounds with אל and compounds with יה. The former are the more ancient, yet even in Judges they are outnumbered by compounds with יה (2 : 1), and this is even more the case in 2 S. ix.-xx. (9 : 2). The characteristic of the following centuries is the rapid proportionate growth of compounds with a divine name, but it is again the compounds with יה that increase most rapidly; among Jeremiah's contemporaries they are six times as numerous as compounds with אל. But subsequently the proportion of compounds with אל greatly increases; among the priestly contemporaries of Ezra (x. 18-22) they are half as numerous as compounds with יה; among the laity as 12 : 31; cf. also the (post-Exilic) proportion in 1 Chr. xxvi. 2-32, xxvii. 16-24, p. 186.

To illustrate the point further I cite the proportions based on Table 3, p. 162.

In Period I.	compounds with יה	: compounds with אל	: :	1 : $2\frac{2}{3}$ [1]
,, II.	,,	,,		1 : 1
,, III. (to cent. 8)	,,	,,		7 : 1
,, III. (from cent. 7)	,,	,,		6 : 1
,, IV.	,,	,,		4 : 1

In connection with the tendency in later literature to suppress the name Yahweh in favour of אלהים, this parallel tendency in proper names is of interest. In ordinary life compounds with יה were never discarded, and for some time after the Exile fresh compounds were freely formed; but there must have been a growing preference in some circles—especially perhaps the priestly circles, for contrast Ezra x. 25-43 with x. 18-22 — for compounds with אל. In artificial later names compounds with אל were created to the entire exclusion of compounds with יה; this is shown by the names of angels in Enoch and the artificial names in P (cf. p. 194 above). Briefly then, the more ancient, and in the very earliest period the more popular, compounds with אל became, from the time of David down to the seventh century, increasingly less numerous in proportion to the compounds with יה, but from that time forward, and especially in certain circles

[1] This proportion is somewhat too high, since some of the compounds with אל are clearly tribal names. But the *personal* names in אל certainly outnumber the *personal* names in יה.

after the Exile, they became again proportionately more numerous.

This leads us directly to consider how far the history of the compounds with יה casts light on the origin of the divine name יהוה. Moses, according to the Old Testament tradition, revealed to the Hebrews the name Yahweh. Whether the name was known before this time, either in other tribes or in Moses' own family or not, has long been matter of dispute; and it is a question which the present investigation cannot decide, but may in one or two points elucidate.

The prior knowledge of Yahweh in the family of Moses has been maintained on the ground of the name of his mother, יוכבד (Ex. vi. 20). This name is known to us only through P; but its genuinely ancient character need not be questioned; for if, as seems most probable,[1] it is a compound with יה, we may infer that it was neither coined by P nor obtained by him from current names. The form (יה prefixed) suggests moreover at least a pre-Exilic origin. Further than this, that the name itself is pre-Exilic and that the statement is therefore presumably derived from a pre-Exilic source, the mere study of names cannot carry us; it certainly does not justify us in accepting, on the other hand it gives us no ground for questioning, the historicity of Jochebed.

The next point to be considered is the infrequency of compounds with יה in the earliest period; for in

[1] Cf. p. 156.

view of two facts—(1) the greater frequency in the same period of compounds with אל, (2) the rapid increase of compounds with יה in the following period—we may safely infer that the infrequency of these names in the literature of the earliest period corresponds to infrequency in actual life. Now this infrequency certainly suggests that the names were of recent origin, and so far therefore supports the view that the Old Testament tradition of the introduction of the name Yahweh among the Hebrews by Moses is based on actual fact.

Further, the only name which is philologically quite certain and unambiguous, and which goes back far beyond the Davidic period, is יהונתן (Judg. xviii. 30), and this, significantly enough, is the name of a member of the family of Moses. The other quite early name is יהושוע, which has been questioned, but on insufficient grounds. Two more ambiguous names of the period of the Judges, יואש and יותם, occur in one family, one being the name of the father, the other of the son of Gideon.

Just before we reach the Davidic period we have in the names of the two sons of Samuel one clear instance אביה, and one doubtful instance יואל, of these names. The precise nature of Samuel's office need not be determined, but he clearly stood in a special relation to the worship of Yahweh, for at his instance both the first and second "Messiahs of Yahweh" received their commission to the monarchy.

Thus, uncertain and ambiguous as most of these early instances are, and incomplete as are the records concerning those who bore them, it has been possible to show that four—two sons of Samuel, one of Gideon, and a descendant of Moses—sprang from families which stood in special relation to Yahweh. With regard to the fathers or ancestors of the other two, Joshua and Joash, we have no definite information. It would be unwise to lay stress on P's account of origin of Joshua's name (Num. xii. 16), though it would be much to the point here if historical; but it is almost obviously not so; cf. p. 155.

The genuine compounds with יה belonging to the Davidic period are also distributed in a manner deserving of detailed attention. These number seventeen in all; one is a son of Saul, three are sons of David, and three[1] his nephews, *i.e.* seven in all or more than a third of the whole are members of the two royal families; four others are directly associated with David's court (see 2 S. viii. 16-18), one is a priest, and another a priest's son. This leaves about four among the ordinary ranks of society, and of these two are textually uncertain, viz. יואל, 1 Chr. xi. 38 = יגאל, 2 S. xxiii. 36, and יהושע, 1 S. vi. 14 (LXX. הושע).

Thus the social distribution of these names in the Davidic period confirms the conclusion suggested by

[1] Provided the relationship asserted in 1 Chr. ii. 16 be accepted, and Jehonadab of 2 S. xiii. 3 be regarded as different from the Jonathan of 2 S. xxi. 21.

their use in still earlier times, that compounds with יה were at first, and indeed for some time, confined to limited circles and special families. It is now generally admitted that the establishment of the monarchy was due to a growing national consciousness, and that with this the worship of Yahweh was closely connected. At this point two facts deserve notice—(1) Samuel, to whom the earliest tradition traces back the conception and establishment of the monarchy, had given two of his sons names, then uncommon, compounded with יה; (2) the term משיח י״י, applied to the king in the earliest sources, testifies to the direct connection even then conceived to exist between Yahweh and the monarch. This same connection between Yahweh and the king is seen reflected in the proper names; compounds with יה, as we have just shown, are almost confined in early and Davidic times to special families and circles, and particularly the royal circles. That this conclusion was sound is shown by these further facts—

1. The names of the twenty-one successors of David—all of his family—on the throne of Judah are, with six exceptions, compounds with יה. The exceptions are Solomon, Rehoboam, Asa, Ahaz, Manasseh, and Amon; one of these, Ahaz, is probably enough only apparent;[1] and an alternative name of Solomon

[1] *KAT*, 263 f. On the other hand note that Eliakim, according to 2 K. xxiii. 34, was the original name of Josiah's son

was ידידיה. The proportion is in any case most striking, and greatly above the normal during the period over which the succession ranges; comparison may be advantageously made with 1 Chr. ii. 35-41, viii. 33-39; cf. pp. 234, 241.

2. The character of the names of the kings of Israel, when closely examined, proves equally significant. Of the nineteen kings from Jeroboam I. to Hoshea inclusive, nine are founders of dynasties, and of these one only (Jehu[1]) bears a name compounded with יה; but of the remaining ten who came to the throne by succession six bear names compounded with יה; the remaining four are (*a*) Nadab, whose elder brother, bearing a יה name (אביה), predeceased his father (1 K. xiv. 1 ff.); (*b*) Elah and Ahab, who, as the first members in succession to the founders of their respective dynasties, may well have been born, and therefore named, before their fathers became king; and (*c*) Jeroboam II. Thus the tendency was as strong in the northern as in the southern kingdom, to give the heirs to the throne a name com-

Jehoiakim; but, further, that Jehoahaz, the name of Josiah's immediate successor, is a compound with יה.

[1] Note that the name of Jehu's father (Jehoshaphat) also contains the divine name; cf. pp. 8 f.

pounded with יה, and it is only on account of the number of usurpers and the brevity of the dynasties that the list of northern kings wears so different a complexion from that of the kings of the southern kingdom.[1]

3. The proportion of compounds with יה is much greater in 2 S. ix.-xx. than in 2 S. xxiii. 24-39. In the former section, which narrates the *court* life of David, these names number *one-fifth* of the whole (nine out of forty-five), in the latter only *one-tenth* (four out of forty).

Now the fact that these names were at first thus largely, or entirely, confined to special circles throws some light on the vexed question of the origin of Yahweh, in so far as it tells strongly against the theory of Fried. Delitzsch that the forms יה and יהוה have no real and original connection, but that the former was in use among the people, the latter among the

[1] The greater prevalence of compounds with יה in royal than in other circles favours the suggestion that the Hezekiah from whom the prophet Zephaniah was descended, was the king of Judah. Of five names in the genealogy (Zeph. i. 1), four are compounded with יה, a large proportion even for the seventh century. Moreover, it has already been observed (Driver, *Introd.* p. 318) that Hezekiah is not a common name; regarding the Hezekiah of 2 Chr. xxviii. 12 as unhistorical—note the names in the context in connection with the discussions above, pp. 226 ff.—we may state the point more strongly: Hezekiah the king is the only pre-Exilic person of the name known to us apart from the prophet's ancestor.

prophets and priests. If the theory in question were sound, how could the fact be accounted for that in the early period this (hypothetically) popular name was so infrequently embodied in the names of the common people, but that it first appears and for some time continued to be all but confined just to those circles where we are able to trace what may, broadly speaking, be termed "priestly and prophetic" influence—to the families of Moses, of Gideon, of Samuel, of the "Messiahs of Yahweh," Saul and David? If the theory were correct, compounds with יה should be distributed with some approach to equality among all classes; just the reverse is the actual case, for everything goes to show that they gradually made their way down from special classes into the ordinary ranks of society, the process of equalisation not being complete even after the Exile, as the contrast between the lay and priestly names analysed above (p. 186) sufficiently shows. It is unfortunate that between the times of David and Ezra we have no quite typical lists of the ordinary people, and, since the Books of Kings deal mainly with persons connected with the court, this fact needs always to be taken into account in estimating the evidence of the tables which have been given above. It is, in particular, to the number of members of the royal and priestly families and generally of the courtly circles mentioned in Jeremiah that I attribute the fact that the proportion of compounds with יה there mentioned is about a mean between the two post-Exilic lists which were analysed, one exclusively of priests, the other exclusively of the common people.

We have seen that a general difference between early and late names is the predominance in later times of sentence-names asserting something concerning יה or אל. The small number of early sentence-names may conveniently be examined in detail and some of the chief characteristics of the very numerous later names.

Of the pre-Davidic names, one יהונתן contains what is the most common thought of their gods embodied by the ancient Semites in their names, cf. *e.g.* in Phoenician אשמניתן, בעליתן, עשתרתיתן = Eshmun (or Baal or Ashtoreth) has given; in Assyrian, Assur-aḫ-iddina = Asshur gives a brother; Marduk-nabal-iddina = Marduk gives a son; in Himyaritic והבאל = El has given. The name Jonathan had indeed a meaning sufficiently elastic to be capable of receiving deeper and fuller meaning, as religious knowledge advanced, and to this fact we may probably ascribe the continued popularity of the name in later periods. The other early and certain name (אביה) has been sufficiently discussed, p. 254, etc. If we sum up the early conception of Yahweh as expressed in the extant early sentence-names, placing in brackets what is inferred from the etymologically or otherwise uncertain names, the statement runs thus: Yahweh is father, gives (or has given, *i.e.* children ?), [is God, is wealth, assists, and is perfect].[1] A similar statement with regard to El would run, El is father, paternal uncle (or has loved, or is Dad), king, help, is He, [is Yahweh]; El has helped, has acquired [and gives life].[1] Two early tribal names (ישראל, ירחמאל) call on him to strive and to have compassion. One or two of the early compounds with אל do not appear to be sentence-names, certainly not מתושאל, probably not שמואל and עתניאל.

The new names in the Davidic period make the following additional statements, Yahweh is brother, is lord, is light, is noble; he knows, judges, builds, and a son of the king is beloved of him.[1] Here, as with the earlier names, some describe the relation in which Yahweh stands to men—as father, lord, etc., but a larger number than before refer to his activity. The actions which this latter class of names asserts are worth recalling—Yahweh has judged (יהושפט and שפטיה); with this cf. 1 S. xxiv. 13-16, 2 S. xviii. 19. The building of Yahweh referred to in בניה is probably that of the house or family,[2] but the name was also frequent in the days of Ezra, when it may have had reference to the building of the walls of Jerusalem or of the Temple. How much is implied in the

[1] The Hebrew names will be found in App. III.

[2] Cf. Gesenius, *Thesaurus*, p. 215, *s.v.* בנה, 4; possibly the Himyaritic בנאל may be compared; on this see Osiander in *ZDMG*, 1856, p. 53. For Assyrian parallels, *ZDMG*, 1872, pp. 120 f.

knowledge that יהוידע ascribes to Yahweh, we cannot say; in itself the ascription of knowledge to the deity is not peculiar to Israel, for we find אלידע in Himyaritic. But it may well be due to the prophetic teaching as to Yahweh's special knowledge of Israel (Am. iii. 2) that this name and the parallel ידעיה were prevalent in later times. The other ideas expressed in these names of the Davidic period continued to be expressed by the same or similar names in later periods, with the exception only of those of the fatherhood and brotherhood of Yahweh, and the somewhat special idea contained in ידידיה. The statements made by the compounds with אל first appearing in the Davidic period are these: El is kinsman, deliverance, wealth, he hides, has been gracious, has heard and has wrought. One of the names—עדריאל, apparently = the herd of God—is not a sentence-name.[1]

It is hardly necessary to continue in the case of the far more numerous names of the following periods a detailed interpretation. But one or two general characteristics are very markworthy. From the tables given on p. 176 it is clear that combinations of יה or אל with a noun were the earliest formations, but that they subsequently became increasingly out-

[1] Unless indeed עדריאל be an Aramaic equivalent of עזריאל; the Greek transliteration of the ע by the soft breathing and not by γ certainly favours connecting the name with عزر = to help rather than غذر, with which latter עדר = a flock appears to be connected.

numbered by verbal combinations. This is important in the present connection, for it means that the tendency, already observed to have been on the increase between Periods I. and II., to refer in the names more to the activities than to the relationships of Yahweh rapidly increased in Periods III. and IV. In other words, the conceptions of the manifold activity and personal character of Yahweh was constantly increasing, and in comparison with this the earlier conceptions of Yahweh's relationships—as father, brother, etc.—were becoming less prominent.

Further, all the statements made in the verbal compounds of Periods I. and II. may, and quite possibly do, refer to particular occasions or to the divine activity in relation to an individual; the gift, for instance, in יהונתן is naturally, on the analogy of other Semitic names, interpreted as a gift of children. But in Period III. (centuries eight and seven) we first find names which appear to assert general activities or attributes of Yahweh—his greatness (גדליה and יגדליה), his might (אמציה) and power (יכליה); and in Period IV. several names which resemble, probably not through mere accident, phrases that are frequent in prophecy and psalms—חסדיה, נחמיה, זרחיה, יזרחיה, פלטיה, רפיה, שכניה, שמריה.[1] Probably enough, also, some of the post-Exilic names

[1] We should add as a striking instance הכליה, if its original pronunciation really was חכליה (see p. 221); for cf. Ps. xxxiii. 20. With the popular post-Exilic name אליועיני cf. Ps. xxv. 15.

refer to Yahweh's activity on behalf of the restored community rather than of any individual; most suggestive is the name אלישיב (= God brings back), which is first found in the post-Exilic period, but then with frequency—five times (also once in 1 Chr. xxiv. 12). Many names coined, indeed, previously, but in this period particularly frequent, may very well have owed their popularity to the fact that they could most naturally refer to the national fortunes; thus יהוחנן is the name of five post-Exilic individuals, בניה of four, זכריה of nine, חנניה of eight, ישעיה of three, מעשיה of seven, מלכיה of five, פדיה of six, שמעיה of five; with מעשיה cf. especially the frequent absolute use of עשה in reference to the divine activity, *e.g.* in Ps. xxii. 31.

One change that has already been indicated remains to be interpreted. It has been shown not only that verbal compounds came to predominate over substantival, but also that verbal compounds in which יה (or אל) stood at the end drove out the earlier formations in which it had stood at the beginning. Now there is certainly a difference between *e.g.* יהושפט and שפטיה, for the first emphasises the subject, the second the predicate, or, more strictly speaking, removes the emphasis from the subject. Now as long as names might consist of a verb with any one of several subjects—אל, יה, אח, אב, עם, אדן, בעל, מלך—there must have been a tendency to emphasise the subject selected by placing it first; gradually as the names confined themselves to assertions about יה or אל, as the *verbal* compounds became so predominantly compounded only with יה, the activity became the main thing, the subject being at once understood. It was but a step to drop the subject at the end altogether, the popular consciousness being trusted to supply it. This change of form thus ceases to be one of mere philological interest, it illustrates the growing sense that "Israel's Yahweh was one Yahweh," who was behind all actions, the source of all welfare, the true object of all worship. It is of course not asserted that the change was consciously made; far from it; the thoroughly gradual way in which it took place would suffice to disprove that; so too would the instance or instances of the same person bearing two names, one with יה prefixed, the other with יה postfixed to a verb;[1] but the more unconscious the process the more does it witness to the general change that came over the popular consciousness in reference to religion during the centuries that have been passed in review. In this respect, indeed, this change is like that to which all the statistical tables testify; we find no class of names suddenly introduced or suddenly abandoned, and it is the net result of these various gradual changes—leading to decay in some cases, to multiplication and increase in others—that throws valuable light on the growth and formation of religious

[1] The one certain instance is יהויכין, 2 K. xxiv. 6 = יכניה, Jer. xxvii. 20.

ideas. Slowly, but surely, the higher teaching, whether of prophet or priest, made way throughout all ranks of society, affecting even the most conservative instincts such as came into play in the choice or creation of a child's name, until at last names which embodied ideas not fully consonant with the more recent but higher conceptions of God, wholly disappear, and those alone survive which briefly set forth certain elements of prophetic doctrine or at least are not manifestly irreconcilable with it.

APPENDICES

I.

APPENDED are classified lists of the names in (1) Judg. ii. 6-xvi., (2) 2 Sam. ix.-xx., referred to on p. 184 and elsewhere in the essay.

I. Names of Israelites mentioned in Judges ii. 6-xvi. exclusive of the names of persons manifestly earlier than the times described.

1. Names compounded with יה, 2.
   - יואש, vi. 11.
   - יותם, ix. 5.
     - [? Ιωβηλ, ix. 26 (LXX.); cf. p. 122.]
2. Name compounded with אל, 1.
   - עתניאל, iii. 9.
3. Other names, 25.
   - *a*. Compound, 3.
     - ירבעל, viii. 29.
     - אבינעם, iv. 5.
     - אבימלך, viii. 31.
   - *b*. Simple, 22.
     - קנז, iii. 9.
     - גרא, iii. 15.
     - יאיר, x. 2.
     - דודו, x. 1.

אהוד, iii. 16.	אבצן, xii. 8.
דבורה, iv. 4.	אילון, xii. 11.
לפידות, iv. 4.	עבדון, xii. 13.
ברק, iv. 5.	הלל, xii. 13,
פרה, vii. 10.	מנוח, xiii. 2.
עבד, ix. 26.	שמשון, xiii. 24.
געל, ix. 26.	כלב, iii. 9.
זבול, ix. 28.	גדעון, vi. 11.
תולע, x. 1.	פואה, x. 1.

Two names שמגר and ענת have been excluded as being probably the names of foreigners (yet cf. Moore on Judges v. 6). Possibly געל and עבד (included above) are also foreign, cf. Moore, *Judges*, pp. 155 f. The name אביעזר has also been excluded as being certainly that of a clan (viii. 2; cf. vi. 11). Probably several of the other names are those of clans, *e.g.* כלב, עתניאל; but it is difficult to feel certain. One of the names classed as simple—אהוד—may be = אביהוד and therefore compound; cf. p. 26 n. 4.

II. Names of Israelites contemporary with David and mentioned in 2 S. ix.-xx.

1. Names compounded with יה, 9.

a. With יה prefixed, 6.	*b.* With יה, post-fixed, 3.
יונתן, (*a*) ix. 1.	ידידיה, xii. 25.
(*b*) xv. 27.	בניה, xx. 23.
יונדב, xiii. 3.	אוריה, "the Hittite," xi. 3.
יואב, x. 9.	
יהודע, xx. 23.	
יהושפט, xx. 24.	

2. Names compounded with אל, 2.

אליעם, xi. 3 (? foreign), עמיאל, ix. 5.

3. Other names, 34.

a Compounds, 11.

מריבעל = מפיבשת, ix. 6.
אדנירם = אדרם, xx. 24.
אבישי, x. 10.
אבשלם, xiii. 1.
אביתר, xv. 27.
אביגל, xvii. 25.
אחיתפל, xv. 12.
אחימעץ, xv. 27.
אחילוד, xx. 24.
בתשבע, (? foreign) xi. 3.
מיכא, ix. 12.

b. Simple, 23.

דוד, ix. 1.
שאול, ix. 1.
ציבא, ix. 3.
מכיר, ix. 4.
נתן, xii. 1.
שלמה, xii. 24.
תמר, (*a*) xiii. 1.
„ (*b*) xiv. 27.
אמנון, xiii. 2.
שמעה, xiii. 3.
צרויה, xiv. 1.
צדוק, xv. 24.
חושי, xv. 32.
שמעי, xvi. 5.
גרא, xvi. 5.
עמשא, xvii. 25.
נחש, xvii. 25.
ברזלי, xvii. 27.
כמהם, xix. 38.
שבע, xx. 1.
בכרי, xx. 1.
שיא, xx. 24.
עירא, xx. 26.

The name יתרא, xvii. 25, is excluded as being almost certainly an Ishmaelite's name, cf. Driver, *Samuel*, p. 252.

Three (אמנון, עמשא, חושי) classed as simple, may possibly be compound: see pp. 64 n. 2, 44 n. 2, 323.

II.

This appendix contains complete lists of the following classes of names found in the Old Testament:—

1. Compounds with אב.

2. Compounds with אח.
3. " " יה.
   A. Names in which יה is prefixed.
   B. " " " post-fixed.
   C. A name " " the second of three elements.
4. Compounds with אל.
   A. Names in which אל is prefixed.
   B. " " " post-fixed.

The object of these lists, on which the statistical tables in Chap. II. and subsequent discussions are based, is to show—(1) what names of the classes were in use; (2) to how many different persons they were given: for this purpose I give a single reference for each different person or family of the name; unless otherwise indicated these references are to Hebrew individuals; the letter F following a reference indicates that the name is that of a family, clan, or tribe; an italicised reference indicates a foreigner. In the case of compounds with אב and אח, I have further distinguished the names of women by placing W after the reference. (3) The third object of the lists is to show at what periods the names were in use, and the nature of the evidence for the usage in the several periods. For this purpose the references are arranged in five main columns; the first four represent the four periods defined on p. 20, the last embraces all occurrences of a name in contexts which do not define the chronology. The first three columns are subdivided so as to show whether the usage of the name is supported by the evidence of the early writings, or only by that of P or Chronicles. In column 3 the Roman numeral in brackets following the reference defines the century to which the name is referred, or rather the century of the (inferential) date of birth.

The following summary of the manner in which I have treated ambiguous passages should be observed.

All the names in 1 Chr. ii.-ix. peculiar to the Chronicles,

either in themselves or in the special application, are classified in the column of uncertain date, with these exceptions:—

1. Names in ii. 14-17 are clearly, in the intention of the compiler, names of individuals contemporary with David, and have therefore been so classed.

2. Similarly in v. 27-41 the names are clearly intended to be those of individuals, and the dates to be as follows:—

   a. Down to Ahitub, verse 33, pre-Davidic, Period I.
   b. From Zadok to Azariah, verses 34 f., Davidic, Period II.
   c. From Johanan to Jehozadak, verses 35-41, Period III.

3. In vi. 1-33 the names are again clearly intended to be those of pre-Davidic individuals, and have been so classed.

In the books of Ezra and Nehemiah the dates are usually clear, but the character of the names—whether personal or family—is often more or less ambiguous; following for the most part Bertheau-Ryssel or Ryle in their commentaries, I have classified the names thus:—

Ezra ii. 2. Personal.
ii. 3-61. Family.
viii. 4-14. The name in the first clause of each statement is that of a family, the (two) following names are of individuals.
x. 18-44. As in viii. 4-14.

Neh. iii. The first names here are clearly of individuals, but the final names are ambiguous; for some, *e.g.* Hakkoz, Pahath-moab (verses 4-11), are well-known family names (cf. Ezra ii. 61; ii. 6, 32); but the terms of verse 30 see to suggest that in other cases we have the name of the actual father and therefore of a second individual. I have therefore indicated these names by F ? after the reference.

viii. 6, 7. Individuals, *vide* Ryssel.

x. 3-27. Families.

xi. 1-23. Probably families, indicated thus, F ?.

xii. 1-9. Families.

xii. 10 f. Individuals.

xii. 12-21. First name family, second individual.

xii. 32. Individuals.

xii. 33-36. Families.

xii. 41. Individuals.

xii. 42. Probably families, marked F ?.

	I.			II.		III.		IV.	Chronologically uncertain.
	P.	Early Writings.	Chronicles.	Early Writings.	Chronicles.	Early Writings.	Chronicles.		
1. אבי[1] .	...	...	...	...	...	2 K. xviii. 2, W (viii.)			
2. אביאל .	...	*a.* 1 S. ix. 1	...	*b.* 1 Chr. xi. 32[2]					
3. אביאסף[3] .	Ex. vi. 24, F								
4. אביגיל[4] .	...	...	...	*a.* 1 S. xxv. 3 W *b.* 2 S. xvii.25 W					
5. אבידן .	Num. i. 11								
6. אבידע .	...	*Gen. xxv. 4*							
7. אביה .	...	*a.* 1 S. viii. 2	...	...	*b.* 1, xxiv. 10	*c.* 2 Chr. xi. 20[2] (x.) *d.* 1 K. xiv. 1 (x.)	...	*e.* Neh. xii. 4, F	*f.* 1 Chr. ii.24 *g.* 1 Chr. vii. 8
8. אביהוא .	...	Ex. xxiv. 1							
9. אביהוד .	...	...	...	...	...	...	...	...	1 Chr. viii. 3
10. אביחיל .	*a.* Num. iii. 35	...	...	...	...	...	*b.*[5] 2, xi. 18, W (x.)	*c.* Esth. ii. 15[6]	*d.* 1 Chr. ii. 29[5] *e.* 1 Chr. v. 14
11. אביטוב .	...	...	...	...	...	...	...	...	1 Chr. viii. 11
12. אביטל .	...	...	...	2 S. iii. 4, W					
13. אבימאל .	...	*Gen. x. 28*							

[1] In 1 Chr. xxix. 1 אביה. In defence of the reading אבי, *vide* p. 24.

[2] Chronicles preserves the correct forms of these names, which also occur, though in an incorrect form, in Kings; *vide* p. 25.

[3] At 1 Chr. vi. 8 אביסף.

[4] Also, and perhaps more correctly spelt אבינל; *vide* Nöldeke, *ZDMG*, 1883, p. 537.

[5] In these cases, some MSS. read אביהיל; *vide* Bertheau on 1 Chr. ii. 29.

[6] Cf. p. 27.

	a. 1 S. vii. 1 *b.* 1 S. xvi. 8 *c.* 1 S. xxxi. 2					
...	*b.* 2 S. xxiii. 27					
...		...	*c.* 1 K. xvi. 34 (IX.)			
	1 K. i. 3, W					
1, v. 30	...	...	...		...	*b.* 1 Chr. viii. 4[3]
...	...	...	...	...	...	1 Chr. ii. 28
...	1 S. xxvi. 6					
...	2 S. iii. 3[4]					
...	...	...	*a.* 1 K. xvi. 28 (IX) *b.* Jer. xxix. 21 (VII.)			

2. Names compounded with אח.

1. אחאב .			...	...		*a.* 1 K. xvi. 28 (IX) *b.* Jer. xxix. 21 (VII.)			
2. אחבן[9] .		...		...		...		...	1 Chr. ii. 29
3. אחומי[10] .		...	...	...	...		...	...	1 Chr. iv. 2
4. אחיאם .		...	...	2 S. xxiii. 33					
5. אחיה .			...	*a.* 1 S. xiv. 3	...	*b.* 1 K. iv. 3 (x.) *c.* 1 K. xi. 29 (x.) *d.* 1 K. xv. 27 (x.)	...	*e.* Neh. x. 27, F	*f.* 1 Chr. viii. 7
6. אחיהוד .	*a.* Num. xxxiv. 27	..	...	...	...	...	...	...	*b.* 1 Chr. viii. 7

[1] Through textual corruption this name is attributed to two other persons: for the one, cf. 1 Chr. xviii. 16, where LXX. rightly reads Ἀχειμέλεχ, see further Bertheau, *ad loc.*; for the other, Ps. xxxiv. 1, on which see *e.g.* Baethgen, *ad loc.*

[2] Cf. Dillmann on Num. xxvi. 29.

[3] LXX. B here reads אבישׁשׁ.

[4] Probably identical with Rehoboam's father-in-law, 1 K. xv. 2.

[5] No doubt the same person as is named in ver. 19 אליאל and in 1 S. i. 1 אליהוא. The variations render the instance an uncertain one

[6] It is possible that this word is not composite, but a derivative from a root; *vide* Nöldeke, *ZDMG*, 1888, p. 477, note 2; cf. above, p. 24. Yet cf. חיאל.

[7] See above, p. 24.

[8] *Vide* note to No. 20 *b.* and cf. p. 26, n. 3.

[9] Uncertain. In Hebrew ἅπ. λεγ. In 1 Chr. ii. 29, Syr. supports *MT*; so virtually Vulg. *Ahobban*, Ar. العابان. But LXX. B reads Ἀχαβαρ, A, Ὀζα.

[10] The versions suggest that the original form was אחימי. Thus LXX. B, Ἀχειμει, A, Αχιμαι; Syr. ܐܚܝܡܝ.

1 K. iv. 12 (x.)			
...	...	...	1 Chr. vii. 34
...	...	...	*b.* 1 Chr. ix. 17
K. iv. 14 (x.)			
K. xxii. 12 (VII.)			
1 K. vii. 13 (*x.*)	...	...	*d.* 1 Chr. viii. 5
...	...	...	1 Chr. vii. 10
K. iv. 6 (x.)			

3. Names compounded with יה. (*A*) יה prefixed.

1. יואב[4] .	... .	...	...	*a.* 1 S. xxvi. 6	...	...	...	*b.* Ezr. ii. 6, F	1 Chr. iv. 14
2. יואח .	...	...	*a.*[3] 1, vi. 6	...	*b.* 1, xxvi. 4	*c.* 2 K. xviii. 18 (viii.)	*d.* 2, xxix. 12 (viii.) *e.* 2, xxxiv. 8 (vii.)		
3. יהואחז .	...	...	...	...	...	*a.* 2 K. x. 35 (ix.) *b.* 2 K. xxiii. 30 (vii.)	*a.* 2, xxxiv. 8 (vii.)[5]		
4. יואל[4] .	...	*a.* 1 S. viii. 2	*b.* 1, vi. 21	*c.* 1 Chr. xi. 38?[6]	*d.* 1, xv. 7[7] *e.* 1, xxvii. 20	...	*f.* 2, xxix. 12 (viii.)	*g.* Joel i. 1 *h.* Ezr. x. 43 *i.* Neh. xi. 9	*k.* 1 Chr. iv. 35 *l.* 1 Chr. v. 4 (?=ver. 8) *m.* 1 Chr. v. 12 *n.* 1 Chr. vii. 3
5. יואש .		*a.* Judg. vi. 11	...	...	*b.* 1, xii. 3.	*c.* 1 K. xxii. 26 (ix.) *d.* 2 K. xi. 2 (ix.) *e.* 2 K. xiii. 13 (ix.-viii.)	...	...	*f.* 1 Chr. iv. 22
6. יהוא .	...	...	...		*a.* 1, xii. 3	*b.* 1 K. xvi. 1 (x.) *c.* 1 K. xix. 16 (ix.)	...	...	*d.* 1 Chr. iv. 35 *e.* 1 Chr. ii. 38

[1] *MT* at 1 Chr. vi. 10 is, in respect of this name, supported by the versions (virtually even by LXX. B Ἀλειμώθ); but in view of the מחת of verse 20 the text is not above suspicion.

[2] On the identity of the forms אחירם, חירם, חורם, חירום, *vide Oxf. Lex. s. vv.*

[3] With *a* cf. *d.*

[4] Uncertain instances owing to ambiguous etymology; see pp. 24, 153.

[5] The name יהואחז as applied to King Ahaziah in 2 Chr. xxi. 17 is probably a textual error, and as such is excluded from the list. Vg. alone supports *MT*; all other VV. reading אחזיה.

[6] Text uncertain; יואל *MT* and VV. in Chr.; in parallel passage in 2 S. xxiii. 36, *MT* Vg. (and virtually LXX.) יגאל; Syr. Ar. בגאל. The reading of Chr. is thus slightly better supported.

[7] Probably = 1 Chr. xxiii. 8; xxvi. 22.

a. 1, xii. 20[1] *b.* 1, xii. 4 *c.* 1, xxvi. 4	*d.* 2 K. xii. 22 (IX.)	*e.* 2, xvii. 18 (IX.) *f.* 2, xxxi. 13 (VIII.) *g.* 2, xxxv. 9 (VII.)	*h.* Ezr. viii. 33[2] *i.* Ezr. x. 22	
...	[(IX.) 2 K. xii. 22			
a. 1, xi. 45	...	...	...	*b.* 1 Chr. viii. 16
a. 1, xii. 4 *b.* 1, xii. 12 *c.* 1, xxvi. 3	*d.* 2 K. xxv. 23 (VII.)	*e.* 1, v. 35 (X.) *f.* 2, xvii. 15 (IX.) *g.* 2, xxiii. 1 (IX.) *h.* 2, xxviii. 12 (VIII.) *i.* 1, iii. 15 (VII.)	*k.* Ezr. x. 6 *l.* Ezr. x. 28 *m.* *Neh. vi. 18*[5] *n.* Neh. xii. 13 *o.* Neh. xii. 22 *p.* Neh. xii. 42 F ? *q.* 1 Chr. iii. 24	
...	*b.* 2 K. xi. 4 (IX.[7])	...	*c.* Neh. iii. 6 *d.* Neh. xii. 10	
...	2 K. xxiv. 6 (VII.)			
	a. 2 K. xxiii. 34 (VII.)	...	*b.* Neh. xii. 10	*c.* 1 Chr. iv. 22 LXX.[9]
	...	...	*a.* Neh. xi. 10, F	*c.* Neh. xii. 6

15. יהוזבד .				a. 2 S. xiii. 3[10]		b. 2 K. x. 15 (IX.)			
16. יהונתן .	...	a. Judg. xviii. 30		b. 1 S. xiii. 2 c. 2 S. xxi. 21[10] d. 2 S. xv. 27 e. 2 S. xxiii. 32[11]	f. 1, xxvii. 25	g. Jer. xxxvii. 15 (VII.) h. Jer. xl. 8[12] (VII.)	i. 2, xvii. 8 (IX.)	k. Ezr. x. 15 l. Neh. xii. 18 m. Neh. xii. 11 n. Neh. xii. 14 o. Neh. xii. 35	p. 1 Chr. ii. 32
17. יער[13] .		...	...	...	...	...	...	...	Neh. xi. 7
18. יהועדה[14] .		...	...	...	...	...	...	...	1 Chr. viii. 36
19. יהועדן[15] .		...	...	...	...	2 K. xiv. 2 (VIII.)			

[1] Two persons of this name are mentioned in this verse; but in one instance the name is very possibly dittographic.

[2] Possibly others of this name are mentioned in Period IV., viz. in Ezra x. 23, Neh. viii. 7, xi. 16; but these may all refer to the same person and be identical with *h*.

[3] An uncertain but probable ἅπ. λεγ. (VV. support). In the parallel 2 Chr. xxiv. 26 *MT* (and VV.) read זבד, a variant which has probably arisen owing to a scribe copying the letters יו once instead of twice (עליו יוזבד), and then reading זבד as זכר, which latter is a familiar name in Chronicles; see 1 Chr. ii. 36, vii. 21, xi. 41; cf. Ezra x. 27, 33, 43.

[4] Textually and etymologically uncertain. It occurs only in 1 Chr. viii. 16, *MT* Vg. (Syr. omits), and xi. 45, *MT* Vg. Syr. and virtually in LXX. B (Ἰωχάν) in the former passage; in xi. 45 LXX. B reads Ἰωδάζαε; and in viii. 16 A reads Ἰωαχά and Ἰεζιά (apparently a doublet). Gesenius (*Thesaurus, s.v.*) suggests that it is a contraction of יוחיה; this is most improbable, מיכה and מיכיהו present no true analogy. Far more probably יוחא is an error for יואח, unless the textual error is deeper still.

[5] An Ammonite; yet cf. Ryle on Neh. ii. 10.

[6] Probably the person here mentioned is identical with the person of 1 Chr. xii. 27 (for cf. 1 Chr. xxvii. 5) and of 1 Chr. xxvii. 34, for see p. 6, n. 1. Otherwise one (or two) instances must be placed in the Chronicle column above.

[7] With this Graf (*ad loc.*) and *Oxf. Lex.* identify the Jehoiada of Jer. xxix. 26; Siegf.-Stade and Ges.-Buhl appear to distinguish them. [8] = B, No. 59.

[9] Ἰωακείμ (= יהויקים, 2 K. xxiii. 34), *MT* יוקים; Syr. and Ar. omit the passage, and Vg. misunderstands it.

[10] Perhaps 15 *a* = 16 *c*; Bertheau also connects 16 *c* with 1 Chr. xxvii. 32; otherwise another entry must be made in the Chronicle column above.

[11] Certainly identical with the Jonathan of 1 Chr. xi. 34; cf. Driver on 2 S. xxiii. 32.

[12] Ewald questions the text, but see Graf.

[13] ἅπ. λεγ. not fully attested; Syr. [Syriac] perhaps = No. 11. Etymology also ambiguous; possibly from root יער.

[14] Text and meaning doubtful. Syr. and LXX. A יהועדן; 1 Chr. ix. 42 *MT* יערה, perhaps originally יעדה; cf. LXX. B in viii. 36 and ix. 42 Ἰαδά.

[15] Some form, otherwise unknown, with יהו prefixed is certainly intended; יהועדן 2 K. xiv. 2, K'ri Vg. Trg. Syr. Ar.; and 2 Chr. xxv. 1, *MT* Vg. Syr., cf. LXX. A; יהועדין 2 K. xiv. 2, K'tib LXX.; and 2 Chr. xxv. 1, Luc.; cf. simple name עדין, Ezra ii. 15.

	I.			II.		III.		IV.	Chronologically uncertain.
	P.	Early Writings.	Chronicles.	Early Writings.	Chronicles.	Early Writings.	Chronicles.		
20. יועזר[1] .	...	...	...	...	1, xii. 6				
21. יועש[2] .	...	...	...	...	*a.* 1, xxvii. 28	...	...	...	*b.* 1 Chr. vii. 8
22. יהוצדק .	...	...	...	...	...	Hag. i. 1 (VI.)			
23. יהורם .	...	...	...	*a.* *2 S. viii. 10*[3]	*b.* 1, xxvi. 25	*c.* 1 K. xxii. 51 (IX.) *d.* 2 K. i. 17 (IX.) [(IX.) 2 K. xi. 2	*e.* 2, xvii. 8 (IX.)		
24. יהושבע[4] .	...	...	...	...	...				
25. יהושע . ישוע	...	*a.* Ex. xxiv. 13	...	*b.* 1 S. vi. 14[5]	*c.* 1, xxiv. 11	*d.* 2 K. xxiii. 8 (VII.)	*e.* 2, xxxi. 15 (VIII.)	*f.* Hag. i. 1 *g.* Ezr. ii. 6, F *h.* Ezr. ii. 36, F *i.* Ezr. ii. 40, F *k.* Neh. iii. 19, F ?	*l.* Neh. xi. 26 (Place)
26. הושמע[6] .	...	...	...	...	...	...	1, iii. 18 (VI.)		
27. יהושפט .	...	...	...	*a.* 2 S. viii. 16	*b.* 1, xi. 43 *c.* 1, xv. 24	*d.* 1 K. iv. 17 (X.) [(IX.) *e.* 1 K. xv. 24 *f.* 2 K. ix. 2 (IX.) [(VIII.)			
28. יותם[2] .	...	*a.* Judg. ix. 5	...	...	...	*b.* Is. vii. 1	...		*c.* 1 Chr. ii. 47
29. יוכבד[2] .	Ex. vi. 20								

(*B*) NAMES WITH יה POST-FIXED.

2. אדניה[1] .	...	...	...	*a.* 1 K. i. 8	...	...	*b.* 2, xvii. 8 (IX.)	*c.* Neh. x. 17	
3. אוריה .	...	...	...	*a.* 2 S. xi. 3	...	*b.* Is. viii. 2 (VIII.)	...	*c.* Ezra viii. 33	
4. אוניה[8] .	...	...	...	...	...	...	..	Neh. x. 10, F	
5. אחזיה .	...	...	...	...	...	*a.* 1 K. xxii. 40 (IX.) *b.* 2 K. viii. 24 (IX.)			
6. אחיה[9] .	...	...	...	*a.* 1 S. xiv. 3	...	*b.* 1 K. iv. 3 (X.) *c.* 1 K. xi. 29 (X.) *d.* 1 K. xv. 27 (IX.)	...	*e.* Neh. x. 27, F	*f.* 1 Chr. viii. 7
7. אליהו .	...	...	...	...	...	*a.* 1 K. xvii. 1 (IX.)	...	*b.* Ezra x. 21 *c.* Ezra x. 26	*d.* 1 Chr. viii. 27
8. אמציה .	...	...	*a.* 1, vi. 30	...	...	*b.* 2 K. xiv. 1 (VIII.) *c.* Am. vii. 10 (VIII.)	...	...	*d.* 1 Chr. iv. 34
9. אמריה[10] .	...	...	*a.* 1, v. 33	...	*b.* 1, xxiii. 19	*c.* Zeph. i. 1 (VIII.)	*d.* 2, xix. 11 (IX.) *e.* 2, xxxi. 15 (IX.) *f.* 1, v. 37	*g.* Ezra x. 42 *h.* Neh. x. 4, F	*i.* Neh. xi. 4
10. אצליה .		...	...	...	...	2 K. xxii. 3 (VII.)			
11. בריה[11] .	...	...	...	...	...	...	...	Ezra x. 35	

[1] ἅπ. λεγ.
[2] Cf. pp. 154, 156, 324.
[3] Text very doubtful; cf. Wellhausen and Driver, *ad loc.*
[4] In parallel 2 Chr. xxii. 11 יהושבעת; variant due to following בת? Syr. here as in Kings reads יהושבע.
[5] LXX. B Ὡσῆε = הושע.
[6] Uncertain ἅπ. λεγ. Vg. Syr. read forms without the prefix.
[7] See note on App. II. 1, No. 7 *c.*
[8] ἅπ. λεγ.; VV. support *MT*, except Syr. [illegible] = No. 43.
[9] Cf. p. 36. [10] Cf. No. 80.
[11] Uncertain ἅπ. λεγ. The elision of ע (pre-supposed by בבנה = עבריה; Olsh. 277 *b*, 4) is without analogy in biblical Hebr. Probably enough the form is a corruption of בר(א)יה, No 17; so LXX. B; cf. Syr.; other VV. support *MT*.

2 S. viii. 18	*c.* 1, xv. 18	*d.* Ezek. xi. 1 (VII.)	*e.* 2, xx. 14 (IX.)	*g.* Ezra x. 25	*l.* 1 Chr. iv. 36
2 S. xxiii. 30			*f.* 2, xxxi. 13 (VIII.)	*h.* Ezra x. 30 *i.* Ezra x. 35 *k.* Ezra x. 43	
...	...			Neh. iii. 6, F ?	
...	1, xii. 5				
...	...		...	Neh. xii. 9	
...	1, xxv. 4				
...	...	...	...	...	1 Chr. viii. 21
...	*a.* 1, xv. 23 *b.* 1, vi. 24	*c.* Is. viii. 2 (VIII.) *d.* Zech. i. 1 (VI.)	*e.* 2, xxviii. 12 (VIII.)	*f.* 1 Chr. iii. 20 *g.* Neh. iii. 4	
	...	...		...	*1 Chr. iv. 18*
	a. 1, xxv. 3	*b.* Jer. xl. 15 (VII.) *c.* Zeph. i. 1 (VIII.-VII.) *d.* Jer. xxxviii. 1 (VII.) *a.* Jer. xxxvi. 10 (VII.) *b.* Jer. xxix. 3 (VII.)		*e.* Ezra x. 18	
	...	...	2, xx. 37 (IX.)		

					F	12 (VII.)		F d.[8] Neh. vi. 10, F (?) e. 1 Chr. iii. 24	
24. הודויה[9] . הודיה .		...				...	...	a. 1 Chr. iii. 24 b. Ezra ii. 40, F c. Neh. viii. 7 d. Neh. x. 11, F e. Neh. x. 14, F	f. 1 Chr. v. 24 g. 1 Chr. ix. 7
25. הושעיה .					...	a. Jer. xlii. 1 (VII.)	...	b. Neh. xii. 32	
26. זבדיה . .					a. 1, xii. 7 b. 1, xxvi. 2 c. 1, xxvii. 7	...	d. 2, xvii. 8 (IX.) e. 2, xix. 11 (IX.)	f. Ezra viii. 8 g. Ezra x. 20	h. 1 Chr. viii. 15 i. 1 Chr. viii. 17

[1] ἁπ. λεγ. fairly well supported.

[2] ἁπ. λεγ. well supported.

[3] ἁπ. λεγ.: VV. all support (Syr. Ar. omit vv. 17-24). Cf. No. 11 n.

[4] On the identity of the forms, *vide* Olsh. p. 621. The full form occurs only in Is. viii. 2, and even there the initial yod lacks the support of any of the VV. Cf. above, p. 216, n. 1.

[5] ἁπ. λεγ. Vg. LXX. A support *MT*; LXX. B Γελιά, Lucian Φαθθουιά. Syr. Ar. omit verses 16-18.

[6] Cf. also No. 46.

[7] Cf. p. 62, n. 1.

[8] Perhaps $d = c$ or a; cf. Ryle on Neh. vi. 10.

[9] It seems unlikely that these two forms were originally, as at present in *MT*, distinguished. Note K'ri and Kt in 1 Chr. iii. 24; further, VV. (1) *Vg. always agrees with MT*, indicating by one of the forms Odouia, Odoia, Oduia, that ו follows ד where *MT* reads הודויה, and by one of the forms Odia, Odaia, that י was read where *MT* reads הודיה; (2) *Syr. always indicates the form* הודיה; cf. also the Arabic; (3) LXX. (with the possible exceptions of 1 Chr. iv. 19 A Ἰουδαιάς, perhaps a Greek error for Ἰδουιάς, and 1 Chr. iii. 24 B Ὀδολια probably an error for Ὀδουία) *always reads* הודויה. Probably, therefore, a single original form gave rise to early variants; Syr. represents one type of early MSS., LXX. another, and *MT* is based on a comparison of both. If the name be early, הודיה is the more probably original; cf. אביהוד, אחיהוד, עמיהוד; if late, הודויה is at least as probably original; on the latter form, cf. Olsh. 277 *i.* and above, p. 221, also Kittel on 1 Chr. iii. 24, etc.

זכריה	...	...	...	...	a. 1, xxvi. 2[1] b. 1, xxiv. 25 c. 1, xv. 18 d. 1, xxvi. 11 e. 1, xxvii. 21	f. Is. viii. 2 (VIII.) g. 2 K. xiv. 29 (VIII.) h. 2 K. xviii. 2 (VIII.)	i. 2, xvii. 7 (IX.) k. 2, xx. 14 (IX.) [(ix.) l. 2. xxi. 2 m. 2 xxiv., 20 (IX.) n. 2, xxvi. 5 (VIII.) o. 2, xxix. 13 (VIII.) p. 2, xxxiv. 12 (VII.)	q. Zech. i. 1 r. Ezra viii. 3 s. Ezra viii. 11 t. Ezra viii. 16 u. Ezra x. 26 v. Neh. viii. 4 w. Neh. xii. 16 x. Neh. xii. 35 y. Neh. xii. 41	z. Neh. xi. 4 aa. Neh. xi. 5 bb. Neh. xi. 12 cc. 1 Chr. v. 7 dd. 1 Chr. ix. 37
חביה	...	...	...	...	...	...	...	Ezra ii. 61, F	
הֲבַצִּנְיָה [2]	...	...	...	...	...	Jer. xxxv. 3 (VII.)			
זרחיה	...	...	a. 1, v. 32	...		...	...	b. Ezra viii. 4	
חַגִּיָּה [3]	...	...	1, vi. 15	...					
חזיה [4]	...	...	...	...	...	...	...	Neh. xi. 5	
יחזקיה [5] חזקיה	...	...	...	...	...	a. 2 K. xvi. 20 (VIII) b.[6] Zeph. i. 1 (VIII.)	c. 2, xxviii. 12 (VIII.)	d. 1 Chr. iii. 23 e. Neh. vii. 21, F	
חכליה	...	...	...	...	...	...	...	Neh. i. 1	
חִלְקִיָּה	...	...	a. 1, vi. 30	...	b. 1, xxvi. 11	c. Is. xxii. 20 (VIII.) d. Jer. i. 1 (VII.) e. Jer. xxviii.	...	f. Neh. viii. 4 g. Neh. xii. 7, F	

						1 (VII.) c. Jer. xxxvi. 12 (VIII.) d. Jer. xxxvii. 13 (VII.)	(VII.) f. 2, xxvi. 11 (VIII.) ...	h. Ezra x. 28 i. Neh. iii. 30 k. Neh. vii. 2 l. Neh. x. 24 F m. Neh. xii. 12 n. Neh xii. 41 o. 1 Chr. iii. 19	24
37. חסדיה[7] .	..	..	...	...	...	...	...	1 Chr. iii. 20	
38. חשביה .	...	...	a. 1, vi. 30	...	b. 1, xxv. 19 c. 1, xxvi. 30 d. 1, xxvii. 17	...	e. 2, xxxv. 9 (VII.)	f. Neh. x. 12, F g. Neh. iii. 17 h. Neh. xii. 21	i. Neh. xi. 15 k. Neh. xi. 22
39. חשבניה ?[8]	...	...	..	...	...	...	...	a. Neh. iii. 10, F ? (b. Neh. ix. 5, F)	
40. טבליה[7] .	..		...	...	1, xxvi. 11				
41. טוב אדניה[7]	. .		...	...	...	...	2, xvii. 8 (IX.)		
42. טוביה .	..	...	...	...	...	...	a. 2, xvii. 8 (IX.)	b. Zech. vi. 10 c. Ezr. ii. 60, F d. *Neh. ii. 10*	

[1] Probably in the intention of the Chronicler identical with the Zechariah of ix. 21.

[2] ἅπ. λεγ. LXX. Χαβασ(ε)ιν: other VV. support termination יה.

[3] ἅπ. λεγ. supported by Vg. LXX. A: cf. Lucian Ἀναά.

[4] ἅπ. λεγ. All verses support a form in יה but Vg. alone agrees with *MT*; LXX. עדיה (=No. 91); Syr. נריה (=No. 87).

[5] For the longer and shorter forms, cf. No. 18.

[6] Probably *b*=*a*; cf. p. 262 n.

[7] ἅπ. λεγ. well supported.

[8] This form, which occurs only in two passages, may be merely a textual corruption of No. 38; in any case No. 39 *b* appears = No. 38 *f*; the Syr. in this case reads חשביה. In Neh. iii. 10, however, VV. support the נ.

a. Jer. xxxv. 3 (VII.)			
b. Ezek. xi. 1 (VII.)			
c.[2] Ezek. viii. 11 (VII.)			
d. 2. K. xxv. 23 (VII.)			
a. 2 K. xxi. 24 (VII.)		*b.* Zech. vi. 10	
...	...		*a.* 1 Chr. ix. 8 *b.* 1 Chr. ix. 8
Jer. xxxv. 4 (VII.)			
		a. Neh. iii. 10 *b.* Zech. vi. 10 *c.* Ezra ii. 36, F *d.* Neh. xii. 6, F	*b.* 1 Chr. iv. 37
		Ezr. viii. 10	
		...	1 Chr. iv. 35
...	...	Ezra x. 25	
...	...	*a.* Neh. xii. 42, F ?	*b.* 1 Chr. vii. 3

58. יכליה	...	...	...	...	...	2 K. xv. 2 (VII.)			
59. יכניהו [11]	...	...		...	...	Jer. xxiv. 1 (VII.)			
60. ? יסככיה [12]			...		...	...	2, xxxi. 13 (VIII.)		
61. ? יעזיהו [13]		...	...	...	1, xxiv. 26				
62. יערשיה [6]	...	...	...	...	...	...	...	...	1 Chr. viii. 27
63. יפדיה [14]	...	...	...	...	...	...	...	...	1 Chr. viii. 25
64. יקמיה			...	...	...	...	a. 1, iii. 18 (VII.)		b. 1 Chr. ii. 41
65. יראייה		...	...		...	Jer. xxxvii. 13 (VII.)			

[1] An abbreviated form יזניה (with which cf. Phoen. יזנאל, Levy. *Sieg.u. Gemmen*, p. 26) also occurs in Jer. xl. 8 = *d* above, and Jer. xlii. 1. In the latter case it is perhaps a textual error for עזריה (No. 94) which is read by LXX. in Jer. xlii. 1, and both *MT* and LXX. in xliii. 2. Syr. however in both cases reads ܝܘܙܢܝܐ. Cf. also No. 4, note.

[2] Possibly $c = b$; cf. Smith's *Dict. of Bible*, s.v. "Jaazaniah."

[3] Cf. No. 52.

[4] The reference of an otherwise unknown name in a single verse to two distinct persons is strange; LXX. B suggests בניה (No. 12)—a name of frequent occurrence; other VV. (with LXX. A) support initial י.

[5] ἅπ. λεγ. Initial yod (*MT*. Vg. Trg.) doubtful; perhaps with Syr. LXX. (Γοδολίου) we should read גדליה, No. 20.

[6] ἅπ. λεγ. well supported.

[7] ἅπ. λεγ. textually (and etymologically) very uncertain; VV. (*e.g.* LXX. Ἰωσεία, Vg. Josaia) suggest that the second vau is not original and that יושיה is a phonetic writing of יאשיה (No. 44); perhaps the manifestly corrupt Syr. form (ܐܘܣܐ) preserves a trace of the א. Some form ending in יה at least seems certain, and the first element was probably an impf.

[8] Uncertain ἅπ. λεγ. LXX. Αζία, etc.; Syr. ܥܘܙܝܐ (= No. 43). Vg. Luc. support Hebrew consonantal text.

[9] Initial yod rather doubtful, note preceding עד in Chr.; LXX. B in Chr., Syr. in Neh. suggest עדיה, No. 30.

[10] ἅπ. λεγ. fairly certain. LXX. Vg. support *MT*; Lucian (influenced by verse 20?) יחיאל and Syr. אחיה both give similar but commoner names.

[11] Abbreviated form כניהו also occurs: cf. Nos. 18, 33. Person so named = A 12.

[12] Uncertain ἅπ. λεγ.; Vg. alone supports *MT*; other VV. read סככיה, No. 89.

[13] ἅπ. λεγ.: VV. suggest עזיה, No. 93. So Kittel.

[14] ἅπ. λεγ.: Vg. LXX. support *MT*; Syr. פדיה, No. 101.

I.		II.		III.		IV.	Chronologically uncertain.
Early Writings.	Chronicles.	Early Writings.	Chronicles.	Early Writings.	Chronicles.		
		...	1, xxiii. 19				
		...	*a.* 1, xii. 4	*d.* 2 K. xxiii. 31 (VII).		*g.* Neh. x. 3, F	
			b. 1, xii. 10				
			c. 1, xii. 13	*e.* Jer. i. 1 (VII.)		*h.* Neh. xii. 34	
				f. Jer. xxxv. 3 (VII.)			
		...	...	...	...	...	1 Chr. iv. 36
		...	*a.* 1, xxiii. 20	...	...	*d.* Ezra. x. 31	*e.* 1 Chr. vii. 3
			b. 1, xxiv. 21				
			c. 1, xii. 6				
	...	...	*a.* 1, xii. 4				
			b. 1, xxvii. 19				
...			*a.* 1, xxv. 3	*c.* Is. i. 1 (VIII.)	...	*d.* Ezr. viii. 7	*g.* Neh. xi. 7
			b. 1, xxvi. 25		...	*e.* Ezra viii. 19	
						f. 1 Chr. iii. 21	
	...	...	*a.* 1, xv. 22	...	*b.* 2, xxxi. 12 (VIII.)		
					c. 2, xxxv. 9 (VII.)		
	...		...	Jer. xxxii. 12 (VII.)			
a. Judg. xvii. 1]			...	*b.* 1 K. xxii. (IX.)	*f.* 2, xvii. 7 (IX.)	*g.* Neh. xii. 41	*h.* Neh. xii. 35
				c. Jer. xxvi. 18, Kt. (VIII.)			

						d. 2 K. xxii. 12 (VII.) e. Jer. xxxvi. 11 (VII.)			
75. מְלַטְיָה[6] .	...	...	...	...	...	...	...	Neh. iii. 7	
76. מַעַדְיָה .	...	...	...	...	...	..	...	Neh. xii. 5, 17, F	
77. מַעַזְיָה			...	...	a. 1, xxiv. 18, F	...	...	b. Neh. x. 9, F	
78. מַעֲשֵׂיָה[7] .	...	..	a. 1, vi. 25		b. 1, xv. 20	c.[8] Jer. xxi. 1 (VII.) d. Jer. xxix. 21 (VII.)	e. 2, xxiii. 1 (IX.) f. 2, xxvi. 11 (VIII) g. 2, xxviii. 7 (VIII.) h. 2, xxxiv. 8 (VII.)	i. Ezra x. 18 k. Ezra x. 21 l. Ezra x. 22 m. Ezra x. 30 n. Neh. iii. 23 o. Neh. viii. 4 p. Neh. viii. 7 q. Neh. x. 26, F r. Neh. xii. 41	a. Neh. xi. 7

[1] In the three passages where this name occurs VV. differ much from *MT*, and from one another.

[2] ἅπ. λεγ. Vg. supports *MT*; LXX. Ἰασουά; Syr. Ar. omit verses 34-37. Etymologically quite obscure.

[3] Initial yod doubtful; all VV. at 1 Chr. xii. 4, LXX. also at xxvii. 19, read שמעיה, No. 122. In latter passage Vg. as *MT*; Syr. Ar. wanting.

[4] *MT* gives three forms—כונניהו in 2 Chr. xxxi. 12 f., xxxv. 9 Kt; כנניהו ib. K'ri; כנניה 1 Chr. xv. 22, 27; xxvi. 29. The first is unquestionably the only genuine form; Vg. always, LXX. except in 1 Chr. xv. 27, indicate long ō after the first consonant; the form כנניה is reflected in the VV. only in LXX. A of 1 Chr. xv. 27 and Syr. of 2 Chr. xxxv. 9 (cf. xxxi. 12 f.). LXX. B א in 1 Chr. xv. 27 and Luc. in 1 Chr. xv. 22 apparently read יכניה.

[5] See above, p. 156.

[6] Well supported ἅπ. λεγ.

[7] By confusion of מ and ב, written בעשיה in 1 Chr. vi. 25; cf. Kittel, *ad loc.*

[8] For the identification of this person with others of the same name, *vide* Graf on Jer. xxi. 1.

. 1, xxiv. 9, F	*c.* Jer. xxi. 1 (VII.) *d.* Jer. xxxviii. 6 (VII.)		*e.* Ezra x. 25 *f.* Ezra x. 31 *g.* Neh. iii. 14 *h.* Neh. iii. 31 *i.* Neh. viii. 4 *k.* Neh. x. 4, F	*l.* Neh. xi. 12
...	...	...	Neh. xii. 12	
. 1, xv. 18	...	...	*b.* Ezra x. 43 *c.* Neh. viii. 4	
. 1, xxv. 4	*b.* 2 K. xxiv. 17 (VII.)	*c.* 2, xxix. 13 (VIII.)	*d.* Ezra x. 26 *e.* Ezra x. 27 *f.* Ezra x. 30 *g.* Ezra x. 37 *h.* Neh. xi. 17, F ?	*i.* Neh. xi. 22
...	...	1, iii. 18 (VI.)		
...	...	...	*a.* Ezr. viii. 33 *b.* Neh. vi. 14	
			a. Ezra ii. 2 *b.* Neh. i. 1 *c.* Neh. iii. 16	
...	...	...	*a.* 1 Chr. iii. 22	*b.* 1 Chr. iv. 42
...	*a.* Jer. xxxii. 12 (VII.) *b.* Jer. li. 59 (VII.) [(VII.)			
. 1, xxv. 2	*b.* Jer. xli. 1 *c.* Jer. xxxvi. 14 (VII.)	*d.* 2, xvii. 8 (IX.)		

90. עֹבַדְיָה .	...	...	...	...	a. 1, xii. 9 b. 1, xxvii. 19	c. 1 K. xviii. 3 (IX.) d. Ob. i. 1 (? VI.)	e. 2, xvii. 7 (IX.) f. 2, xxxiv. 12 (VII.)	g. Ezra viii. 9 h. Neh. x. 6, F i. Neh. xii. 25 k. 1 Chr. iii. 21	l. 1 Chr. vii. 3 m. 1 Chr. viii. 38 n. 1 Chr. ix. 16
91. עֲדָיָה . .	...	..	a. 1, vi. 26	...	...	b. 2 K. xxii. 1 (VII.)	c. 2, xxiii. 1 (IX.)	d. Ezra x. 29 e. Ezra x. 39	f. Neh. xi. 5 g. Neh. xi. 12 h. 1 Chr. viii. 21
92. ? עֲזַזְיָהוּ[7] .		...	...	..	a. 1, xxvii. 20 b. 1, xv. 21	...	c. 2, xxxi. 13 (VIII.)		
93. עֻזִּיָּה[8] .	...	...	a. 1, vi. 9	...	b. 1, xxvii. 25 c. 1, xi. 44	[? d. 2 K. xv. 13 (VIII.)]	...	e. Ezra x. 21	f. Neh. xi. 4
94. עֲזַרְיָה .	...	...	a. 1, vi. 21	...	...	b. 1 K. iv. 2 (X.) c. 1 K. iv. 5 (X.) d. 2 K. xiv. 21 (VIII.) e. Jer. xliii. 2 (VII.)	f. 1, v. 37 g. 1, v. 39 h. 2, xv. 1 (X.) i. 2, xxi. 2 (IX.) k. 2, xxiii. 1 (IX.) l. 2 xxiii. 1 (IX.) m. 2, xxvi. 17 (VIII.) [(VIII.)] n. 2, xxviii. 12 o. 2, xxix. 12 (VIII.) [(VIII.)] p. 2, xxxi. 10 q. Dan. i. 6 (VII.)	r. Neh. iii. 23 s.[9] Neh. vii. 7 t. Neh. x. 3, F	u. Ezra vii. 1 v. Ezra vii. 3 w. 1 Chr. ii. 8 x. 1 Ch. ii. 38

[1] Very uncertain ἅπ. λεγ. *MT* מְרָיָה suggests connection with מרה, but that yields no probable sense. Were the name ancient we might point מְרִיָּה, cf. מְרִיב־בַּעַל. But probably the form is an error (or abbreviation) for אמריה, No. 9; cf. Syr. and Luc. (Ἀμαριά): but א AB = *MT*.

[2] ἅπ. λεγ. well supported. [3] Cf. No. 86.

[4] Uncertain; LXX. (except Luc. which = *MT*.) Νωαδειά = No. 84.

[5] Cf. No. 32. [6] ἅπ. λεγ. (well supported); cf. No. 60.

[7] This name occurs only in three passages, and is always identified by LXX. (except perhaps by A in 2 Chr. xxxi. 13), and in 2 Chr. xxxi. 13 by Syr. also, with No. 93. Kittel reads עזיהו in 1 Chr. xxvii. 20, rejects the name in 1 Chr. xv. 21, and reads עזיה as doubtful in 2 Chr. xxxi. 13; see his note on 1 Chr. xxvii. 20.

[8] Cf. Nos. 32, 61, 92. *c* appears in *MT* as עזיא. For *d* (= No. 94 *d*) the form עזיה is an error; cf. Stade, *Geschichte*, i. 569 n.

[9] Text doubtful. In Ezra ii. 2, שריה; 1 Esdr. v. 8, *Ζαραίου*.

xvii. 16 (IX.)		
...	*a.* Neh. viii. 4	
	b. Neh. x. 23, F	
...	*a.* Neh. iii. 23, ? F	*b.* Neh. xi. 32, *place*
...	...	*c.* 1 Chr. iv. 36
		d. 1 Chr. ix. 5
...	...	Neh. xi. 5
...	*b.* Ezr. viii. 7	*c.* 1 Chr. viii. 26
1, iii. 18 (VI.)	*d.* Neh. iii. 25	*f.* Neh. xi. 7
	e.[4] Neh. viii. 4	
...	Neh. x. 11, F	
	b. Neh. x. 23, F	*d.* 1 Chr. iv. 42
	c. 1 Chr. iii. 21	
	1 Chr. iii. 24	
	...	Neh. xi. 12

107. פתחיה .	...	...	..	...	a. 1, xxiv. 16[4]	...	...	b. Ezra x. 23 c. Neh. ix. 5 d. Neh. xi. 24 e. Neh. x. 2	
108. צדקיה .			...		...	a. 1 K. xxii. 11 (IX.) b. Jer. xxvii. 3 (VII.) c. Jer. xxxvi. 12 (VII.) d. Jer. xxix. 21 (VII.)	...		
109. צפניה .			a. 1, vi. 21	...	...	b. Zeph. i. 1 (VII.) c. Jer. xxi. 1 (VII.) d. 2 K. xxv. 18 (VII.) e. Zech. vi. 10 (VI.)			
110. קליה[7] .			...	...	...	a. Jer. xxix. 21 (VII.)	...	b. Ezr. x. 23	c. Neh. xi. 7
111. ק(ו)שיה?[8]	...	...	...	...	1, xv. 17				
112. ראיה .	...	...	...	...	..	...	...	a. Ezr. ii. 47, F	b. 1 Chr. iv. 2 c. 1 Chr. v. 5

[1] ἅπ. λεγ. fairly supported. For עבד in proper names, cf. Phoen. עבדאשמן, בעליעבד, CIS, 564, 719.

[2] LXX. in Neh. viii. 4, Syr. and variants of LXX. in Neh. x. 23, identify עניה with No. 97.

[3] A very uncertain ἅπ. λεγ. The parallel, 1 Chr. ix. 4, reads עמיהוד.

[4] Possibly Neh. xiii. 13 should be added as a distinct instance.

[5] ἅπ. λεγ. well supported. Probably it is a mere phonetic variant from 102; cf. also next note.

[6] ἅπ. λεγ.; VV. support *MT* except Syr. ܦܠܛܐ = 104.

[7] Vocalised in *MT* of Ezra x. 23 קְלִיָה; but LXX. Κωλειά; cf. Ar

[8] Very uncertain; = קִישִׁי (1 Chr. vi. 29) which is perhaps philologically preferable. Kittel reads קִישָׁיָהוּ.

	I.			II.		III.		IV.	Chronologically uncertain.
	P.	Early Writings.	Chronicles.	Early Writings.	Chronicles.	Early Writings.	Chronicles.		
113. רחביה .	...	...	...	...	1, xxiii. 17				
114. רמיה[1] .	...	...	...	...	...	...		Ezra x. 25	
115. רמליה .	...	...	...	...	...	Is.vii.1 (VIII.)			
116. רעליה[2]	...	...	...	...	...	...	...	Ezra ii. 2	
117. רפיה .	...	...	...	...	...	...	...	*a.* Neh. iii. 9 *b.* 1 Chr. iii. 21	*c.* 1 Chr. iv. 42 *d.* 1 Chr. vii. 2
	...	...							*e.* 1 Chr. ix. 34
118. שבניה ?[3]	...	...	...	...	*a.* 1, xv. 24			*b.* Neh. ix. 4, F *c.* Neh. x. 5, F	
119. שחריה[1].	...		...	...	...		...	...	1 Chr. viii. 26
120. שכניה[4].			...		*a.* 1, xxiv. 11, F	...	*b.* 2, xxxi. 15 (VIII.)	*c.* Ezr. viii. 3 *d.* Ezr. viii. 5 *e.* Ezr. x. 2 *f.* Neh. iii. 29, F ? *g.* Neh. vi. 18 *h.* Neh. xii. 3, F	
121. שלמיה[5]. משלמיה	...	...	...	...	*a.* 1, xxvi. 14	*b.* Jer. xxxvi. 14 (VII.) *c.* Jer. xxxvi. 26 (VII.) *d.* Jer. xxxvii. 3 (VII.) *e.* Jer. xxxvii. 13 (VII.)		*f.* Ezr. x. 39 *g.* Ezr. x. 41 *h.* Neh. iii. 30, F ? *i.* Neh. xiii. 13	

122. שמעיה .	...	...	...	..	a. 1, xv. 8 b. 1, xxiv. 6 c. 1, xxvi. 4	d. 1 K. xii. 22 (x.) e. Jer. xxvi. 20 (vii.) f. Jer. xxix. 24 (vii.) g. Jer. xxxvi. 12 (vii.)	h. 2, xvii. 8 (ix.) i. 2, xxix. 14 (viii.) k. 2, xxxv. 9 (vii.) ...	l. Ezr. viii. 13, F? m. Ezr. viii. 16 n. Ezr. x. 21 o. Ezr. x. 31 p. Neh. iii. 29 q. Neh. vi. 10 r. Neh. x. 8, F s. Neh. xi. 15, F? t. Neh. xii. 36, F u. Neh. xii. 42, F?	v. 1 Chr. iv. 37 w. 1 Chr. v. 4 x. 1 Chr. ix. 16
123. שמריה .	...	...	...	...	a. 1, xii. 5	...	b. 2, xi. 19 (x.)	c. Ezr. x. 32 d. Ezr. x. 41	
124. שעריה[6].	...	...	...	...	...	...	...	...	1 Chr. viii. 38
125. שפטיה .	...	...	...	a. 2 S. iii. 4	b. 1, xii. 5 c. 1, xxvii. 16	d. Jr. xxxviii. 1 (vii.)	e. 2, xxi. 2 (ix.)	f. Ezr. ii. 57, F g. Ezr. ii. 4, F	h. Neh. xi. 4 i. 1 Chr. ix. 8
126. שרביה .	...	...	...	...	...	...	...	a. Ezr. viii. 18 b. Neh. x. 13, F	

[1] ἅπ. λεγ. well supported. [2] = רעמיה, Neh. vii. 7. VV. slightly favour רעליה; cf. 1 Esd. v. 8 (A).

[3] Somewhat uncertain: שבניה Neh. xii. 14 (=c) = שכניה verse 3; the LXX. also reads ב for כ in some cases. Possibly, therefore, שבניה is a corrupt form of No. 120. Yet cf. Levy, *Sieg. u. Gemmen*, p. 40.

[4] Cf. No. 118. On *c*, *d*, see Ryle's notes on Ezra viii. 2, viii. 5. Possibly $h=f$; but Neh. xii. 3 mentions *priestly* houses, and Ryle (note on Neh. iii. 29) considers that iii. 29 refers to a levite. Further, is the Shemaiah son of Shechaniah mentioned in the latter passage identical with the person in 1 Chr. iii. 22? If not, add another in column IV. both for this name and שכניה.

[5] Possibly $h=i$: see Ryle on Neh. xiii. 13.

[6] ἅπ. λεγ. fairly well supported.

	I.			II.		III.		IV.	Chronologically uncertain.
	P.	Early Writings.	Chronicles.	Early Writings.	Chronicles.	Early Writings.	Chronicles.		
127. שריה[1]		...	...	...	...	*a.* 2 K. xxv. 18 (VII) *b.* 2 K. xxv. 23 (VII) *c.* Jer. xxxvi. 26 (VII.) *d.* Jer. li. 59 (VII.)	...	[*e.* Ezr. ii. 2] *f.* Neh. x. 3, F	*g.* 1 Chr. iv. 13 *h.* 1 Chr. iv. 35

(*C*) Name with יה forming the second of three Elements.

אליהועיני אליועיני	...		...	...	*a.* 1, xxvi. 3	...		*b.* Ezr. viii. 4 *c.* Ezr. x. 22 *d.* Ezr. x. 27 *e.* 1 Chr. iii. 23	*f.* 1 Chr. iv. 36 *g.* 1 Chr. vii. 8 *h.*[2] 1 Chr. viii. 20

4. Names compounded with אל.

(*A*) With אל Prefixed.

	...	...		...					
4. אלדד[6] . אלידד	a. Num. xxxiv. 21	b. Num. xi. 26							
5. אלידע .	...	...	...	[a. 2S. v. 16][7]	...	b. 1 K. xi. 23 (x.)	c. 2, xvii. 17 (ix.)		
6. אליהו .	...	...	...		...	a. 1 K. xvii. 1 (ix.)	...	b. Ezra x. 21 c. Ezra x 26	d. 1 Chr. viii. 27
7. אליהוא .	...	a. 1 S. i. 1[8]	...	...	b. 1, xii. 20 c. 1, xxvi. 7 d. 1, xxvii. 18	...	...	...	e. Job. xxxii. 2
8. אליחבא[9] .	...	...	...	2 S. xxiii. 32					
9. אליחרף .	...	...	...	...	...	1 K. iv. 3 (x.)			
10. אלימלך .	...	Ruth i. 2							
11. אליסף .	a. Num. i. 14 b. Num. iii. 24								
12. אליעזר .	...	a. Gen. xv. 2 (For. ?) b. Ex. xviii. 4	...	...	c. 1, xv. 24 d. 1, xxvii. 16		e. 2, xx. 37 (ix.)	f. Ezra viii. 16 g. Ezra x. 18 h. Ezra x. 23 i. Ezra x. 31	k. 1 Chr. vii. 8

[1] שריה is also read by *MT* in 2 S. viii. 17 (=1 Chr. xviii. 16), but this is an error for שישא 1 K. iv. 3, cf. 1 Chr. xviii. 16 and 2 S. xx. 25. See the notes of Wellhausen, Driver, and Budde on 2 S. viii. 17; 127 *c* = 94 *s* (which see, with note).

[2] Kittel no doubt rightly restores this name here.

[3] On 1 Chr. vi. 12, see below, n. 8. Another Eliab is mentioned among the remote ancestors of Judith, Judith viii. 1.

[4] On 1 Chr. vi. 19, see below, n. 8.

[5] In 1 Chr. xxv. 27 spelt אֱלִיָּתָה.

[6] Both forms are transliterated by LXX. Ἐλδαδ. Perhaps *a* = *b*.

[7] Probably a scribal correction for בעלידע, 1 Chr. xiv. 7; in 1 Chr. iii. 8, however, אלידע appears as above.

[8] The precise form of the name of Samuel's great-grandfather is uncertain; in 1 Chr. vi. 12 it is אליאב, probably enough the correct form. The form אליאל in 1 Chr. vi. 19—a name peculiar to the Chronicler—is improbable, and may be a mere textual error for אליאב; cf. *MT* and LXX. B in 1 Chr. xii. 11.

[9] This name is read only in 2 S. xxiii. 32, and the parallel, 1 Chr. xi. 33; Vg. in both passages, LXX. A in Chr., support *MT*. Otherwise the forms individually differ from, yet perhaps collectively support, *MT*. LXX. A in Sam. Ἐλιάβ is manifestly an incorrect easier reading. On the punctuation, see p. 217, n. 3.

2 S. xi. 3 (For. ?) 2S. xxiii. 34					
...	...		...		*b. Job ii. 11*
...	1, xv. 18				
2 S. v. 16[2] 2 S. xxiii. 34[3]	...		...	*c.* Ezra viii. 13, (F ?) *d.* Ezra x. 33	*e.* 1 Chr. viii. 39
S. xxiii. 25					
...		*a.* Is. xxii. 20 (VIII) *b.*[6] 2 K. xxiii. 34 (VII.)	...	*c.* Neh. xii. 41	
S. v. 15					
...	*a.* 1, xxiv. 12			*b.* Ezra x. 6[7] *c.* Ezra x. 24 *d.* Ezra x. 27 *e.* Ezra x. 36 *f.* Neh. iii. 1 *g.* 1 Chr. iii. 24	
2 S. v. 16[8]	...	*h.* Jer. xxxvi. 12 (VII.)	*c.* 2, xvii. 8 (IX.)		

25. [illegible] .	–	..	...	...	...	1 K. xix. 16 (ix.)			
26. אלישפט[9] .	...	...	...	...	...	...	2, xxiii. 1 (ix.)		
27. אלנעם[10] .	...	...	...	...	1, xi. 46				
28. אלנתן .	...	...	...	...	...	a. 2 K. xxiv. 8 (vii.) b. Jer. xxvi. 22 (vii.)	...	c. Ezra viii. 16 d. Ezra viii. 16 e. Ezra viii. 16[11]	
29. אלדעה[12] .	...	*Gen. xxv. 4*							
30. אלזבד[13] .	...	...	...	...	a. 1, xii. 12 b. 1, xxvi. 7				
31. אלחנן .	...	...	...	a. 2 S. xxi. 19 b. 2 S. xxiii. 24					

[1] On the genuineness of this rare name, see p. 44, n. 3.

[2] At 1 Chr. xiv. 5 אֱלִיפָֽלֶט (pausal), but LXX. B Ἐλειφάλεθ; ℵ and A very similar.

[3] In 1 Chr. xi. 35, the word has lost its final letter אֱלִיפָל; LXX. B Ἐλφάτ, A Ἐλιφάλ.

[4] At Ex. vi. 22, Lev. x. 4, אלצפן, but LXX. Ἐλισαφάν. 1 Chr. xv. 8, 2 Chr. xxix. 13, presumably refer to a family derived from the person (?) named in Ex. vi. 22: cf. *Oxford Lex.* s.v. See also n. 9.

[5] A strange form read only in 2 S. xxiii. 25, and even there textually doubtful; LXX. (B. Luc.) and Syr. (?) omit; so also *MT* in the parallel 1 Chr. xi. 27 (cf. 1 Chr. xxvii. 8 ff.).

[6] Also called יהויקים, 2 K. xxiii. 34. See App. II. 3 A, No. 13.

[7] For the relation of this Eliashib to others of the same name, see Ryle on Ezra x. 6.

[8] 1 Chr. iii. 6 cites as bearing this same name another son of David, but this is certainly a mere textual corruption for אליפלט, which is read both in 2 S. v. 15 and 1 Chr. xiv. 5.

[9] Read only in 2 Chr. xxiii. 1, where VV. support *MT* except LXX. B which reads Ἐλεισαφάν = אליצפן = No. 18.

[10] Read only in 1 Chr. xi. 46 (in a section of the list peculiar to the Chronicler); Syr. (cf. Ar.) reads ܐܠܝܥܕܐܝܠ; but LXX. and Vg. virtually support *MT*. In spite of differing punctuation, cf. אחינעם, אבינעם. In Phoen. somewhat analogous names occur, *e.g.* גרנעם, *CIS*, i. 383, נעמלכת, *CIS*, 41.

[11] The occurrence of three Elnathans in a single verse is strange, since no other post-Exilic Elnathan is mentioned. LXX. and Syr. possibly indicate a variant in the case of the first.

[12] In spite of the curious variant (Θεργαμά = תרגמה) in LXX. A, this name, which occurs only in Gen. xxv. 4, 1 Chr. i. 33, must be considered well supported; with the exception just mentioned, *MT* in both passages has the entire or substantial support of all VV. Cf. further 1 Chr. vii. 20, Syr. See also p. 222 above.

[13] Read only in the two passages above, but the form is fairly certain. VV. on the whole support *MT*. In 1 Chr. xii. 12 LXX. B Ἐλιαζέρ, perhaps represents a further stage of a familiar corruption (ר for ד) in Syr. ܐܠܙܒܪ. In 1 Chr. xxvi. 7 the Syr. itself has perhaps reached its present form through the same initial corruption combined with a faulty division of words.

	I.			II.		III.		IV.	Chronologically uncertain.
	P.	Early Writings.	Chronicles.	Early Writings.	Chronicles.	Early Writings.	Chronicles.		
32. אלעד[1] .		...	...		...	...	...	...	1 Chr. vii. 21
33. אלעדה[1] .	...	...	...	...	...				1 Chr. vii. 20
34. אלעוזי[1] .	...	...	...	...	1, xii. 5				
35. אלעזר .	...	*a*. Judg. xx. 28	...	*b*. 1 S. vii. 1 *c*. 2 S. xxiii. 9	? *d*. 1, xxiii. 21	...		*e*. Ezra x. 25 *f*. Neh. xii. 42, F *g*.[2] Ezra viii. 33	
36. אלעלה . אלעלא .		...	...	...			..	...	Is. xv. 4, *place*
37. אלעשה .	...	...		...	...	*a*. Jer. xxix. 3 (VII.)		*b*. Ezra 10, 22	*c*. 1 Chr. ii. 39 *d*. 1 Chr. ix. 43
38. אלפעל .	...	...	...	...	...	...	...	...	1 Chr. viii. 11
39. אלקנה .	*a*. Ex. vi. 24	*b*. 1 S. i. 1	*c*. 1, vi. 20[3] *d*. 1, vi. 21	...	*e*. 1, xii. 6 *f*. 1, xv. 23	...	*g*. 2, xxviii. 7 (VIII.)	...	*h*. 1 Chr. ix. 16

(*B*) NAMES WITH אל POST-FIXED.

						bolic name (VIII.)			
6. אשראל .						...		...	1 Chr. iv. 16
7. אשריאל .	Num. xxvi. 31								
8. בצלאל .	*a*. Ex. xxxi. 2							*b*. Ezra x. 30	
9. גאואל .	Num. xiii. 15								
10. גבריאל .	...	...						Dan. ix. 21	
11. גדיאל .	Num. xiii. 10								
12. גמליאל .	Num. i. 10								
13. דניאל[6] .				...	*a*. 1, iii. 1[7]	*b*. Ezek. xiv. 14[8]		*c*. Ezra viii. 2 *d*. Neh. x. 7, F	
14. דעואל[9] .	Num. i. 14								
15. זבדיאל .	...			...	*a*. 1. xxvii. 2			*b*. Neh. xi. 14	
16. חזיאל[10] .	. .			...	1, xxiii. 9				
17. חיאל[11] .	...			...	...	1 K. xvi. 34 (IX.)			

[1] Nos. 32-34 are all ἅπαξ λεγ. Etymologically they are intelligible and not without tolerably close analogies. Textually they are a little uncertain; Vg. and LXX. A in each case closely resemble *MT*; LXX. B and Syr. diverge. The most noticeable variant is the Syr. [illegible] (=No. 29) for No. 33. אלעד is probably enough dittographic from אלעדה; cf. the repetition of תחת and תחת in the same passage, 1 Chr. vii. 20 f.

[2] Ryle on Ezra viii. 33 appears to identify *g* with *f*. The name Eleazar was also popular in the Maccabaean period (1 Mac. ii. 5; viii. 17; 2 Mac. vi. 18), and later. In Pirke Abhoth are mentioned seven different persons of this name, ii. 9, iii. 7 *a*, iii. 11, iii. 17, iii. 18, iv. 12, iv. 32 (Strack's ed.). For other later names see דור ודורשיו, ii. p. 53.

[3] Several Elkanahs are mentioned in the confused passage, 1 Chr. vi. 7-13, but apparently they are identical with one or other of those distinguished above; thus Elkanah in verse 8 = *b*; in verse 11 = *c*; in verse 10 = *d*. See further Bertheau's *Chronicles*, pp. 60 f.

[4] Chr. here preserves the original of the corrupt reading of 2 S. xxiii. 31; Driver, *Samuel*, p. 283.

[5] Cf. further the late angelic name Uriel, Enoch xix. 1.

[6] Spelt also דנאל; *e.g.* Ezek. xiv. 14.

[7] Text probably not original; cf. Bertheau on the passage.

[8] Certainly before sixth century; how much earlier is uncertain. Cf. A. B. Davidson, *Ezekiel*, p. 96, note on xiv. 14.

[9] The first letter is read ר always in LXX. and Syr. and in the Hebr. of Num. ii. 14 (yet with variants דעואל). If LXX. and Syr. are correct the name is identical with No. 70.

[10] A doubtful ἅπ. λεγ. Vg. LXX. A (and Lucian) support *MT*; LXX. B Ἐιειήλ; Syr. (and Ar.) [illegible] = יחיאל, No. 94.

[11] A well supported ἅπ. λεγ. in spite of Syr. [illegible].

	I			II.		III.		IV.	Chronologically uncertain.
	P.	Early Writings.	Chronicles.	Early Writings.	Chronicles.	Early Writings.	Chronicles.		
18. חמואל[1] .	...	...	...		...	...	...	...	1 Chr. iv. 26
19. חניאל .	*a.* Num. xxxiv. 23	...	...		...	...	...	...	*b.* 1 Chr. vii. 39
20. חנמאל[2] .	...		...	...	...	Jer. xxxii. 7 (VII.)			
21. ידיעאל .	...	...			*a.* 1, xi. 45[3] *b.* 1, xxvi. 2	...	...		*c.* 1 Chr. vii. 6
22. יהללאל .			...	...	...	...	*a.* 2, xxix. 12 (?F) (VIII.)		*b.* 1 Chr. iv. 16
23. יואל . .	*vide* יה, *A*, No. 4								
24. יזיאל[4] .	...			...	1, xii. 3, K'ri				
25. יחדיאל[5] .	...			...	...	...	...		1 Chr. v. 24
26. יחזקאל .	...			...	*a.* 1, xxiv. 16	*b.* Ezek. i. 3 (VII.)			
27. יחזיאל .					*a.* 1, xii. 4 *b.* 1, xvi. 6 *c.* 1, xxiii. 19	...	*d.* 2, xx. 14 (IX.)	*e.* Ezra viii. 5	
28. יחיאל .				...	*a.* 1, xv. 18 *b.* 1, xxiii. 8 *c.* 1, xxvii. 32		*d.* 2, xxi. 2 (IX.) *e.* 2, xxxi. 13	*h.* Ezra viii. 9 *i.* Ezra x. 2 *k.* Ezra x. 21	

	b. Num. xxvi. 9								
32. יעיאל . יעואל .					*a.* 1, xi. 44 *b.* 1, xv. 18		*c.* 2, xx. 14 *d.* 2, xxvi. 11 (VIII.) *e.* 2, xxix. 13 (VIII.) *f.* 2, xxxv. 9 (VII.)	*g.* Ezra viii. 13 *h.* Ezra x. 43	*i.* 1 Chr. ix. 6 *k.* 1 Chr. v. 7 *l.* 1 Chr. ix. 35
33. יעזיאל[7] .	...			...	1, xv. 18				
34. יעשיאל .	...			...	*a.* 1, xi. 47 *b.* 1, xxvii. 21				
35. יקותיאל[8].	...		...		...	...		...	1 Chr. iv. 18
36. ירואל . יריאל	...		...		...	...		...	*a.* 1 Chr. vii. 2 *b.* 2 Chr. xx. 16, place
37. ירחמאל .		*a.* 1 S. xxvii. 10[9] (Clan)	...	...	*b.* 1, xxiv. 29	*c.* Jer. xxxvi. 26 (VII.)			

[1] A well supported ἅπ. λεγ.; cf. p. 64. Syr. (Ar.) [illegible] is no true variant but a corruption.

[2] Owing to the etymological obscurity of this name it has been suggested that it = ימואל. Textually this is uncalled for. The name occurs four times, and always with the support of VV.

[3] The person here mentioned is usually identified with 1 Chr. xii. 20; so Ges.-Buhl, Siegf.-Stade, *New Oxf. Lex.*

[4] A very doubtful ἅπ. λεγ. K'tib יעואל; LXX. *B*, Syr. Ar. suggest יעיאל; LXX. *A* יעזיאל, No. 16. But some form ending in אל was certainly read.

[5] ἅπ. λεγ. fairly well supported.

[6] The orthography, נמואל, of Eliab's son, mentioned only in Num. xxvi. 9, is supported, so far at least as the initial letter is concerned, by all VV. The name of the Simeonite family is spelt in *MT* ימואל in Gen. xlvi. 10, Ex. vi. 15, נמואל in Num. xxvi. 12 (*bis*), 1 Chr. iv. 24. The Syriac in all five cases has initial י; otherwise the VV. support *MT* in the several passages. Epigraphically the form with י appears to me more probably a corruption in Gen. xlvi. 10 than the form with נ in Num. xxvi. 12. Either form is etymologically obscure.

[7] In 1 Chr. xv. 20, עֲזִיאֵל. Each form occurs but once; VV. differ. Both forms are probably errors for עֻזִּיאֵל, No. 56. Cf. LXX.

[8] ἅπ. λεγ.; but the name is probably identical with יקתיאל (No. 85), which form is on the whole best attested by the various transliterations of the LXX.

[9] According to the LXX. in 1 S. i. 1 an early individual bore this name.

...	...	Prov. xxxi. 1, 4, ? For.
...	*b*. Neh. vi. 10	
...	...	*b*. Neh. xi. 4
2, xxi. 2 (IX.)	*f*. Ezra viii. 8, ? F *g*. Dan. x. 13	*h*. 1 Chr. v. 13 *i*. 1 Chr. v. 14 *k*. 1 Chr. viii. 16

עבדיאל					...	26 (VII.)	...	...	15
54. עדיאל .	...			...	a. 1, xxvii. 25		...	...	b. 1 Chr. iv. 36 c. 1 Chr. ix. 12
55. עדריאל[8] .	...		...	1 S. xviii. 19					
56. עזיאל[9] .	a. Ex. vi. 18		...	...	b. 1, xxv. 4[10]		c. 2, xxix. 14 (VIII.)	d. Neh. iii. 8	e. 1 Chr. iv. 42 f. 1 Chr. vii. 7
57. עזראל .					a. 1, xii. 6 [b. 1, xxv. 18][10] c. 1, xxvii. 22		...	d. Ezr. x. 41 e. Neh. xii. 36. F	f. Neh. xi. 13[11]
58. עזריאל .				...	a. 1, xxvii. 19	b. Jer. xxxvi. 26 (VII.)		...	c. 1 Chr. v. 24
59. עמיאל .	a. Num. xiii. 12			b. 2 S. ix. 4	[c. 1, iii. 5][12] d. 1, xxvi. 5				
60. עמנואל .	...			...	...	Is. vii. 14 (VIII.)			
61. עשהאל .	...			a. 2 S. ii. 18		...	b. 2, xvii. 8 (x.) c. 2, xxxi. 13 (VIII.)	d. Ezr. x. 15	
62. עשיאל[13] .	...	...	...	...	...	...	...	...	1 Chr. iv. 35
63. עתניאל .	...	Jos. xv. 17							

[1] ἅπ. λεγ.; Vg. Iamiel; LXX. A Ἰσμαήλ. Syr. and Ar. omit verses 34-37.

[2] An uncertain ἅπ. λεγ. Vg. *Iathanael;* LXX. B Ἰερουήλ. Possibly the correct reading was נתנאל—so Lucian, Syr. Ar.—a name common in Chronicles.

[3] Doubtful ἅπ. λεγ.; see Dillmann, *ad loc.*

[4] Probably a foreigner; cf. De Wette-Schrader, *Einleitung* (1869), p. 536.

[5] Etymology uncertain. If אל be here a divine name (cf. Ges.-Buhl, *s.v.*) the name should be excluded from the present list.

[6] ἅπ. λεγ.; LXX. (and Ar.) read Μαθουσάλα = מתושלח; otherwise VV. support *MT;* etymology also ambiguous. See Dillmann, *ad loc.*

[7] Cf. No. 41 with footnote.

[8] In the only two places where this name occurs Syr. identifies it with No. 58.

[9] Cf. also No. 33.

[10] 56 *b* = 57 *b*; in one case the text must be corrupt.

[11] Ges.-Buhl, Siegf.-Stade identify *e* and *f*.

[12] = A, No. 13.

[13] ἅπ. λεγ.

	I.			II.		III.		IV.	Chronologically uncertain.
	P.	Early Writings.	Chronicles.	Early Writings.	Chronicles.	Early Writings.	Chronicles.		
64. פגעיאל .	Num. i. 13								
65. פדהאל[1] .	Num. xxxiv. 28								
66. פוטיאל[1] .	Ex. vi. 25								
67. פלטיאל[2]	*a.* Nu. xxxiv. 26	...	...	*b.* 2 S. iii. 15					
68. פנואל .	...	*a.* Gen. xxxii. 31 (place)		...		...		...	*b.* 1 Chr. iv. 4 *c.* 1 Chr. viii. 25
69. פתואל[3] .	...	...		...	...		...	Joel i. 1	
70. צוריאל[4] .	Num. iii. 35								
71. קדמיאל .	...	...			...		...	Ezr. ii. 40, F	
72. קמואל .	*a.* Nu. xxxiv. 24	*b. Gen. xxii. 21*			*c.* 1, xxvii. 17				
73. רעואל[5] .	*a. Gen. xxxvi. 4*	*b. Ex. ii. 18*			...			...	*c.* 1 Chr. ix. 8
74. רפאל[6] .	...	...	...	...	1, xxvi. 7				
75. שאלתיאל	...	...	...	...	...	Hag. i. 1 (VI.)			
76. שבואל[7] שובאל	...	...	...	...	*a.* 1, xxiii. 16 *b.* 1, xxv. 4 *c.* 1, xxiv. 20				
77. שלומיאל .	Num. i. 6								
78. שמואל .	*a.* Nu. xxxiv. 20[8]	*b.* 1 S. i. 20	...	...	...	...	...	...	*c.* 1 Chr. vii. 2

[For Nos. 79-97 see the following pages.]

In addition to the preceding, the following names occur only as those of towns or foreigners.

Eight occur as names of towns in pre-Exilic writings, viz. :—

79. בית אל, Gen. xii. 8 (JE).

80. בית אל ברית, Judg. ix. 46.

81. בית ארבאל, Hos. x. 14.

82. יזרעאל,[1] *a.* 1 K. xviii. 45, Jos. xix. 18.
b. 1 S. xxv. 43, Jos. xv. 56.
c. 1 Chr. iv. 3.
d. Hos. i. 4 (Hosea's son).

83. יקתאל,[2] *a.* 2 K. xiv. 7.
b. Jos. xv. 38 (P).

84. נחליאל,[3] Num. xxi. 19 (JE).

85. קבצאל, *a.* Jos. xv. 21 (JE).
יקבצאל, *b.*[4] Neh. xi. 25.

86. חננאל, Jer. xxxi. 38.

The following five are names of towns mentioned only in P :—

87. יבנאל, *a.*[5] Jos. xv. 11.
b. Jos. xix. 33.

88. גיא יפתחאל, Jos. xix. 14.

89. ירפאל,[6] Jos. xviii. 27.

90. מגדלאל, Jos. xix. 38.

91. נעיאל,[7] Jos. xix. 27.

The following five names occur only as those of foreigners :—

92. אדבאל,[8] referred by P to Period I., Gen. xxv. 13.

---

[1] In spite of usages *c*, *d*, this name is essentially geographical.

[2] Cf. No. 35 with note.

[3] ἅπ. λεγ. well supported.

[4] Perhaps *b* = *a* : cf. Ryle on Neh. xi. 25.

[5] = יבנה 2 Chr. xxvi. 6.

[6] ἅπ. λεγ. well supported ; but the Syr. identifies the name with No. 74.

[7] ἅπ. λεγ. well supported.

[8] LXX. both in Gen. and Chr. Ναβδαιήλ, otherwise VV. entirely or substantially support *MT.*

93. מגדיאל, referred by P to Period I., Gen. xxxvi. 43.
94. חזאל, 1 K. xix. 15, Period III. 9.
95. טבאל, *a*. Is. vii. 6, Period III. 8.
    b. Ezr. iv. 7, Period IV.
96. ברכאל, Job xxxii. 2.

Finally—

97. בתואל is the name of a Syrian (Period I., Gen. xxii. 22, JE) and a place, 1 Chr. iv. 30.

APPENDIX III

This appendix tabulates the compounds with יה or אל according to the periods to which they are severally first referred in the literature; on the left hand the tables are constructed with regard to the evidence of the approximately contemporary writings only (cf. pp. 11 f., 21), on the right hand with regard to all O.T. literature. In each case the compounds in which the divine name precedes are placed in separate columns from those in which it follows. In Period III. the number following the name indicates the century to which it is first referred.

1. Compounds with יה

The Names assigned to Period I. (early literature).		Names assigned to Period I. (all writings).[1]	
A = 5.	B = 1.	A = 7.	B = 14.
יואל	אביה	יואל	אביה
יואש	(? מיכיהו)	יואש	(? מיכיהו)
יהונתן		יהונתן	
יהושוע		יהושוע	אמציה
יותם		יותם	אמריה
			זרחיה
		יואח	חגיה
		יוכבד (P)	חלקיה
			חשביה
			מעשיה
			מלכיה
			עדיה
			עזיה
			עזריה
			עשיה
			צפניה

[1] Names in this section brought over from the parallel section of the table stand at the head of the columns, separated from the remainder by a space. Of the remaining names Chronicles is the source, except when otherwise indicated. This applies also to pages 316 f.

First appearing in Period II. (early literature).		First appearing in Period II. (all writings).			
A=4.	B=5-6.	A=11.	B=41-42.		
יואב	ארניה	יואב	ארניה	? ישויה	? קישיה
יהונדב	אוריה (foreign)	יהונדב	אוריה	יְחִדיה	רחביה
יהושפט	אחיה	יהושפט	אחיה	יְחִיה	? שבניה
יהורע	בניה	יהורע	בניה	? יְעִזיה	שבניה
	ידידיה		ידידיה	יְריה	שְׁלֶמיה
	שפטיה	יהוא	שפטיה	יְרמיה	שמעיה
		יהוזבד		יִשִּׁיה	שמריה
		? יוחא	בעליה	? ישמעיה	
		יהוחנן	בְקיה	ישעיה	
		יועֶזר	בֶּרֶכיה	כונניה	
		יועש	גדליה	מַעֲזיה	
		יהורם	דליה	מַתתיה	
			זבדיה	מַתניה	
			זכריה	נתניה	
			חנניה	סמכיה	
			טבליה	עובדיה	
			ידעיה	? עוזיה	
				פדיה	
				פתחיה	

First appearing in Period III. (early literature).				First appearing in Period III. (all writings).		
A = 12.	B = 45.			A = 8.	B = 30.	
יואח, 8	אחזיה, 9	יגדליה, 7 ?	פדיה, 7	יהואחז, 9	אחזיה, 9	פקחיה, 8
יהואחז, 9	אליה, 9	יכליה, 7	פלטיה, 7	יחבר, 9	אליה, 9	צדקיה, 9
יהוא, 10	אמציה, 8	יכניה, 7	פקחיה, 8	יהרכין, 7	אצליה, 7	קוליה, 7
יהחבר, 9	אמריה, 8	יראיה, 7	צדקיה, 9	יהרקים, 7	גמריה, 7	רמליה, 8
יחבר, 9	אצליה, 7	ירמיה, 7	צפניה, 7	יהועדן, 8	הושעיה, 7	שריה, 7
יהחנן, 6	[י]ברכיה, 8	ישעיה, 8	קוליה, 7	יהצדק, 6	חבצניה, 7	
יהרכין, 7	גדליה, 8	מחסיה, 7	רמליה, 8	יהושבע, 9	יחזקיה, 8	רודיה, 9
יהרקים, 7	גמריה, 7	מיכיהו, 9	שלמיה, 7		יאזניה, 7	טוב אדניה, 9
יהועדן, 8	דליה, 7	מעשיה, 7	שמעיה, 10	הושע, 6	יאשיה, 7	טוביה, 9
יהצדק, 6	הושעיה, 7	מלכיה, 7	שריה, 7		יגדליה, 7 ?	יסמכיה, 8 ?
יהרם,[1] 9	זכריה, 8	מאניה, 7			יכליה, 7	יקמיה, 7
יהושבע, 9	חבצניה, 7	נריה, 7			יכניה, 7	נדביה, 6
	יחזקיה, 8	נתניה, 7			יראיה, 7	עמסיה, 9
	חלקיה, 8	עובדיה, 9			מחסיה, 7	
	חנניה, 7	עדיה, 7			מיכיהו, 9	
	יאזניה, 7	עזריה, 10			נריה, 7	
	יאשיה, 7	עשיה, 7			עתליה, 9	
		עתליה, 9			פלטיה, 7	

[1] Possibly in Period II. as foreign name.

First appearing in Period IV. (early literature).				First appearing in Period IV. (all writings).		
A=1.	B=42.			A=1.	B=30.	
יויריב F	אוניה F	יזיה	פתחיה	יויריב F	אוניה F	מריה ?
	בְּרָיה ?	יורחיה ? F ?	ראיה F		בריה ?	נועדיה
	בְּסֹדְיה F ?	יחויה	רמיה		בסודיה F ?	נחמיה
	בַּקְבֻּקְיה	ישיה	רעליה		בקבקיה	נעריה ?
	הודויה F	מלטיה	רפיה		הודויה F	עניה ? F
	זבדיה	מ(ו)עדיה F	שבניה ? F		חביה F	ענניה F ?
	חביה F	מַעֲזיה F	שכניה F		חכליה	פלאיה F
	זרחיה	מריה ?	שמריה		חסדיה	פליה
	חכליה	מתתיה	שרביה F		חשבניה ? F ?	ראיה F
	חסדיה	נועדיה			ידיה	רמיה
	חשביה F	נחמיה			יוספיה	רעליה
	חשבניה ? F ?	נעריה ?			יזיה	רפיה
	טוביה F	עֻזִּיה ?			יורחיה ? F ?	שרביה F
	ידיה	עניה ? F			יחויה	
	ידעיה F	ענניה F ?			מלטיה	
	יוספיה	פלאיה F			מ(ו)עדיה F	
		פליה				

2. COMPOUNDS WITH אל.

Names assigned to Period I. (early literature).		Names assigned to Period I. (all writings).[1]		
A = 7.	B = 8.	A = 11.	B = 33.	
אליאב	אביאל	אליאב	אביאל	יחציאל
אלדד	יואל ?	אלדד	יואל ?	נמואל
אליהוא ?	ירחמאל	אליהוא ?	ירחמאל	לאל ?
אלימלך (Ruth)	ישראל	אלימלך	ישראל	מהללאל
אליעזר	מחויאל ?	אליעזר	מחויאל ?	מיכאל
אלעזר	עתניאל	אלעזר	עתניאל	מישאל
אלקנה	שמואל	אלקנה	שמואל	מלכיאל
	מתושאל ?		מתושאל ?	נתנאל
		אליסף		עזיאל
		אליצור	אשריאל	עמיאל
		אליצפן	בצלאל	פגעיאל
		אלישבע	גאואל	פדהאל
			גדיאל	פוטיאל
			גמליאל	פלטיאל
			רעואל ?	צוריאל
			חניאל	קמואל
			יחלאל	שלומיאל

[1] The names brought over from the opposite section of the table stand at the top of the respective columns (A, B) : of the remainder on this page P, on pages 320 f. Chronicles, is the source.

Names first appearing in Period II. (early literature).		Names first appearing in Period II. (all writings).		
A = (8) 7.	B = 4.	A = (15) 14.	B = 20.	
(אלידע) ?	עדריאל	(אלידע) ?	עדריאל	עזראל
אליחבא	עמיאל	אליחבא	עשהאל	עזריאל
אליעם	עשהאל	אליעם		רפאל
אליפלט	פלטיאל ?	אליפלט	אוריאל	שובאל
אליקא ?		אליקא	אליאל	
אלישוע		אלישוע	[רניאל]	
אלישמע		אלישמע	זבדיאל	
אלחנן		אלחנן	חזיאל	
			ידיעאל	
		אליאל	יויאל	
		אליאתה	יחזקאל	
		אליפלהו	יחזיאל	
		אלישיב	יחיאל	
		אלנעם	יעואל	
		אלזבד	יעזיאל	
		אלעוזי	יעשיאל	
			יתניאל	
			עזריאל	

Names first appearing in Period III. (early literature).		Names first appearing in Period III. (all writings).	
A = 6.	B = 9 (10).	A = 8.	B = 8 (9).
אלידע, 9	חיאל, 9	אלידע, 9	חיאל, 9
אליחרף, 10	חנמאל, 7	אליחרף, 10	חנמאל, 7
אליקים, 8	עבדאל, 7	אליקים, 8	עבדאל, 7
אלישע, 9	עמנואל, ?8	אלישע, 9	עמנואל, 8
אלנתן, 7	שאלתיאל, 6	אלנתן, 7	שאלתיאל, 6
אלעשה, 7	דניאל, ?7	אלעשה, 7	דניאל, 7?
	יחזקאל, 7		ישמעאל, 7
	ישמעאל, 7	אלידע? 9	(אריאל), 8?
	עזריאל, 7	אלישמע, 9	
	(אריאל), ?8		יהללאל, 8

First appearing in Period IV. (early literature).		First appearing in Period IV. (all writings).	
A=1.	B=17.	A=0.	B=7.
אלישיב	אואל		אואל
	אריאל		אריאל
	בצלאל		גבריאל
	גבריאל		מהיטבאל
	זבריאל		פתואל ?
	יחויאל		קרמיאל F
	יחיאל		משיזבאל F
	יעיאל		
	מהיטבאל		
	מיכאל (F ?)		
	מישאל		
	נתנאל		
	עזיאל F		
	עזראל		
	פתואל ?		
	קרמיאל F		
	משיזבאל F		

ADDENDA

P. 26. Dr. Gilbert contributes to the number of *Hebraica*, dated April-July 1895, but only just published (Aug. 1896), an article on Old Testament proper names. It contains some very serviceable comparative tables of many of the compound names. Among compounds with אב Dr. Gilbert includes כלאב. The etymology here presupposed is far from certain; if accepted, the name increases by one the Davidic instances of this class.

P. 44. Wellhausen's suggestion that עֲמָשָׂא (= עמשי) should be pointed עֲמָשַׂי gains support from the LXX. $A\mu\epsilon\sigma\sigma\alpha\iota$, which is exactly parallel to $A\beta\epsilon\sigma\sigma\alpha\iota$ = אבישי. For the reduplication of the σ, cf. p. 23; the single μ is the regular LXX. equivalent for the dagheshed ם in compounds with עם.

It is possible that חושי may be a parallel compound with אח, the א being dropped as in חירם. But the Greek transliteration does not favour this view.

P. 56 (and 52). The non-Babylonian origin of the names of the first Babylonian dynasty is disputed by Jensen in *Zeitschr. für Assyr.* x. (Jan. 1896) 342 ff.; but he thinks it worth considering whether a common North Semitic divine name may not be represented in *Ammi*; *ib.* p. 343.

P. 64, l. 5. Since, however, the LXX. always represents the dagheshed ם of עם by the single μ, the form $A\mu o\iota\eta\lambda$ is indecisive as to the incorrectness of *MT*.

P. 100. For a modern Bedouin instance of giving an animal name to a child, see Burckhardt, *Notes on the Bedouin and Wahâbys*, i. 97.

P. 110. With גֻּדְגֹּדָה (the name of a place in the Wilderness, Dt. x. 7) we may compare جُدْجُد, which signifies a cricket, and is the exact phonetic equivalent of the Hebrew. The Greek transliterates Γαδγαδ after the גִּדְגָּד of Num. xxxiii. 32.

P. 127. The term following Beth in place names is so frequently of a divine character as to lead us to expect it to have been the same even in names where this is no longer manifestly the case. It seems probable, therefore, in the light of the general discussion (pp. 126 ff.) that many forms like Beth Reḥob are abbreviations of forms with Ba'al—*e.g.* Beth Baal Reḥob. Cf. actual cases like Beth Maon and Beth Baal Maon.

P. 134. "Der Name (בעל צפון) bedeutet 'Herr des Nordens,' erscheint hebr. Ursprungs" (Jensen, as cited above, p. 366).

P. 155. The LXX. transliteration (Ιωας) does not favour connecting the עש of יעש with a root beginning with غ.

P. 277 (No. 9). The LXX. never recognises the form אביהוא, but always gives Αβιουδ = אביהוד (except in Ex. vi. 23 A, Αβισουρ = אבישור).

INDEX I

OF MATTERS

(Supplementary to the Table of Contents.)

INDEX II

OF SOME BIBLICAL PASSAGES

Old Testament

New Testament

INDEX III

OF NAMES

References are not given to names merely mentioned in the course of discussion in the sections to which they naturally belong; and to names in the Appendix only when some note on the text, etc., is to be found there.

An asterisk * is attached to a few forms that have been *decisively* rejected as due to textual (or scribal) corruption.

A few forms restored from the versions, and a few names not found in the Old Testament but discussed in the book, are included in the index and enclosed in square brackets.

Of two parallel forms (*e.g.* יהונתן, יונתן) one only, as a rule, is entered in the index; and references to compound expressions with בית, חצר, etc., will be found under the second term.

THE END

Printed by R. & R. Clark, Limited, *Edinburgh*

www.ingramcontent.com/pod-product-compliance
Lightning Source LLC
Chambersburg PA
CBHW032354230426
43672CB00007B/699
* 9 7 8 3 3 3 7 3 1 6 2 5 9 *